THE CODE
OF THE
RIGHTEOUS
WARRIOR

THE CODE
OF THE
RIGHTEOUS WARRIOR

10 Laws of Moral Manhood
for an Uncertain World

REV. DR. ALYN E. WALLER

Howard Books
New York   London   Toronto   Sydney   New Delhi

Howard Books
An Imprint of Simon & Schuster, Inc.
1230 Avenue of the Americas
New York, NY 10020

First Howard Books hardcover edition May 2019

HOWARD and colophon are trademarks of Simon & Schuster, Inc.

For information about special discounts for bulk purchases,
please contact Simon & Schuster Special Sales at 1-866-506-1949
or business@simonandschuster.com.

The Simon & Schuster Speakers Bureau can bring authors to your live event.
For more information or to book an event, contact the Simon & Schuster Speakers Bureau at
1-866-248-3049 or visit our website at www.simonspeakers.com.

Interior design by Davina Mock-Maniscalco

Manufactured in the United States of America

10   9   8   7   6   5   4   3   2   1

Library of Congress Control Number: 2018039848

ISBN 978-1-5011-7718-7
ISBN 978-1-5011-7720-0 (ebook)

This book is dedicated to my father and mother,
Rev. Dr. Alfred Waller and Belva Jean Waller,
for giving me life and for setting me on the road to manhood;
my wife, Dr. Ellyn Jo Waller, and daughters, Morgan and Eryka,
for loving and supporting me through the stages of manhood;
and to all the men who are trying to be Righteous Warriors.

Contents

Introduction

I SAW THE movement out of the corner of my eye. A guy getting out of a car that I hadn't noticed. *What is a car doing in the desert? And who is that?* Suddenly, not just one, but two, three, four, five men were running toward me through the darkness, shouting. I stopped jogging, my vision tightly tunneling around them.

What the . . . ?

"You probably thought that you'd made it, didn't you?" one of them yelled. "Well, it ain't over yet!"

Shoot!

I may be a pastor but I wasn't thinking about pacifism as I fought off my attackers—experts in Krav Maga, the martial art practiced by the Israeli Defense Forces—in the darkness of the Negev Desert. I was taking my test to become a Level 8 Instructor, the level that tests your ability to endure extreme exhaustion and pain. The test required me to stay awake for sixty hours straight, braving all sorts of endurance tests—endless push-ups under the one-hundred-degree sun, running up and down dunes carrying thirty-pound sandbags, doing countless sit-ups along the shore of the Mediterranean with the surf crashing over my face. I was participating along with five other Kravists, as we are called. (*Krav maga* means "contact combat.") Now I was being jumped at three a.m. at the end of a seven-kilometer run.

The first attacker tried to punch me in the gut. My arms flew up and blocked him. I pummeled his torso, then I pushed him around to shield myself from the other attackers as he rained blows into my rib cage.

"OOOOF!"

I ducked an elbow but took a kick to my thigh as one tried to take my legs out from under me.

"We're taking you down!"

Over two and a half days of excruciating pain, I'd been deprived of sleep and permitted to eat only one orange, three dates, two almonds, and a couple of figs. It would have been easy to allow the expletives and racial slurs they threw at me along the way to bait me into losing my composure. But I knew not to think about them or the misery; I could not quit. So I called on one of my favorite passages of scripture: *I can do all things through Christ who strengthens me.*

More than an hour earlier, Moni Aziks—a former commando with the Israeli Special Forces who had later founded the self-defense system Commando Krav Maga—had started a group of us on our run, ten to fifteen minutes apart. Back home and under normal conditions, I ran a nine-minute mile. This wasn't normal. I could barely lift my legs and my lungs were on fire. My chest, my arms, my quads, my calves, the soles of my feet—everything burned.

Every hundred meters or so I'd reach one of the glow sticks Moni had placed along the trail, and each time I dragged myself to the top of yet another sand dune, I could see another glow stick glimmering.

Do not quit.

That was about the only thought I'd allowed myself.

I'd known from enduring previous CKM tests that any thought of my wife, Ellyn; daughters, Morgan or Eryka; food; or any other creature comfort might make my mind wander. Give the Devil a foothold. Make me return to Philadelphia short of the goal it had taken almost ten years of training to achieve. Something important about my manhood depended upon my ability to complete this test. I was a successful pastor, but had also made some big mistakes during my life. Some that still haunt me. I needed this.

Don't quit.

I slogged up yet another sand dune, then I saw Moni standing with his arms folded over his chest.

Hallelujah! You're almost there!

I was on the verge of meeting a goal I'd set for myself when I was forty years old and overweight and had vowed to get my body back.

Don't quit.

I was only about fifty yards from Moni when the car had come into view and the guys had jumped out.

Unexpectedly engaged in the fight of my life, I had no time to think "He's swinging, let me put up my hand"; I relied on my body to do instinctively what I'd trained it to do. My hands went up in time to block the blows without my thinking or directing them to do so. I'd reached the point Bruce Lee once described as "I don't hit; it hits itself."

As another attacker came at me, I used the first guy as my shield and kicked my assailant's legs out from under him.

Don't quit.

Suddenly, my pants were down around my ankles and I couldn't move my feet!

Uh-oh!

Then someone threw sand in my face. As I blinked and tried to spit it out of my mouth, a freight train slammed into my gut.

"OOOOF!"

My hand reached for my belt buckle and I pulled my belt free and began to swing it like Okinawan nunchucks. I heard the leather whistle through the air, and saw it slice one attacker's face.

"You punk!"

I swung the lash again, this time backing two of them up.

A thought arose: *This is the hardest thing I've ever done, but I'm doing it—I can do this!*

But there was no time to dwell on it. Fingers closed around my neck from behind.

Don't let him choke you out!

I clenched my teeth into his arm as hard as I could.

"AAAARGH!" he yelled as my bite penetrated his protective arm pads.

His hands loosened around my neck.

Then Moni's voice: "Okay, stop. That's enough!"

I'd done it!

No Longer Running

I have been in ministry for more than thirty years. I hold both a master's degree and a doctorate. But I also like to fight. The truth be told, I love to fight. I *really, really* love to fight! In fact, I have been engaging in fights of one form or another since my mother signed me up for judo when I was eight years old and got me a G.I. Joe with the kung-fu grip. I know, this may not make sense to you. If you're like most people, you have been raised to see ministers as mild-mannered, even weak—the kind of guys who turn the other cheek. So it's probably hard to imagine a man of the cloth who also likes to throw and take blows. But I do and I stand unabashedly in that truth about myself. Perhaps knowing a little bit about my background will help you understand.

I grew up outside of Cleveland, in Shaker Heights, Ohio, the son of a prominent minister. From my earliest recollections, when I was three or four until I was in the fifth grade, I was always the shortest boy in the class, and thin. You could have called me shy, timid, or something politically incorrect, but the truth of the matter is, despite my father's position, there were ways in which my life was rough. Among them, Derrick, Michael, Mark, and Jeff bullied me, and when people pick on you, you don't soon forget. I was afraid of them, and I was scared a lot. Until I started fifth grade, that is.

You may have seen the TV show *The Fresh Prince of Bel-Air*, starring Will Smith, which was popular back in the early nineties. That was my life in a nutshell, and I would have been Carlton, not the Fresh Prince. But in the fifth grade, my cousin Lonnie relocated to Cleveland from Philadelphia. Lonnie was "West Philadelphia born and raised," just like the Fresh Prince. He, too, had gotten in trouble, and Aunt Willa Mae wanted him out of their neighborhood.

But as soon as Cousin Lonnie showed up in the CLE, my life got a whole lot better. Lonnie was five years older than me and he promised that he would have my back. Then he "handled" Derrick, Michael, Mark, and Jeff; they didn't bother me anymore. Lonnie taught me how to protect myself: He took me into the garage and taught me how to fight. To my surprise, I kind of liked fighting. Before long, I was able to hold my own and dish out "a two-piece and a biscuit" whenever the situation required it. Knowing how to protect myself changed something inside of me. I was no longer scared, no longer always running. A few years after that I discovered wrestling, and I was good at it; and over time I became very accomplished. Finally, I could "handle myself" when it came to the aggression I experienced from other males.

Then one day Lonnie handed down to me an Army shirt with cut-off sleeves and Bruce Lee spray-painted on the back that one of his uncles who had served in Vietnam had brought back and given to him. He might as well have awarded me a black belt; when I wore it you couldn't tell me anything. The movie *Enter the Dragon* had just come out and Bruce Lee was its star. After that came David Carradine and *Kung Fu*. Everyone was into karate. Martial arts became my world.

Fast forward to my freshman year in college. I got distracted by parties and booze and quit the wrestling team. I didn't know it then, but I was born with a gene that predisposes me to alcoholism, a battle I'd fight for the rest of my life. To help pay for school I enlisted in the National Guard, and for six years served as a weekend warrior as a 19 Delta Calvary Scout, part of the Emergency Response Team. It was there that I learned military values, as well as how to box and handle a weapon. I received my call into the ministry while I was in the Guard. During my final year, I became a chaplain's assistant. In 1994, several years after graduating from seminary and after pastoring the First Baptist Church in Donora, Pennsylvania, God presented me with the opportunity to become the senior pastor at Enon Tabernacle Baptist Church in Philadelphia. Unbeknownst to me, I was arriving during what would become known as the mega-church movement. Our congregation grew from several hundred to more than fifteen thousand members.

It was a tremendously fun and exciting time; the work was also extremely demanding. I struggled to balance my family life and our rapidly growing ministry with self-care. My blood pressure, cholesterol, and weight began to creep up; I started to feel weird. After being so physically active and fit during my youth, I became the classic middle-aged man struggling with his weight. During my late thirties, I finally started going to the gym, where I faced the sobering reality that, in addition to gaining around thirty pounds, I'd lost a tremendous amount of strength, flexibility, and fitness. Working out was a struggle. Not only that, the more I fought to regain what I'd lost, the more I felt haunted by what I'd left on the table. I'd departed for college with the intention of wrestling and excelling academically. Truth be told, I had done neither. I was a fair student at best until I attended seminary. What would my life have been like if I had been a scholar during my undergraduate years? What would my life have been like if I hadn't thrown in the towel on the wrestling team? How good could I have become? Could I have made it to the Pan-Am Games or the Olympics? Regrets started eating away at me.

During this time, I learned that an older member of our church, Hamilton Robinson, was an expert in Naphtali, a martial art with a Christian overlay that had originated among the Berber people of North Africa. I knew that I needed to work toward a goal. I also wanted to be held accountable. Fortunately, Master Robinson was at a point in his life where he was looking to share what he knew with younger men. A small group of guys who attended the church and loved fitness and martial arts started training intensively under him several times a week. Everyone's health improved as we took better care of ourselves. Along the way, our band of brothers, as we'd begun to call ourselves—Leroy, Jerry, Jerome, Mark, Rich, and Vernell—promised each other that we would stay fit and practice martial arts for the rest of our lives. We joked that we would become like SEAL Team Six, forty-year-old style. I started telling the guys that when I turned fifty, I wanted to be like Jason Bourne, the CIA assassin in the Bourne spy-thriller movie series. I was laughing as I said it, but from a self-defense standpoint, I really wasn't kidding. I reimmersed myself in the martial arts, earning an advanced ranking in four: CKM, American Kenpo karate, Muay Thai, and Naphtali. I've also picked wrestling back up. Individually, we began to set goals to really challenge ourselves, then we held each other to them. We have trained together to run in the Penn Relays, the world's largest track-and-field competition, as well as participated in endurance events like the Tough Mudder, Spartan Race, and GORUCK Challenge. We've also engaged in extreme adventures—from a Navy SEALs BUD/S experience in North Carolina, to Muay Thai training in Thailand, to Greg Jackson's MMA training in New Mexico, to a survivalist adventure in the Amazon. I do something extreme at least once a year.

I realize that these are not activities you'd normally associate with a minister; however, they help me to remove myself from the strange world of ministry, where people often defer to me to an extent that makes me extremely uncomfortable. Instead, experiences like these allow me to connect with my inner "man's man" and experience a lot of variety and adventure. They equip me with skills I need in other areas of life: in my marriage and in my relationships with my adult daughters; during daily life as an African-American man, as I minister to people on the best and worst days of their lives; and as I serve God in various ways in Philadelphia, around the nation, and, increasingly, as I travel the world. They also push me past my limitations and give me the chance to live the scripture: *I can do all things through Christ who strengthens me.*

As I engaged in these activities and martial arts practices, I found myself becoming fascinated by the lives of warriors in different cultures, and began to study them. This caused me to think seriously about manhood—particularly in the years around the recession, as I spoke with so many men who had been shaken to their core and challenged to call upon every weapon they possessed to protect themselves and their loved ones—and not always successfully. The experiences have also allowed me to talk about difficult topics with a wide variety of men, often because these contexts allow men to put their guard down. For example, in my martial arts life, during extreme adventures, and in my work as a chaplain for the police and FBI, I have spoken with many White men about their lives and concerns—from fears of job loss and the demographic change taking place in the United States, to a perceived loss of status as men, to the typical family struggles, to the opioid crisis, to school shootings, and so on. Of course, I was already well aware of the trials that many Black males experience, as they have experienced both economic challenges and society's racism, being "last hired and first fired," as well as daily struggles to participate in the American Dream, the police brutality being caught on cell phone videos, and in inner-city contexts, underfunded schools and gun violence. I interact frequently with Philadelphia's Islamic community as well as with rabbis and religious leaders of other faiths and have learned a bit about their concerns. Over the past several years, I have also traveled the world. I was once invited to preach in Korea, where I learned more about that nation as well as a bit about the struggles that Korean Americans and other Asian Americans face. Our own church missionary activities and my leadership of the Lott Carey Baptist Foreign Mission Society helped me to connect the dots between men's experiences in the United States and all over the world, as I've traveled to places as varied as Mexico, Italy, Israel and Palestine, South Africa, Kenya, India, and beyond.

Along the way, life happened to the brothers and me as we trained and got to know each other. God blessed us with children and our families grew together. The church snowballed in size and began to impact both the city and the world. We bought houses, got new jobs, and won promotions. Somehow our children grew up. Some have gone off to college and others have even graduated. But tragedy struck, as well. Between all of us we have lost parents, children, siblings, and other people we loved. Some of us enjoyed the golden years with our parents; others nursed elders through sickness and watched them pass away. Some of us excelled professionally; others have struggled. Some of us have wives who have surpassed us professionally and financially. Our daughters started facing sexism, sexual harassment, and other struggles we didn't want them to face. Some of us had sons who were not only experiencing the difficulties inherent to life as a Black male, but also competition and new rules and expectations from girls and women that we knew we hadn't prepared them for.

As we engaged in these issues, we realized that society didn't have much to offer us in terms of guidance. There was little that we'd learned about manhood that could help us navigate this brave new world, which was so different from that of our parents. So we learned to trust and share with and lean on each other, each of us finding in the other something that we didn't know we were missing. We read and studied together—the Bible, Christian literature, leadership, money and finance, self-help, martial arts philosophy. As we experienced skirmishes in the world, we had each other's back. In time, we recognized that each of us needed to dial back in order to reconcile the parts of ourselves that had been hurt or we'd left behind or overlooked, so we could move forward as more fully developed men. Together, we learned more what it means to be a middle-aged man, as we absorbed lessons around teamwork, taking care of ourselves, dealing with adversity, and how we could grow in our fellowship and, as Christians, in our witness for Christ.

A Man's Fight

Even though I try to prepare myself to fight any battle, as I write this book at age fifty-four, I don't ever want to have a physical fight. In fact, you can fight me if you want, but even though I know how to drop you, I'll be calling the police and pressing charges. That said, I believe that every man should know how to defend himself and his loved ones. The martial arts and extreme experiences have given me many contexts in which to grow and develop that most other guys don't have. Indeed, I wish every man had the ability to undergo some sort of ritualistic manhood training, as I have, to prepare him to respond to the demands of life as instinctively and effectively as a fighter responds to an incoming punch. Because the fact of the matter is, every guy will have to fight. He will have to fight for his job, fight for his marriage, fight for his children, and at some point, each of us will probably have to fight for our life. We also have to persevere when we're hurt and afraid and the demands of life push us past our current capabilities.

Whether in my church, on a martial arts mat, or as I travel the country and world engaged in various forms of pastoral leadership, many men I talk to are feeling uncomfortable and insecure, even as the economy has strengthened. As the rich get richer and increasingly wall themselves off from the rest of society, many of the jobs and career paths that traditionally allowed working- and middle-class guys to make a good living are either going up in smoke or have already vanished. Many Millennials struggle to get a foothold in a workforce full of adults doing jobs—working at Starbucks, delivering advertising circulars, selling at stadium concessions, and the like—that once were held by young people. Even some careers populated by professional men—think accounting, finance, law, and medicine—are being partially outsourced and automated. Experts project that in the coming years, many jobs and even entire career paths will be taken over by robots.

So it's no wonder that an increasing numbers of guys have been telling me that, even though they were raised to believe that they should protect and provide, they find themselves at least somewhat reliant upon women. Men talk about how the women in their lives are not only becoming more powerful, they're also excelling in areas where they didn't expect to compete with them. Most of the guys I know want their wives and sisters and daughters to do well. They also admit that it's hard to know what the women need from them and where they stand in their relationships with women. (Been there, done that, bought the T-shirt.) Many guys are struggling with the belief that the gains women and people of color have experienced are coming at their expense—a perception that's particularly challenging in an era during which men's roles in society and family life have become so unclear. And let's not forget about the #MeToo movement. Lots of guys are struggling to understand the new rules; some even feel as though they are under attack. Untold numbers of men have revised their expectations downward. Then they worry because they don't know how low the bottom is. That's really scary! Even among very successful men, you'd be surprised how many guys feel isolated, inadequate, vulnerable, anxious, and depressed. Unfortunately, many of them think they're the only ones having those feelings.

The Way of the Warrior

I don't know about you, but I'm a movie guy. The Brad Pitt movie *Fight Club* is one of my favorites, and I believe that Brad Pitt's character, Tyler Durden, expresses the way a lot of men feel: "We've all been raised on television to believe that one day we'd all be millionaires, and movie gods, and rock stars. But we won't. And we're slowly learning that fact. And we're very, very pissed off."

I get it. Many of us have reason to feel betrayed and afraid.

But I have to admit that a lot of guys don't handle change particularly well, either.

Many of the men I talk to don't know how to channel fear, frustration, anger, and grief into positive emotions and action. If I'm going to be perfectly honest, I've been that dude—and still am sometimes. The truth of the matter is, there's no place for a man to talk about what's going on with him. So instead, we do things like grab a cigarette, a brew, a blunt, an Oxy, or a Xanax; retreat to our man cave; watch porn and/or have sex; put our head under the hood of our car; or head to the electronics store for our fix—not realizing that by not sharing we're not only isolating ourselves further, we're undermining our health. More often than many of us might like to admit, in ways large and small, men are throwing in the towel and giving up the fight. Many of us are falling short of our goals and waving the white flag—whether at work, in relationships, family life, finances, health, spiritually, or other areas where succeeding would require us to dig deeper than we ever have and actually show up as our best selves. Some of us are becoming abusive, violent, and destructive, whether toward ourselves, our loved ones, or other human beings. Sadly, many of us are failing to demonstrate the type of fortitude that was common among men of previous generations.

Yet, while unacceptable, some of what we're witnessing actually makes sense. Because aside from being initiated into sports, drinking, street fighting, and sex, only a handful of American men have ever engaged in any formal manhood ritual to prepare us for the challenges of modern life—least of all, physically, mentally, emotionally, and spiritually healthy approaches. The one exception I'd make is among men who've joined the military, who learn a set of values around manhood, order, valor, and fighting that prepare them to excel, though active duty leaves many men mentally, physically, emotionally, and spiritually debilitated.

With this as the backdrop, it's no wonder that many of us flail, fail, or even implode when we encounter demands that could equally have strengthened, transformed, or even propelled us to the next level had someone merely prepared us to handle them. It's no surprise that so few of us demonstrate a mind-set that would prepare us to thrive, rather than just survive, amidst difficulty, if we only knew it. Absent these skills, perhaps it shouldn't even surprise us that we are witnessing so many men taking on life's challenges in morally questionable—or, worse, cynical, corrupt, or even depraved—ways.

Unlike those of us who live in the industrialized world, many young men in more traditional cultures engage in ritualistic manhood training that prepares them to take on life's trials and tribulations. Indeed, in every traditional society that I'm aware of, the fighting class of men—from British knights, to the Maasai *morans*, to Maori warriors—once lived or currently lives according to a Bushido, the Japanese word for the code of conduct that governed ancient samurai fighters. In English, "bushido" means "way of the warrior." A bushido not only trains a man how to fight, it teaches him leadership, spiritual development, fiscal responsibility, a positive mental attitude, as well as other productive masculine values. Importantly, it provides guidelines for engaging in fruitful relationships—with God, himself, the woman in his life, children, extended family, other men, or the entire nation.

Warriors who adhere to a bushido abide by a different set of rules than other males in that same society. They value morality, truth, honor, integrity, and justice above all else, as members of our modern military are trained to do. They pursue excellence throughout their lives and perfect their character in order to achieve it. And as they challenge themselves to live by these rigorous virtues they find tremendous power. I believe that modern-day men could learn a lot about life's fight from the values of warriors in other cultures.

Christianity offers its own bushido and, as a minister who is also a martial artist, I believe that Jesus role-modeled it during his life. I believe that understanding these principles can help Christian men, men who practice other faiths, men who describe themselves as spiritual but not religious, as well as men who are agnostic and atheist learn skills to help them live into their manly promise and potential. Far too many of us have been socialized to equate Christianity with peace. I believe that peace is important, but the Bible also includes plenty of imagery of battle and war, particularly in the Old Testament.

Indeed, I believe that Jesus Christ was a warrior.

Of course, this bumps up against the Church's historical portrayal of Jesus as a namby-pamby type of guy. I think this weak representation of Jesus is one of the reasons you find more women in church than men no matter what denomination or where in the nation you go. Most of the men I know don't relate to this milquetoast version of Christ, nor should they. As I will explain, the way I interpret the Bible, that story is fundamentally inaccurate. As a minister who is also a martial artist, it is evident to me that as Jesus was aggressed against on the way to Calvary, where he was crucified, his approach to defending himself was consistent with the tenets of a warrior's code. As Jesus lived a warrior's life, Jesus not only fulfilled his destiny but also transcended the limitations society had placed on him and overcame the world's way of thinking.

Cracking the Code

In *The Code of the Righteous Warrior,* I share the blueprint that Jesus provided and propose a bushido that Christian and other religious, spiritual, and moral men can live by in order to access their best selves. When I use the term "righteous," I am not referring to a man who is sinless, beyond fault, or perfect. I mean a man who strives to do the next right thing and in the process to sin less. For the record, when I use the word "sin," I refer to the term originally derived from archery that means "off the mark." In other words, off the spiritual path God intended you to follow through life.

The appropriate response to sin is to acknowledge your mistake, make any reparations that may be necessary to the offended party (if there is one), make an adjustment, and ask God to help you get back on track.

In Part One of this book, I describe the bushido that Christ set forth and discuss how following it can help any man begin to live into his destiny. In Part Two, I set forth what I call "The Code of the Righteous Warrior," a bushido consisting of ten laws based on Judeo-Christian principles that I've developed for men who desire to understand and fulfill the journey through their destiny. The Code explores what it might look like for a spiritual, moral, and masculine man to embrace the rules of martial arts conduct in the six areas of fitness I believe modern-day men must master to thrive: spiritual, physical, mental, emotional, relational, and financial. I believe every man should know how to defend himself and his loved ones. Not only is every principle consistent with Christianity—as well as with the other Abrahamic religions: Judaism and Islam—every principle also reflects a tenet of Naphtali, the only martial art completely consistent with Jesus's teachings on self-defense. We teach Naphtali at our church.

Each tenet of the Code is accompanied by real men's stories. In the interest of transparency, I include a few of the lessons I've learned during my own manhood journey, including my personal, professional, martial arts, and extreme experiences. Several of the fellas who engage in extreme adventures with me—Revs. Jerome Glover and Leroy Miles, who are both now pastors at Enon, as well as three members of our church: Vernell Bailey III, Jerry Pendergrass, and Richard Walls—have shared their stories in the hope that by being transparent about their lives and making themselves vulnerable, they might touch and help change another man's trajectory.

As you consider these stories I invite you to locate yourself within them and think: "He is talking to me." I also encourage you to get a notebook or create a journal to take notes and capture your thoughts as you consider how these ideas relate to your own life. As you read, I invite you to imagine how your life could look under ideal circumstances, no matter how things look today. Ask yourself questions like:

+ What makes me tick?

+ What do I really like?

+ What does it take for me to feel happy?

+ What works well in my life right now?

+ What isn't working well that I'd like to change?

+ Who and what are inspiring me?

+ How might I need to change in order to live a more inspired life?

Pay attention to the answers and record them. As you read the stories of our adventures, also imagine some manhood rituals you could engage in to help you live into this higher vision of yourself.

I See You

As I write this book during the first eighteen months of the Trump administration, I would be remiss not to acknowledge that we are facing challenging racial times.

I approach this book about manhood as an African-American man. Men of different races, ethnic and socioeconomic groups, and cultural backgrounds tend to experience some aspects of manhood differently. I believe that my life experience and perspectives will not only bless men of African descent, but also White men and men of other races and ethnicities—whether Asian, Latino, mixed-race, or Native American— who share the challenges that people of color face in their effort to be seen as fully human. I also believe this book will provide all men with the opportunity to consider life and manhood through a different lens, and, in the process, access some new and different tools and approaches to life that might help them to create new possibilities and options.

While I do not take up the issue of race specifically, I do not run from it, either. Our oppressive society has stripped some of the warrior from African-American men, and those of us who identify as such need to think about what we need to do to get it back. Some White men knowingly or unknowingly oppress Black and other men of color, stripping us of our manhood. The dynamic of stripping and being stripped deprives all men, indeed all of humankind, of our full humanity and promise. So when I address race, I make an effort to show how much all men have in common, even in our diverse ways of understanding and experiencing manhood.

I also want to call out the fact that I tend to look at the world from an Afro-sensitive perspective. In other words, not only am I Christ-centered, I am also sensitive to the African experience of Jesus and understand my relationship with God through God's revelation through African people. I look at Africa as a place of rich history, culture, and humanity, not as a "dark continent" devoid of humanity and culture—a position that has been strengthened by my travels and work with our sister church, partners, and fellow ministers in South Africa, Kenya, Uganda, and beyond. I do not view people of African descent as minorities, outsiders, or "others," as we are typically viewed within the United States and throughout Western culture. Instead, I place people of African descent as a significant source of the conversation. Importantly, African thought tends to rest in the belief that a person's humanity comes first—before their race, ethnicity, class, or other dimensions of who they are. This often runs counter to the typical Western approach, where a person's value is often determined by what they have or what they do. African values tend to be very human-centered. From an Afrocentric perspective, one of the greatest things I can do is see you—see you, acknowledge you, and respect you. In South Africa—a nation where our church engages in a lot of ministry work—one of the words for hello, *sawubona*, a Zulu word, carries the connotation "I see you."

In general, people of African descent do not look at or value people according to either their accomplishments or sins; they tend not to be overly impressed with or disgusted by anyone—no matter what they've done. From this perspective, "I see you" has a human-first approach, whether you do things that are great or have done things that are terrible. I bring that worldview to this book. I believe that if diverse humans can see each other, we can learn to love each other. A person who truly sees you cannot nullify or ignore you. A police officer who sees your humanity will not be quick to kill you. A young man on the street who sees your humanity will not shoot you. Learning to see each other opens the door to loving each other. You will see this belief system reflected throughout the book.

Another significant way African thought tends to differ from Western thought is that, in the African worldview, difficulty is expected in life and the presence of evil is certain. As a result, people who interpret life through an Afrocentric lens learn to be comfortable with life however it comes and to let it roll off of them. This differs from traditional Eurocentric thought, where difficulty and evil are viewed as aberrant. When things don't go well, a person interpreting a difficult or evil event through an African-centered framework might ask "What is to come of this?," where someone approaching the same happening through a more Eurocentric framework might ask "Why did this happen to me?" One is not better or worse than the other; they're just different and create different outcomes. There are many ways of thinking that we all should explore. I believe we can all learn from one another.

In addition to being African American, I am also a conservative Christian. That means that I believe Jesus Christ was the Son of God and accept him as my personal Savior. I also accept the Bible as the word of God. I believe it means what it says, but also that it must be interpreted in order to carry the principles, rather than the literal meaning, across the ages. The Black conservative Christian tradition means I am theologically conservative but socially liberal. I believe in the Bible as it is; however, I struggle to understand the socio-grammatical questions of the text. By that I mean that I wrestle to understand: What does it say? What did it mean to the original hearers? What has the church said? What does it mean to me? How does that apply to today? Whenever there's a question between the truth in the Bible and other truths, for me the Bible wins out. However, though I believe the Bible, I do not have what we might consider to be right-wing beliefs.

One of Christianity's many wonderful teachings is that it tells us that God loves everyone. That means Christians ought to love and honor all of humankind. A well-developed Christian respects people whether or not they believe they are behaving honorably. They also love other people whether or not those persons love them back. What's more, a Christian who is also mature ought to demonstrate a sense of self that extends beyond his family, gender, race, ethnicity, socioeconomic status, political party, geography, or any of the ways that people think of themselves as different. They also ought to be content with the fact that many Christian beliefs run counter to popular culture and consumer capitalism. Consequently, Christians tend to sit angularly to the world. But I believe we ought to accept that "angledness" without becoming closed off or narrow-minded.

Having said that, all of the world's major religions teach good information and I respect them. In fact, Judaism, Islam, and Christianity all contain some form of the Golden Rule and have a code of ethics that monitors marriage and families; describes who you can and cannot have sex with; identifies what you can and cannot eat; distinguishes between good and bad behavior; and provides some sort of reckoning day when God makes everything make sense. Indeed, they're very similar except in what can help us wrestle with our brokenness and wash away our sin. That's where Jesus becomes important to the Christian. As you read, you will see these values among those reflected in my approach. You will also note that as often as possible I refer to God as God and Jesus as Jesus rather than He or Him. I do this because trapping God in a masculine pronoun limits our understanding and appreciation for the masculinity and femininity of God. Many of us know God as Our Father, but we may not be aware that God is also El Shaddai, the many-breasted one. In other words, God is a motherly father.

But rather than approach you merely from my position as minister, I come before you as both a man who has developed himself spiritually in order to lead and as an imperfect one who has struggled—and continues to struggle—to get it right and become the best man I can. For example, among the stories I share is the fact that I am an alcoholic, and like many recovering alcoholics I wrestle with that weakness. It was not God's creational intentionality for me to be an alcoholic, but in his permissive will, I was born that way. That said, God allows me to live, love, and function although I am one. The degree to which I wrestle with and overcome my addiction is the degree to which God opens up more opportunities in my life; whereas, the degree to which I have succumbed to it has just led to frustration. Early in my ministry I'd imagined myself leading a neighborhood church of just a few hundred people; however, God had something different in mind. Despite alcoholism and other weaknesses, I lead and teach thousands of people. Often, the fact that I stand in front of so many makes me even more aware of my faults and areas where I fall short and feel unworthy. In my struggle to be my best self, I am aware that my loved ones, my staff, my congregation, and the larger world meet me at the intersection between my ugliness and my awesomeness. Now you will as well.

So in the pages of this book, I share what I know with tremendous humility. I have intentionally stepped away from some of the traditional Christian language I use in the pulpit to adopt a brotherly tone that reflects my personal struggles and hope that these ideas will reach men of all religious backgrounds, as well as guys who define themselves a spiritual, atheist, agnostic, or nothing at all. I respect different religious traditions and we all wrestle with very similar issues in life no matter what god we call on.

No Re-dos

If you are a man, we have some things in common despite any other differences between us. That's why I hope that men of all races, ethnicities, and spiritual and religious beliefs (or no spiritual beliefs) will consider how the ideas I share might help you navigate the tumultuousness and uncertainty of modern life and help you experience possibilities that few men are able to access by adhering to the norms of modern society and popular culture.

Indeed, life is not a dress rehearsal. Most of us don't get a lot of do-overs and second chances. I know that I am not trying to leave life with too many "I wish I hads" remaining on my bucket list; I hope you don't, either. And why should you? God wants you to experience your full potential and fulfill the reasons that you were placed on this planet. Indeed, you were born both with a destiny and the ability to achieve it. When I use the term "destiny," I mean a hidden power and a spiritual assignment to accomplish specific things in the world that no one who ever has lived or is ever to come will be able to accomplish. This destiny was assigned to you before you were born and is connected to every other person's destiny. The decision of whether to fulfill it or how much of it you fulfill is in your hands; it is up to you.

Our planet is facing many serious challenges and you have been wired with the ability to help the world overcome at least one of them. This mission, if you choose to accept it, will challenge you, provide the sense of adventure that many men complain is missing from their lives, and fill your existence with great meaning and joy; even a sense of victory. Though we may hold different spiritual or religious perspectives, I believe that at least some of the Code of the Righteous Warrior will not only resonate with you but also help you become the man you long to be, just as it is helping me. Because the time has come for men to overcome our differences so we can participate in our lives and the world in a much greater way.

Your brother,
Alyn E. Waller

PART ONE

How a Righteous Man Fights

MY FATHER ALWAYS told me never to fight an ugly man.

"An ugly man is going into the fight ugly, and he's going to come out ugly," my father would say. "You never fight an ugly man because an ugly man has nothing to lose."

As a Baptist minister, it was not unusual for my dad to use stories to teach me about life and about manhood. Despite what we might now call his political incorrectness in talking about people's appearances, he wasn't really talking about looks or even fisticuffs. He was schooling me about the importance of understanding what's at stake. Dad was helping me to know that you don't get "down and dirty" with just anyone; that part of knowing when and when not to fight, in any form or fashion, is understanding whether it's worth it.

But implicit in my father's warning was the understanding that there are times when every man has to roll up his literal or metaphorical sleeves and stand up for himself, for his loved ones, and for the principles or ideals he believes in. But how do you do that without jeopardizing your principles, your position, your loved ones, or even your life? We have to sift out the useful from the harmful manhood messages we've received and ground ourselves in a righteous approach to life's fights.

The Messages of Manhood

Like most fathers and father figures, my dad taught me lessons about life—lessons about hard work, about getting a good education, how to treat women, managing my emotions, ways of dealing with authority figures, and many other aspects of a guy's existence. In addition to my dad, there were many other people and entities influencing my perceptions of manhood, including my uncles and cousins, my dad's minister peers, the men who attended our church, guys who lived in our neighborhood, coaches and teachers, my classmates, friends, and teammates, and the movies and TV shows I was watching.

Many of the manhood messages I learned helped me grow and prosper. I learned about the importance of family, the value of education, doing chores, working hard, and respecting authority. I learned what it means to have self-respect, the importance of teamwork, how to compete, how to treat women and girls, and more. Because of my family's religious focus, I learned why it's so valuable for a male to have a healthy and vibrant spiritual life.

But other manhood messages I received—from "men don't cry" to a lack of emphasis on self-care—turned out not to be helpful at all. Indeed, many traditional rules of manhood have boxed me and other men into an uncomfortable and unhealthy corner. Take, for example, the image of the strong but silent type. Depending upon your age group, you may have grown up thinking it was cool to behave like Luke Cage, James Bond, Shaft, Rambo, Clint Eastwood, or the Marlboro Man. Luke Cage has tremendous and valuable superpowers; however, he's a loner. Luke doesn't get close to anyone or even truly understand his own powers. Shaft was "fly," but he didn't speak much, and no one understood him except his woman. The Marlboro Man looked real cool smoking a cigarette on his horse against the landscape of the American West, but the guy never spoke at all. This raises the question of whether the image of manhood that has been presented to us is actually what we want for ourselves. Even if it is, is it good for us physically, mentally, emotionally, and spiritually?

No matter where you grew up or what your background is, you may be among the many men who have internalized beliefs like: there is a difference between being a man and being a male; men don't cry; men keep their emotions in check; men never back down; some women don't deserve our respect; men don't go to church; real men don't change diapers; and so on. Yet in many cases beliefs like these are not only inaccurate, but increasingly they are not helpful. For instance, try telling your female boss or peers that you don't respect them and see how far forward you advance at work. Disrespect them by sexually harassing or assaulting them and you'll join the growing list of men who are being dropped by the #MeToo movement.

Indeed, the fact of the matter is, guys do cry, dudes definitely have feelings, brothers had better back down sometimes, men who honor their woman feel more connected, fellas find fulfillment at church, and I know a heck of a lot of men who are very hands on in raising their children and would have it no other way. Indeed, today's men engage in a long list of behaviors that defy both long-held masculine traditions and society's narrow expectations of us. It is highly likely that you engage in them, and I do, too.

Whether in my church, in my community, as I travel and minister to others, and on my extreme adventures, I have repeatedly observed that when men confine ourselves to conventional stereotypes, we tend to live frustrated, painful lives. Indeed, every day I speak with guys who are feeling adrift. As I dig into what they're feeling, beneath their discomfort I often uncover that limiting beliefs about manhood are keeping them stuck. For instance, I may discover that they need to return to school to remain relevant in the workplace, but wrongly perceive that classrooms are spaces for women. Or that they feel anxious and perhaps even depressed about their family life yet hunker down into their man cave rather than face the facts and develop new skills. Or that they've been ignoring the advice to take care of themselves and have gained weight, have high blood pressure, are worried about diabetes, and are struggling to "get it up." I meet guys who never developed their spiritual life because they were socialized to believe that church was for women, men whose wallets are empty and their credit cards are maxed but who continue to spend so they can appear "large and in charge." Guys who feel lonely and disconnected from their children and loved ones, yet don't do the inner work required to develop loving relationships.

All of these guys are living beneath their "pay grade" in life. Each needs to update his manhood operating system to experience a more fulfilling existence. In fact, if I take my own halo off, I have to admit that I, too, have bumped my head against my traditional masculine socialization—not the least of which included the drinking during my college years that showed me to be an alcoholic. But even as a grown man, I allowed my insecurities to lead me to compete against some of my close minister peers whose gifts I greatly admire. At one point, because I envied them, I even distanced myself from them. As I've dealt with my insecurities and reexamined some of the messages I've received about competition, I've confessed that behavior to my friends and apologized for my shortcomings.

Indeed, socialization that has outlasted its expiration date tends to come with a very high price. Among our strong-but-silent movie heroes, Shaft died of a heart attack, a typical outcome for men who internalize their frustration and anger. James Bond no longer smokes and has even had a woman boss, but he's also become more dangerous, emotionally damaged, and narcissistic now that Daniel Craig portrays him. Luke Cage's indestructible skin and super strength don't mask his pain or isolation. Not a lot of people know that all six of the actors who portrayed the Marlboro Man died of smoking-related diseases. Sadly, the only time the public ever heard them speak was when they testified before Congress about the dangers of cigarettes.

The Tough Get Going

By warning me about ugly men and implying that I was going to have to fight during my life, my father attempted to arm me with information about a particularly important area of masculine socialization: handling life's aggressions. Every man must figure out how to respond when his own well-being or that of the people he cares about come under attack. We need to know how to fend for ourselves when we are facing a custody battle, how to protect our loved ones when our job is on the chopping block, how to engage in self-defense when the drunk guy at the bar suddenly wants to fight. Closer to home, we need to learn how to fight fairly and productively with our own partner. We also need to know when to go for the win and when to back down when our teenagers and young adults get testy. The capacity to ward off various turbulence and violence is a particularly important skill men must possess. Indeed, though we're often warned against it, I disagree with the idea that fighting is always a bad thing to do. Instead, what I think we need to understand is how a righteous man fights.

Because not only may we not have learned the most productive rules about when and when not to and how to fight, it isn't always clear how to fight back when you're besieged by intangible factors like economic disruption, changing gender norms, health challenges, and political correctness. How should you update your socialization and what should be your new rules? I'd like to suggest that if we want to do more than white-knuckle our way through life, we must root ourselves in timeless practices that transcend the economy, materialism, changing gender norms, and popular culture.

I believe that Jesus role-modeled a set of guidelines that not only show us the ideal way to live under normal conditions, but also what we should do when the going gets tough and it's time for the tough to get going. Indeed, when I consider Jesus through the lens of a martial artist, it is clear to me that Jesus Christ took a principled approach to violence—one consistent with the warrior codes practiced by the fighting class of men found throughout traditional societies. Of course, as a Christian, I believe Jesus was God in the flesh. That said, I believe that Jesus can teach men of all backgrounds, Christian or not, how to find purpose in our lives, as well as meaning and victory as we engage in life's fights.

I disagree with the traditional church teaching that people should not ever fight. To the contrary, not only do I believe that fighting is often necessary, but also, approached righteously, that fighting is not the immoral activity people often claim it to be. For example, fighting can also be a way of protecting oneself. Beyond that, it can be a method of delivering justice.

There are three different places in the Bible where Jesus faced violence. In each instance, he had to choose how to respond. It's important that we understand them.

Real Men Run

The first story occurs during the final days of Christ's short thirty-three-year life. By this point, Jesus has already performed many miracles, including turning water into wine, healing sick and disabled people, and feeding more than five thousand people from two fish and five loaves of bread. Back then, the rumor was beginning to circulate that Jesus might be the Son of God or some sort of deity. In fact, word had traveled back to the Roman politician and general Caesar, who controlled what we now know as the Holy Land and felt threatened by anything claiming to be as powerful as he was. Indeed, Caesar felt the need to get rid of Jesus.

On this particular day, Jesus had come to the Mount of Olives to a town called Bethany, outside of Jerusalem, in Israel. He'd ridden there on a colt, and crowds had praised him along the way. Once he arrived, he started teaching in the courtyard of the Temple. The ideas he taught challenged the authority of the scribes and Pharisees, the religious rule-keepers of Jewish society and the region's religious leaders. In the process, Jesus's teachings exposed the leaders' hypocrisy. Many people had begun to follow Christ and wondered openly if he was the Messiah, the "anointed" or "chosen" one the Old Testament had prophesied. Feeling threatened, the scribes and Pharisees attempted to set Jesus up with a series of tests designed to trick him into breaking Jewish law. If he broke the law they would have him arrested.

The debate between Jesus and these religious leaders went on for quite some time. As part of their test, these authorities brought a woman who had committed adultery to him and asked if she should be stoned. Those of us who live in Western society don't typically spend much time thinking about stoning. But having a crowd of people throw rocks at you is the equivalent of the death penalty. It is a cruel punishment but back then it wasn't unusual. What's more, parts of the Temple were still under construction, so there were plenty of rocks lying around. Once confronted, rather than answering the leaders directly, Jesus issued a challenge: "He that is without sin among you, let him first cast a stone at her." In other words: "If you're so perfect, why don't *you* kill her?" Called out on the carpet, everyone left, beginning with the elders, who had lived long enough to be humble about their shortcomings.

Once everyone was gone, Jesus forgave the woman; however, his interactions with her had turned the area's religious, political, social, and gender customs on their head.

While teaching in the Temple courtyard, Jesus also debated religious leaders about whether he was the Son of God. The leaders charged Jesus with blasphemy, or speaking profanely against God. Since the penalty for blasphemy was death, they started to stone Jesus.

Now, Jesus already knew that what he was teaching was going to cause problems. He had willingly taken on this fight. Jesus also knew that this was not the place where he was supposed to die. He was to be crucified on a cross at Calvary. Getting stoned to death in Bethany didn't make any sense.

So Jesus ran and hid.

Biblical scholars debate whether Jesus outran his attackers, was hidden by members of the community, or if, miraculously, he simply escaped. But no matter whose version you believe, it's fair to say that Jesus got "ghost."

As Jesus demonstrated and my father tried to teach me, understanding time and place is a very important part of manhood. Every guy needs to recognize when he is overpowered, outnumbered, or in a fight that he cannot win. In this story, Jesus reminds us that we don't necessarily have to fight back when we're aggressed against. There are times when we should de-escalate to reduce or even eliminate the level of conflict. That is to say, fleeing is an honorable and morally acceptable option. Indeed, running and hiding can demonstrate both our strength and a sense of purpose.

In China, the legendary martial arts strategist Sun Tzu, the author of *The Art of War,* taught warriors to retreat if your enemy is greater than you; fight, if your enemy is equal to you; attack if your enemy is lesser than you. Country-music legend Kenny Rogers also conveys this idea clearly: *You've got to know when to hold 'em / Know when to fold 'em.* Even men who consider themselves masculine run.

Fight the Power

Jesus's second response to violence took place not long after the first incident. Large numbers of people had traveled to Jerusalem to commemorate the Jewish observance of Passover. Many of them had stopped at the Temple upon their arrival. Now, Jerusalem's Temple was a place where everyone came to pray, whether the region's Israelite Jews or people of various religious beliefs who had come from other nations. Commerce was conducted in the Temple's outer courtyard, where money changers converted foreign currencies into the local money, shekels. It was in the Temple's sacred inner courtyard that prayer took place.

When Jesus went to the inner courtyard to pray, he noticed that commerce was going on in this holy part of the Temple. Jesus also witnessed merchants and money changers shortchanging vulnerable travelers. Jesus was outraged by what he saw. The Temple was God's house—his Father's house—a place Jesus believed he had a moral duty to protect. So Jesus wove several ropes into a whip and started flogging the merchants and money changers. They ran. Jesus then dumped out their money and turned over their tables and chairs. In other words, Jesus went "off"!

The way most American theologians interpret these scriptures, Jesus's whip never actually touched anyone. Indeed, most of them teach that Jesus merely disrupted commerce. But that interpretation doesn't make any sense to me. Why would the money changers leave their money behind and run if the whip wasn't actually landing on them?

I believe Jesus is showing us that there are times when a man must stand up for what is right. He is saying that righteous men speak truth to power. They respond aggressively to the violence perpetrated by exploitive systems; in this case, the unjust financial system perpetrated by the money changers, but we could just as easily be talking about unfair political, educational, labor, or criminal justice systems that exist in society today. God wants us to challenge injustice, even when we seem to be outnumbered or overpowered.

Jesus's skirmish in the Temple shows us that a man can stand up to power and win.

Taking One for the Team

Not long after his fights at the Mount of Olives, Jesus experienced a season of struggle as God removed the urge to quit from Jesus's spirit to prepare him to die on the cross and fulfill his destiny. Ultimately Jesus knew that he would soon be crucified so he went to the garden of Gethsemane, a place whose name means "place of pressing" or "oil press." He was despondent and needed to pray to his Father about his impending reality.

Jesus left Gethsemane a changed man—no longer ambivalent, resistant, or afraid of what was to come—a testament to the power of prayer. In fact, when Roman soldiers came to arrest Jesus, his disciple Peter defended him by cutting off one of the soldiers' ears with his sword; however, Jesus told Peter to put his sword away, for he had already decided to let Rome win. Christians believe that three days after he died for our sins, Jesus rose from the grave and later ascended to heaven.

Sometimes a righteous man takes a courageous stand even though he knows he will lose. When a man takes one for the team, his position powerfully demonstrates his belief that his life is part of a narrative that is greater than himself. The willingness to take the loss becomes a symbol of his strength. Indeed, a weak man is unable to walk away from a fight because he believes he must defend his fragile ego. In other words, sometimes the fight is about something or somebody else.

When we "man up" we can rest assured that on a spiritual level, when we are walking in our Purpose, everything works together for good. I'll talk more about Purpose later. For now, understand that this doesn't merely mean that everything is gonna work out, it means that angels have been assigned to you, nature will work for you, and circumstances will bow down to create the outcome God has projected for your life. Everything will be okay in the end—and if it ain't okay, it ain't the end.

Jesus Is Not a Punk

These three passages teach us that there are times when it's important for a man to stand up and fight, but also how to fight in a very principled way.

Jesus knew when to run, when to fight, and when to let things go.

Consistent with this, real manhood says: I can fight; I can run; I can let the other side win. But real *spiritual,* or righteous, manhood checks in with God by asking: I am capable of doing all these things; which approach do you want me to take?

The righteous warrior engages in analysis, but he also interacts with God. In other words, he says: I'm man enough to run from something I know I could win; I'm man enough to fight when I know I can win; I'm also man enough to fight when I don't think I can win. Then he listens to what God tells him to do and moves forward accordingly. To the righteous warrior, being a real man is about the relationship between himself and God, not his interaction with another man or entity. This approach is far more complex than the traditional Christian religious advice to "turn the other cheek," which, in my experience, is typically set forth as putting up with more mistreatment. Furthermore, I believe the conventional interpretation and teaching around "turn the other cheek" is both morally wrong and fundamentally inaccurate. I don't believe that any human being should surrender to harm or abuse. No man should allow another human being to beat him up or behave violently or inhumanely toward him without doing two things: first, defending himself, and second, getting the aggressor off of him. Consistent with this, no man should behave passively when he's being harmed by heartless institutions or world systems— whether economic systems, criminal justice systems, or educational systems.

But if "turn the other cheek" doesn't mean that a man should stand there and take it, what does it actually mean?

The first thing that it's essential to understand is that "turn the other cheek" is not an in-the-moment teaching. It is a lifestyle that you should engage in *only after you have stopped the violence, and the threat of aggression is over.* In other words, a man turns the other cheek *only after he is safe.* I believe that a physically, mentally, spiritually, and emotionally healthier interpretation of this passage essentially says: We have bumped heads and you hurt me, but I won't label you "enemy." I forgive you, and I am offering you the opportunity to reconcile and start over. However, so we can begin anew, I will move you to a part of my life where our relationship can work.

Said another way, every single one of us must guard our personal boundaries and borders. Once we are safe—and only after we are safe—we should eventually bury the hatchet, demonstrate the love of God toward the person, and give them another chance. But I want to make sure that I emphasize this: You should not "turn the other cheek" while you are still mad. Give yourself time to heal first. That said, it's important that you make a very serious attempt to forgive. A relationship that can't withstand a misunderstanding or fight is not a relationship at all. We should all make room for other people's humanity just as they make room for ours. However, if too much conflict is taking place, the relationship may need retooling.

I also want you to understand that though you may decide to resume interacting with the person after your disagreement is over, you do not necessarily need to allow the person to be as physically or emotionally close to you as they once were—not unless or until you feel safe. You should only interact with the person to the extent and in a way that the relationship works. In fact, depending upon the nature of the disagreement, it may not be possible for both parties to be their authentic selves and pick up the relationship where it left off. Eventually, your goal should be to get to the point where you can carry out Christianity's foundational principle to love your neighbor as you love yourself; however, you may need to relate differently to do that. You cannot love some people to that degree if you allow them so close that they continue to hurt you. If you do that you are not loving yourself. In fact, you may need to reposition yourself in order to be loving toward them. And if I take it further, there are some instances in which it may be best not to be in a relationship at all. The time may have come to go separate ways, and that's okay. Some relationships are for a reason and others just a season. Only a few will last for our entire lifetime.

So how did Jesus practice the principle "turn the other cheek"? Not long after he ran and hid from the people who tried to stone and kill him, Jesus stated his intent to return to Bethany to raise his dear friend Lazarus, who had died, from the grave. Jesus's disciples were in disbelief. In a nutshell, they said: "A short while ago, the Jews there tried to stone you, and now you are going back?" Only the apostle Thomas was "ride or die" with him; even then, he wasn't optimistic. Thomas said: "Let us also go, that we may die with him."*

Despite the grave danger, Jesus was committed to performing an act of love for his friend. So he returned to Bethany to bring Lazarus back from the dead. When he actually did that he caused even more people to believe he was God's son.

Jesus may have been a skinny guy. But he definitely wasn't a wimp.

Onward, Righteous Warrior

By now, you may be wondering why so many theologians teach "turn the other cheek" in a way that leaves people vulnerable to abuse. That's a very complicated question, but I'll do my best to address what I believe to be part of it. I think it's for the same reason that they also interpret Jesus's fight with the money changers as nonviolent: so they can teach that Jesus was a pacifist, or someone who believed that violence and war can never be justified.

Why would they want to do that? Let me explain.

The Bible consists of sixty-six books in which one oppressed person is addressing other people who are living under oppression. The Gospel, a word whose translation means "Good News," is actually a good word to

---

*John 11:1–16

oppressed people. However, over time—from the Vatican, to evangelical leaders, to people who run schools of religious education, to leaders of religious think tanks and foundations, to prominent ministers—many religious leaders have become very powerful. So has the Christian church as an entity. When I refer to the Church, I'm referring to all Christians, regardless of their denomination. In other words, many of these people and institutions no longer fall or do not consistently fall in the category "oppressed."

For all the good we do—and let's not get it twisted; these organizations often do wonderful work—the Christian church and many of its more powerful leaders are now not so different from the power structure that the oppressed once fought against. So it's no wonder that many ministers and religious leaders leave out oppression when they teach the scriptures, or the Bible's sacred writings. At various points throughout history, the Christian church specifically and Christianity in general has also been used to oppress people. In the United States, the Bible was used to justify the slavery and segregation of people of African descent and dropping the atomic bomb on the people of Japan during World War II. In Europe, the Christian church failed to respond to Hitler's fascist policies that, among other atrocities, led to the mass murder of some six million Jews during World War II. In Africa and Asia, Christian missionaries have helped to justify the plundering of people and resources. In both Catholic and evangelical Protestant churches, we've witnessed allegations of abuse get silenced the world over. All of these atrocities and more have taken place because the traditional Christian church's imperialistic perspective has made room for dominating others. Dictionary.com defines imperialism as "1. the policy of extending the rule or authority of an empire or nation over foreign countries, or of acquiring and holding colonies and dependencies; 2. advocacy of imperial or sovereign interests over the interests of the dependent states."

As a reflection of this position, I believe that many people who interpret the scene in the Temple as nonviolent and teach that Jesus is a pacifist are, perhaps unknowingly, looking through the lens of Christianity's imperialist history. Indeed, dating as far back as the Roman emperor Constantine, wherever Christianity has been the religion of the majority culture, the Church has taught the vanquished people that Jesus was both passive and a pacifist. As a reflection of this, many theologians teach that Jesus was "meek and mild." Perhaps they either don't know or don't take the time to explain that in Greek, one of the original languages of the New Testament, the word *praus,* which is typically translated as "meek," actually means "controlled power." The image of the letter is that of a stallion with a bridle in its mouth, suggesting that his strength is being restrained. In other words, biblical meekness is not the same as weakness. Jesus had power, but "checked" how he used it.

I also find it interesting that many religious teachers promote pacifism even though one of the Bible's primary messages is to encourage oppressed people to develop their relationship with God so that God can help them break free from their bondage. The truth of the matter is that the Church has often had a vested interest in discouraging persecuted people's natural urge to fight back. I think we need to be honest with ourselves: If oppressed people could imagine Jesus fighting back, perhaps they would want to fight back as well. Wouldn't you? I believe that portraying Jesus as a pacifist helps to maintain the status quo between victor and vanquished.

Fortunately, the Bible is a story of redemption. God not only identifies with oppressed people, he also wants them to hear the Good News that Jesus loves them and overcame the world and its oppressive systems—and they can, too. We can, too. However, sometimes we must fight to do it.

So, once Jesus fled, once Jesus stood his ground, and once Jesus died for something greater than himself by taking one for the team, he decided how to respond to violence on a case-by-case basis. That makes Jesus a pragmatist, or someone who takes a commonsense approach to aggression, not a pacifist.

These three principles—run, fight, and take one for the team—form the core of a Christian warrior's code and the foundational set of responses that a righteous man selects from when he is under any type of attack. Instead of succumbing to his emotions, a well-developed man demonstrates self-mastery over them. Having choice allows him to feel empowered, and his communication with God tells him which option to choose.

This is the hallmark of a righteous warrior and the foundation beneath the Code of the Righteous Warrior.

The Code of the Righteous Warrior

Principle 1
Keep your as life simple as possible so you can handle the important things well, survive life's battles, and fulfill your destiny.

Principle 2
Learn to tell the difference between things that are essential, important, interesting, and distracting so you can channel your energy into things that matter, identify and categorize risks quickly, and deal with challenges appropriately.

Principle 3
Anchor yourself in enduring truths rather than in pop culture or fads, then stand on those principles even through difficult times, so you can experience meaning, joy, and success in all circumstances.

Principle 4
To thrive in the middle of challenge and change, take life as it comes, accept both the truth of the situation and your limitations, and handle whatever circumstances life serves you, rather than fantasizing about or ruminating over what could or should have been.

Principle 5

Identify and protect your assets so you can invest in your goals and protect yourself from society's seductive attempts to part you from your money and pull you into narrow definitions of manhood that can limit you and keep you from fulfilling your dreams.

Principle 6

Remain focused on your goals and dreams, always doing what's right even during confusion and difficulty; refuse to allow yourself to become distracted. God will work things out over the long term.

Principle 7

Understand that you must fight both to have a family and to keep your family. This is an uphill battle, but you have the tools to turn the fight.

Principle 8

Come to terms with your weaknesses and imperfections, work on them, live in the tension of their existence, and stay engaged in the fight even when you're hurt—it's possible to live your best life both with and because of your shortcomings, heartbreaks, and pain.

Principle 9

Commit to reaching a high enough level of development that you fight for others to enjoy the same rights, privileges, and opportunities that you want for yourself and your loved ones.

Principle 10

Persevere and strive for excellence even during the difficult, exhausting, and unfair phases of your life—you will obtain results that men who give up early do not know are possible and cannot access.

PART TWO

Keep It Simple

Keep your as life simple as possible so you can handle the important things well, survive life's battles, and fulfill your destiny.

WE FLEW IN a thirteen-seat Cessna Caravan about 150 feet above the canopy of the Amazon rain forest. It was midafternoon. The deep green trees stretched from horizon to horizon. I felt very small and insignificant by comparison—the humbling kind of feeling my soul desperately needed. Earlier that morning, back in Philadelphia, I had kissed my wife and two daughters good-bye. Then the fellas and I had flown from Philly to Dallas, and from Dallas to Georgetown, Guyana, a country that is located along the northern coast of South America. Now we were flying out to the remote airport where our tour guide would meet us. When our flight had first taken off, we'd been talking a lot of trash. But as the distance between us and modern-day conveniences increased, everyone got very quiet.

This was not the first time Leroy, Jerome, Vernell, Mark, Jerry, and I had left the relative safety of our lives to go on a "man trip" or undertake an adventure. We had begun ten years earlier as a ragtag band of brothers struggling with our weight, high blood pressure, diabetes, ED, depression, and other problems common to middle-aged men. We had steadily gotten more physically fit, over the years participating in things like the Penn Relays, Tough Mudders, Spartan Races, and Navy SEAL Basic Underwater Demolition (BUD/S) training together to challenge ourselves. We'd also studied martial arts; several of us held various black belts. Now we were on the brink of our most difficult test. We would spend ten days in the Amazon, including thirty hours during which each of us would be alone. On a scale of difficulty, this would be a big step up from our other adventures. If something went wrong in the wild, we could get seriously hurt.

Once we landed, a rugged-looking, deeply tanned White man greeted us, wearing the type of brown leather hat you might see on Crocodile Dundee.

"I'm Ian," he said, shaking everyone's hands. "Welcome to the Amazon."

That would be Ian Craddock, the former British Special Forces member who trained Bear Grylls, host of the reality TV show *Man vs. Wild*, the show where Grylls and his film crew get dropped off in a wilderness somewhere in the world and he figures out how to survive. Watching the show had taught me how to save myself if I fell into quicksand, got attacked by an alligator, found myself cornered by a snake, and some other unfortunate circumstances—theoretically, at least. I hoped that I had retained some of what I'd learned.

"Hey, man, how you doing? I'm Alyn," I responded. "Glad to be here."

"We're glad to have you," Ian offered. "This is Derrick and Phillip," he added, gesturing to two men whose appearance I (inaccurately) associated with Mexicans. "They are part of our team and will be our guides." I immediately took to Derrick and Phillip; they were shorter than I am. At five feet eight, I'm often the most vertically challenged guy in the room. Being around short people makes me feel better. I try not to "hate" on them, but some of the guys in our group are tall, muscular, and handsome, and the truth of the matter is: I don't like it.

Ian motioned us into Jeeps, and told us we had to get to base camp before dark. Once we arrived Derrick and Phillip showed us to our cabins: thatched huts a lot like those on *Gilligan's Island*, the TV show I'd watched as a kid. Each hut had a bed, a mosquito net, and a bathroom. The mosquito net would be critical. I'd gotten my shots but was afraid of malaria and yellow fever—and I didn't want to be itching and scratching all night.

As we unpacked, Derrick and Phillip cooked our dinner over an open fire. We'd been provided a list of gear to bring: a first-aid kit, a head torch, mosquito repellent, clothes, a sun hat, jungle boots. A knife hadn't been on our list, but I was really excited about using my khukuri, a curved-bladed Nepalese machete I'd brought along that can serve both as a weapon and a tool. I have been fascinated by knives ever since I was a Boy Scout. I own Bowie knives, switchblades, swords, a Rambo knife that has been signed by Sylvester Stallone, and a sword like the Green Destiny in *Crouching Tiger, Hidden Dragon*. Whenever I travel internationally, I buy the knife that comes from that region.

My khukuri was one of my prized possessions, and in the weeks leading up to the trip, I'd let all the guys know it. "I'm bringing my own knife, I don't need their machete," I'd boasted. I'd even brought my khukuri to church so the guys could see it. I'd told them the history of the knife and the story of where I'd bought it. I'd joked about how nobody better mess with me or I'd slice and dice them—like one of those ginsu knives you used to see infomercials for—because every now and then every guy has to talk a bit of trash. And because I often get catered to while doing my job, I had the need to remind them that I'm not the dainty preacher type. Of course, none of the fellas really cared, so I'd just bring it up for laughs.

After unpacking and spraying ourselves with mosquito repellent three layers thick, we joined Derrick and Phillip for a dinner of fish and some kind of goo. After you've gone on a few extreme trips, you learn to eat just about anything. As the sun went down, and we talked about our lives, Derrick and Phillip told us that they were members of the Macushi, people indigenous to the region. The Macushi were *baaad!* Back when European settlers had tried to enslave them, the Macushi had fought back with poisonous darts projected through blowpipes, and other exotic weapons I'd only seen in the movies. My mind drifted to a few people back home I wouldn't mind blowing poisonous dart at. If I got lucky, maybe Derrick and Phillip would teach me.

Once we wrapped up our meal, they laid out the agenda for our trip. We would spend several days living close together learning various survival skills. Ultimately, we would separate and fend for ourselves for almost three days.

"I suggest you get to bed early," Ian told us. "We will get up at sunrise and head into the Amazon."

Back in my cabin, I inspected my mosquito net for holes, placed my khukuri on my nightstand, applied more bug repellent, then climbed into bed with my clothes on. I tucked the edges of the mosquito net beneath my mattress to secure the perimeter. Then I thanked God for the day and our safe travels, prayed for my family back home, and closed my eyes, expecting to conk out. But I found it very hard to relax. It might have been my imagination, but I kept hearing mosquitoes buzzing. I even started itching as though they were biting me. It took me a while to calm down and feel comfortable.

Just when I started to doze off, I heard a roar so loud that I thought it was inside my hut. *What the heck is that?* I yelled to no one in particular, reaching for my khukuri, sitting up, and doing my best not to wet my pants.

"Don't worry, they're just howler monkeys," came a measured response.

"That wasn't a howl, that was a roar!" I yelled. The other guys started speculating that it might have been a big cat.

"We have a lot of howler monkeys around here," the voice calmly told us. "Don't worry, they're harmless."

"You should have told us that before we got into bed," I said, with a little edge in my voice. I hoped he was right; they sounded like lions to me. Thank goodness, I didn't have high blood pressure; I might have had a stroke.

Then it started. "Hey, Alyn, I hope you have a spare pair of underwear . . ." Now that they knew we were safe, everybody had jokes.

Eventually I fell asleep.

The following morning, we were awakened before dawn.

"You will only need four items in the rain forest: a canteen, some io-dine, the means to make a fire, and a machete," Ian instructed as we ate breakfast. "The jungle contains everything else you'll need. When we set up our campsite, we are going to teach you how to identify those things."

We'd need the canteen, obviously, to carry water. I already knew from being in the military that you can put three drops of iodine into almost any water and after three minutes it will be safe to drink, though it may not taste like Fiji Water. We would use flint to make sparks, and cotton to catch the sparks so we could start a fire. Just before we set off, they handed out our machetes.

"Thanks, but I have a knife of my own," I said, showing off my khu-kuri.

"That's a nice knife, but you really need this machete."

"You can hang on to that," I said. "I'm cool."

"I strongly suggest that you take a machete," Ian said.

"Thanks, but I'm good."

"Okay, if you say so."

After we loaded up our knapsacks, we trekked through the jungle for about an hour. When we finally reached the area where we would camp, Derrick and Phillip showed us how to identify the four trees we'd each need to set up our hammocks. They wanted us to position ourselves about thirty feet apart—close enough to hear each other, but not right on top of each other. I found my four trees and staked out the spot where I would sleep. Then I pulled out my khukuri and admired the menacing curve of its blade with five holes drilled through it. I'd bought a *bad* knife! And be-cause I had a *bad* knife, I figured I'd start with the biggest tree first.

I drew back my arm, then swung it toward the tree, imagining how cleanly it would make its first cut. The knife felt light and aerodynamic as it sliced through the air. Then it hit the tree trunk.

Clunk!

Huh?

The khukuri's exquisite handle remained in my hand, but the blade was laying on the ground.

What the . . . !?

I picked up my blade and tried to put my knife back together. No luck; the blade was broken. I thought back to the guy who had sold me what was suddenly dawning on me was a piece of crap. I was furious—I'd been had! My knife that had been so beautiful in its sheath had turned out to be worthless in the wild. I hoped that no one had seen me. Of course, one of the guys had.

"Check out Alyn's khukuri!" he hollered, barely able to get the words out of his mouth as he doubled over laughing.

I couldn't play it off; the guys all saw me holding one piece in each hand.

"It *broke*?!"

"That's what happens to those little plastic knives you get from McDonald's."

"My daughter's Barbie doll has knives that are stronger than that!"

I was mad at them for laughing at me. But there was nothing I could do but look sheepish and take it. Eventually, I played it off and started laughing so they'd stop and I wouldn't get my feelings too hurt. Needless to say, the jokes didn't stop. It seemed like it took me about an hour to finish what I had started. And the whole time I was sweating and chopping, all of the fellas were grinding me.

So much for my fancy khukuri!

The rain forest had just reminded me of a very important lesson that I also knew to be true in the martial arts and in life: To survive, you don't need a lot of stuff, but the few things you need, you really need. The jungle, as Derrick and Phillip would teach us, would bring us everything else.

Simplicity Is Genius

In a world that measures manhood by things like how much money you make, what kind of ride you drive, how beautiful your woman is, and the size of your flat-screen, it's easy to get caught up in consumerism, materialism, and other mindless distractions. Now, before you think I sound self-righteous, I'll be the first to admit that mindless pursuits can be fun. I enjoy cars; I accumulate chess sets; I own a few guns. And as a knife collector, I have to admit that I accumulated lots of cool points when I was showing off my khukuri and fantasizing with the fellas about how I would use it—until it didn't work and I was literally left holding the handle. It's good to have hobbies and personal interests, and everyone needs a little entertainment and to blow off steam. But diversions and distractions can also complicate life, depending upon how we engage them.

For instance, if we spend time and money on our diversions that we would be better off investing elsewhere, they can interfere with our ability to accomplish things that are really important: getting an education, finding a fulfilling career path, developing an intimate relationship with our partner, raising our children to the best of our ability, and demonstrating leadership in our families, communities, nation, and the world, among other things. As a minister, I know that during quiet moments or within a counseling context, lots of men will confess that they are following the dominant themes and trends in our society or somebody else's script for their life, rather than forging their path forward based on their own goals and dreams. It's not unusual for a guy to pull me aside and tell me that he's doing the right things but in what feels like the wrong way. He may have a respectable or even high-flying career, be a supportive partner, and have an amazing family—the kind of life most guys aspire to—yet more men than you might imagine fantasize about creating a life that would feel more satisfying in their souls. A smaller number of guys seem to do all the wrong things; sadly, some even do them really well.

Indeed, as entertaining as both capitalism and materialism can be, at some point most men become disenchanted with the superficial things. They want their life not merely to look good but also to work for them. Eventually, guys want to know the answers to some of life's deeper questions, like: Why am I alive? What have I been put on this earth to do? What's important and what's not? Why are certain things happening to me? Does God even care what goes on in my life? Though these simple but powerful questions are difficult for any man to handle, the growth and insights that occur as you wrestle with them can transform your entire life.

In no small part because of the failure of my fancy khukuri, in the Amazon I grew to truly appreciate that simplicity is genius. As we struggled to survive in the wilderness, keeping life uncomplicated helped us to focus on the important things, take on the challenges we faced and handle them well, and ultimately complete what we set out to accomplish. By seeking simplicity and clarity a man can find meaning, fulfillment, and joy. This means a righteous warrior must be discerning.

Man vs. Male

Now, as we engage in this conversation, it's important to establish what I mean when I'm talking about manhood. There is a difference between being a man and being a male. Genetically, all it takes to be a male is to have both an X and a Y chromosome. In most states you legally become a man at eighteen or twenty-one years of age. Sociologically, however, you start to become a man when you begin to take responsibility for your life, your loved ones, and the world. Righteous manhood entails a lifelong spiritual journey of becoming more of yourself—more of who you were created to be—and doing the things that you, uniquely, have been put here to do.

You were made to enjoy your journey as it unfolds over the course of your life cycle. Most men's lives take place over several predictable phases.

The late theologian Isaac Green, the former pastor of Central Baptist Church in Pittsburgh, used to say that it takes a man about thirty years to grow up, another thirty years to accumulate knowledge, and the rest of his time to give back what he's discovered. Or as I like to summarize it, first a man learns, then he earns, and later in life he should return to the wisdom he has garnered. Born in 1922 and living until 1999, Reverend Green lived during the greatest economic period in American history. Back then, a man could pretty much guarantee that he would have some place to work, and that if he worked hard this year, he would get a raise the next year. If he lost his job, there was another one to be found. Not only that, he would receive a gold watch and a pension when he retired. Well, that's likely what would have happened if he was White. During that same era, Black men were subject to Jim Crow segregation, which aborted and stunted their possibilities, and many (if not most) Latino, Asian, and Native American males experienced discrimination and exploitation as well. Of course, cradle-to-grave employment is unlikely today no matter your background, and men of color continue to bump up against racism and other obstacles. Nevertheless, the general principle applies: a righteous man learns, earns, and returns.

Another clear way to think about life is to divide it into quarters. My apologies if you're a soccer fan because I will use football for this metaphor. Every team plans to play well during the first quarter and to head into halftime with a lead. In fact, many times, as a fan, you have a good sense of who's going to come out on top by the time the third quarter comes around. If all goes well, during the third quarter, coaches whose teams have a lead often run their best plays in order to maintain their advantage. Ideally, they want to play conservatively during the fourth quarter, holding on to or building upon their advantage until the clock runs out.

So since the average American man's life expectancy is about eighty years—seventy-two if you're Black—let's consider birth to age twenty as the first quarter of life. If you are a caregiver, ideally the game plan for boys and adolescents should include priorities like creating a loving and caring family life, helping him develop a strong identity and self-esteem, establishing high expectations for him academically and holding him accountable for achieving them, helping him figure out his God-given gifts, and discovering what he likes and is good at. If you are a young man living in this season, I encourage you to master your lessons; get a summer job or kick-start a side-hustle if you can; earn your high school diploma; begin to identify and develop relationships with mentors and people who can help you get a foothold in life; start working your way through college, or begin your training and certification if you're not college bound; travel a bit if you can; and start building your résumé. If you can afford to take an internship, or offer to volunteer for someone you admire, go for it! Right now, experience is worth more than money because over the long term, learning who you are, what you're good at, and what you love will be priceless! Generally, you want to lay down the foundation for the rest of your life. In other words, first quarter is a time to put your head in the books, learn about yourself, and explore and seek out experiences, whether or not those experiences come with a paycheck. I cannot emphasize enough the importance of your education, even if your schools are not great and you have to teach yourself things by learning them online. As you move through your adulthood, your knowledge will become like your fire-starter and machete.

From age twenty-one to forty is the second quarter, when all your learning ought to begin to transform itself into the ability to go out into the world, start a life of your own, earn a living, get your business up and running, and perhaps marry, have children, and help provide for your family. The game plan now should be to graduate from college or your certification program and establish a foothold in the world so you can create some momentum. The combination of your education, your hustle, and your work ethic will help increase the size of your canteen. So go out and "slay the dragon" by getting your first real job, working hard and going after what you want in all areas of life, and really stepping fully into your career or area of interest. I cannot recommend strongly enough that you sidestep the temptation to spend everything you earn and, instead, learn how to save and take care of your financial resources so they accumulate over the course of your entire life and into the next generation. If you aspire to have them, start to build your family and perhaps even purchase a house now. Consider somewhere between thirty-five and forty as halftime. Though it may be hard to imagine that your life is likely half over, don't fool yourself! Age thirty-five is the sweet spot of life. If you aren't living a healthy lifestyle already, it's time to make some major adjustments and commit to taking good care of yourself.

The third quarter unfolds between the ages of forty-one and sixty. These tend to be a man's peak earning years, so try to establish yourself accordingly. It's also a time to celebrate the first half of your life; for instance, your children will likely graduate high school, start college, and even begin their own families. But that's not all. Don't be surprised if issues you thought you'd put to bed resurface, giving you the opportunity to consider them from a more mature perspective. It's not unusual during your forties for the choices you made during your twenties to arise again. You may discover that decisions about education, or who you married or had children with, or how well you have taken care of yourself, or who you've made friends with, or the state of your spiritual life arise; old girlfriends may even come back around, and so on. In fact, it's during the forties that decisions we made during our youth tend to become either a blessing or a curse.

The typical male midlife crisis occurs at age forty-four. This is a time when for many men, their identity and self-confidence shift, as the superficial no longer satisfies, some of the deeper questions of life bubble up, and guys start to wonder "Is this all there is?" We all know the stereotype of the man who buys a red sports car, gets a toupee, and ditches his family to run off with a younger woman. And while new cars and affairs are not at all unusual, just as commonly men get bored with their lives, begin to compare themselves to other guys, get depressed, reminisce about the past, regret some of their choices, spend a lot of time in front of the mirror, head back to the gym, get a makeover, worry about their health, and otherwise feel the hands of time's relentless march forward. If we dig into and explore these issues, this period of uncertainty, too, shall pass; if we don't, life is likely to become increasingly painful and dissatisfying. Indeed, the fifties can be particularly satisfying for men who share their knowledge and stories in order to help others. Because by now they have lived long enough that some of their hard work and struggles have yielded results. It's also likely that God has saved them from a difficult situation or two.

Then the time comes when the "slaying the dragon" era is over and many men begin to wrap up their working and child-raising years and slow down and enjoy their senior years. Though Isaac Green's norm of getting a gold watch is increasingly unlikely, ideally, from age sixty on, you want to be putting a metaphorical bow on your life. Whether you're privileged enough to retire and kick back or you've got to continue to "grind," it's time to package some of what you've earned and everything you've learned—the good *and* the bad—and make beauty out of it by pouring it into a younger person and seeding their potential. It's your job to open doors for somebody else just like your parents, mentors, and other elders helped create opportunities for you.

Use this model just as you use the map on the kiosk at the mall. Orient yourself within your life cycle by looking for the "red dot" that identifies "You are here."

Call It a Comeback

But while these standards may provide you with some guidelines and structure, the average man's life doesn't play out like it does in the textbook. Whether a guy was born into a difficult family situation or social context, experiences the death of a parent or other unexpected tragedy, or just makes some bad choices or mistakes, every fella doesn't get early points on the scoreboard and many guys get off to a rough start in life.

For instance, with many public school systems failing to deliver the education they promise, the cost of college sky high, and the crushing weight of student loans, it's increasingly common for men's struggle to get an education to extend through their twenties and even their thirties; for them to experience starts and stops, periods of work and un- and under-employment, to bring children into the world before they are fully able to support them, and so on.

In fact, within our own band of brothers, early challenges were common. Vernell's father experienced a seizure and died when Vernell was just three years old. Though his grandparents rallied around his mom in order to raise him—and they reared him well— his life hasn't been easy.

"After I graduated high school, for a very long time I was lost. School was difficult for me because I'm mechanically inclined and a visual person—if I see somebody else do it, I can do it, too, but I didn't like all the lectures. I also have more than one talent. And school seemed to require me to completely focus on one thing. I didn't have that in me, so I didn't go to college.

"I started out working at the waterfront driving a truck and trailer and a forklift part-time. You had to go down there five thirty, six in the morning and sell yourself. Whether you got hired or not, you had to continually come back. That part wasn't hard, but the work just wasn't paying the bills. So I latched onto other things. I would do second shift driving a tow truck. I was also an exterminator, I did personal training here and there, and I cut hair. At one point I went to restaurant school, so for a while I worked as a cook. But the jobs just paid the bills; nothing more.

"I got married along the way and we had two sons to provide for. Every day, I would get down on my knees and pray for the strength to make it through the day. It just became second nature to 'grind.' I could get paid on a Thursday and be broke on Friday. I was trying my hardest but going nowhere. I thought, 'This is my life. This is just where I'm at.' I believed that was all I was gonna be, I wasn't gonna be anything else, and that was just that. A lot of the people that I went to high school with had gone to college. They took different routes, didn't really have those type of struggles."

Leroy also ran into challenges during his adolescence and early adulthood.

"I was only sixteen when my brother had a car accident. It was his thirty-fourth birthday and he had been drinking and was showing off his new Camaro, which looked like the car in the movie *Smokey and the Bandit*. The glass was out of the roof and he wasn't wearing a seat belt. Somehow, he drove up an embankment and was ejected from the car. One year later my dad died of cancer. That left just me and my mom and two sisters. I was in my senior year of high school but wanted to drop out to provide for them. I had been a serious athlete in several sports. Instead of pursuing those ambitions, which would have taken me away for school, I went to college close to home. My sports career was ruined; I never put a helmet on again. For years I was mad at my dad. I also longed for a man who was a blood relative that I could connect with. Since I didn't have one, I made my own way."

Experiences like these are more common than you think. If this describes your life, know that your hurt can propel you forward rapidly and contribute to your development. We will talk about that more when we discuss Principles 6 and 8, about dealing with life's chaos and playing hurt.

One of my early blunders involved not being serious about school. I'm not proud to admit this, but until I attended seminary, I was a very marginal student. In fact, I have spent some of my adult life compensating for that. I drank and partied during my first year in college. I loved drinking so much that during my first semester I decided to quit the wrestling team so I could party. Not too far down the road that decision led to alcoholism, but I wouldn't understand that until much later. Quitting also deprived me of the opportunity to discover who I could have become athletically.

Thirty years later—well into the third quarter of my life—the decision to throw in the towel still haunts me. To this day I still wonder whether I've maximized my physical potential. Whether a trophy for a national wrestling championship or even an Olympic medal could have been in my trophy case. Sadly, I'll never know. Even in my third quarter, I haven't let wrestling go because I'm still trying to answer the unanswerable.

Though this is not typical, some guys are fortunate enough to turn their slow start or pain early in life into an advantage—Jim Carrey, Shawn Carter (Jay-Z), Woody Harrelson, Shia LaBeouf, Kendrick Lamar, George Lopez, Donnie McClurkin, Marshall Mathers (Eminem), Dylan McDermott, and Mark Wahlberg are among them. So you should know that it's possible. The high trajectory of these men's lives reminds me of what happens when you shoot a bow and arrow. In the sport of archery, the farther the archer draws back the bowstring the more tension he places on it. The more tension he places on the bowstring, the farther and faster the arrow flies. In a similar fashion, the pain and pressure experienced by men who have had a rough start in life can also give them a work ethic, drive, and clarity that men who have lived more comfortable lives tend to lack. Vernell's work ethic, for instance, would put many men's to shame. In other words, the determination and hustle that result from their pain can propel them farther.

So if you have made some mistakes or fallen behind in the first, second, or even third quarter, as discouraged as you may feel right now, please hear me when I beg you not to throw in the towel. If you bring your A game, there is still lots of time left on the clock. No basketball fan is worried when a team led by Steph Curry, Kevin Durant, James Harden, or LeBron James is down fifteen points in the second quarter, even though they face an uphill climb. You are the LeBron of your own life. So, though there may be days when you despair, if you were dealt a bad hand, are a late bloomer, or made mistakes early on, don't give up. Just as in sports, it's not unusual for a team to recover from turnovers and fumbles made during the first half. Slip-ups in the third quarter and beyond? Well, they tend to have more significant consequences. It gets much harder to win when you're making first-quarter mistakes during the second half. There's also less time left on the clock to outlive them. That said, some teams have a reputation for getting off to a slow start, during a game or even the season, then getting it together and earning the win. And comebacks can be the most thrilling and satisfying parts of sport.

Just think about it: Some of the greatest games you've ever watched—the greatest thrills—have been the come-from-behind wins. For instance, many African-American men who are living in their third quarter remember Doug Williams's Super Bowl 22 comeback against John Elway and the Denver Broncos. Williams was the first Black man to play quarterback in a Super Bowl. He found himself down ten points at the start of the second quarter, then scored thirty-five points—the most ever for a single NFL postseason quarter—as he mounted one of the greatest comeback stories in pro football history. And he did it while he was playing against America's sweetheart, John Elway.

Love him or hate him (and the New England Patriots), how about Tom Brady's fourth-quarter comeback in Super Bowl 51? You can't deny that he's a fourth-quarter guy. Give him two minutes and a scare and Tom Brady can win the game. And who can forget the time Tracy McGrady scored thirteen points in thirty-five seconds when the Houston Rockets came back in the final seconds against San Antonio? Or when Reggie Miller scored eight points in nine seconds? Or when the Sacramento Kings came back thirty-five points against the Chicago Bulls in 2009? Or in 1996, when the Utah Jazz came back from thirty-six points behind the Denver Nuggets—the greatest NBA comeback of all time? And of course, I'll never forget when LeBron James and my hometown team the Cleveland Cavaliers came back from 3–1 down against Steph Curry and the Golden State Warriors in the 2016 NBA Finals. Later on, I will tell you why LeBron is not only one of my favorite athletes, but why I also consider him a righteous warrior.

As you will learn about Vernell and some of the other fellas, even if a man has fallen behind, if he steadily chips away at his deficit—or finds his stride and goes on a run or strings together several bursts of progress—he can live a very fulfilling and rewarding life. A regular guy can rally and, in the process, become a person not only who experiences the victory but who also is admired and inspires others. You can find purpose and satisfaction as you put points on the board. Any man can find his most memorable victories and greatest joy in the comeback fight.

Keep It Simple, Son

Whether you're off to a great start or mounting a comeback, it's important to focus your time and resources upon what's essential and important. In the military we used the acronym KISS, short for "keep it simple, stupid." I prefer the more righteous way of saying this: "Keep it simple, son." In this context, "simple" merely means that you build your life upon basics. It may sound simple and sophomoric, but this is one of the most important principles in life.

Whether or not you recognized it, you have already seen KISS in action. Football players master fundamentals related to factors like speed, quickness, agility, balance, and strength. Musicians learn notes, major and minor scales, melodies and harmonies. And in the Amazon, you carry your canteen, iodine, flint, cotton, and, yes, a machete. These are the basics, and only if you master them can you build more complex things on top of them.

One of the easiest ways to keep your life simple is to resist the temptation to organize it around material possessions. As my broken khukuri reminded me, men often relate to the world through stuff—our title, our salary, our electronics, our car, our home, and so on. But we are not our stuff. In fact, every physical aspect of life will change: Our job and title will change; we will relocate to a different home or even city; at some point, almost all of us will replace a car. That's because things come and go. They go out of date, we lose interest, or we misplace and even lose them. Possessions also change in value as well as in how we value them. Think about it: Could you even give away an old flip phone (if you could even find one)? Not likely. But I'm sure you remember back in the day when everyone had to have one. Your relationship to your body will change as well. So though I am a big proponent of physical fitness, most of us will probably be better off not defining ourselves by how many heads turn when we walk into a room, the number of push-ups we can do, or whether or not we can dunk. The guy who defines himself by his physicality sets himself up to experience a tough time at midlife, as his hair thins and grays, his belly grows, his stroke count declines, or he blows out his ACL. At that point he is going to be left asking: "Who am I now if I don't turn heads in the same way? I'm not as strong as I was, and don't possess the same physical stamina as I once did."

You can cut through all the nonsense by following a strategy from management guru Stephen Covey: Keep the main thing the main thing. In other words, organize your life around principles that can stand the test of time. As you learn each principle of the Code of the Righteous Warrior, I encourage you to explore two complementary lines of thought that can help to answer the difficult questions that most men must face. I learned the first from Dr. G. Peter Schreck, a professor at Eastern Baptist Theological Seminary (now Palmer Theological Seminary) in Philadelphia. The second model is my own.

Dr. Schreck suggests that a well-developed person regularly reflects upon questions related to four concepts: Identity, Industry, Intimacy, and Integrity. When Dr. Schreck talks about Identity, he's referring to the human quest to answer the question: Who am I? When he mentions Industry he means we should also explore: What productivity do I contribute to the world? Questions involving Intimacy ask: Who loves me and matters in my life? And explorations of Integrity investigate: How can I make sense of everything that happens to me during my life?

I call my model the 5Ps of Personhood. The 5Ps come from the story of Adam and Eve, which is found in the Bible within the Book of Genesis.* Whether you take the story of Adam and Eve literally or interpret it as a metaphor, biblically Adam was the original man. As I have attempted to understand through my studies what God meant in the beginning, this text has helped me gain clarity about things that were true about Adam before Eve came into the picture. I believe that men today can learn from the experience of Adam, the original man.

Four things were true about Adam before God created Eve, the first woman, to be his partner. God had breathed Power into his nostrils in order to bring him to life. God had also given Adam a Place within which to fulfill his destiny (the Garden of Eden), a Purpose for his life (working the Garden), and specific Parameters to live within (don't eat the fruit of the Tree of Life). Eve became the fifth P, his Partner. Consistent with this, over the course of his life, a righteous man should engage in a dialogue about his Power, Place, Purpose, Parameters, and his Partner. I recommend that you do this by considering the following questions:

1. What is the Source of my Power and the state of my relationship with my Source?

2. Where is my Place in the world?

3. What is my Purpose while I'm living on earth?

4. What Parameters do I need to observe and what is off limits to me?

5. Who is my ideal Partner?

The answers you uncover will help you to anchor your life in substance and meaning while at the same time keeping it uncomplicated. Reflecting upon these questions and the issues they raise will help you focus on what's important and live in a way that helps your daily existence make sense. Indeed, if your life is anything like my life, you don't have time to do everything that crosses your mind, captures your attention, or lands in your

*Genesis 2:7–3:22

in-box. Though it may seem on paper as though you have a lot of time, the 168 hours in every week fly by very fast. At least 40 of them you will probably spend doing some form of work; another 40 or so you will likely spend sleeping. That leaves about 88 waking hours—and that includes things like doing the laundry, getting ready for work, commuting, going to the grocery story, making dinner, and other chores. Days, months, and even years can fly by if you aren't thoughtful about how you spend them. If you focus on what's important, you are far more likely to get the results you want in your life. And as more seasoned men will tell you, time seems to speed by faster and faster with age. Remember that childhood car trip that you thought would never end—you know, the one where your sibling kept touching you? Time doesn't move anywhere near that slowly as you grow older.

Time management is one of Jerry's strong suits. A soldier in the U.S. Army for thirty-one years, his training helps him to organize his life, make the most out of his time, and keep things simple.

"In the military, discipline is the lifestyle everything revolves around," he says. "The order and structure make life simpler. We're trained to prepare on the front end to prevent failure on the back end. They teach us that 'prior planning prevents piss-poor performance.' For instance, I have to go to work tomorrow, so to prevent all the confusion, rushing, and stress, I prepare by laying my stuff out the night before. I also think through the next day. That way, I can rest in peace knowing that I'm prepared.

"In the military mind-set, punctuality is key. If the mission requires getting there at nine thirty, someone that you have to relieve is waiting. If you arrive at nine thirty-two, that person could be dead. If you get there at nine twenty-nine, they're safe. Military life is punctual down to the millisecond. If you don't get there, they're dead because you were late."

Jerry is clear about what's important to him and how he manages his time.

As society tries to distract you with its endless options, remember that everything people try to persuade you to do and that companies want to sell you is not necessarily good for you. Constantly ask yourself this simplifying question: "Is this thing or idea that someone's pushing going to develop me or distract me?" The quicker you differentiate between what's essential, what's important, what's interesting, and what's foolishness, the easier it will be to choose among your options, build a life that makes sense, and achieve outcomes you can feel proud of.

An additional strategy to keep your life simple is to sort it into boxes or categories that help it make sense. I organize the vast majority of my life into what I call the five Ms: Manhood, Marriage, Ministry, Music, and Martial arts. These five Ms inform my life in that order of priority. For instance, I'm consistently asking questions like, "If I make this decision right now, what does this mean for me as a man?" The next question I ask is, "What impact would it have on my marriage?" I put my marriage second because I can't have a good marriage if I'm not a good man. My marriage comes before my ministry because my ministry is informed by my marriage. After my ministry, I enjoy and engage in music. My martial arts and survival activities come last. If a thing doesn't fall into one of these five categories, I probably won't do it—because a man can't do everything. Making certain decisions precludes other decisions. Choosing this means I won't be able to do that. And at some point, life is going to come back and ask, "Are you sure you want to leave this aspect of me unfinished?" It's important to make sure that this doesn't happen with the deep stuff.

Make the Connection

The Schreck and the 5Ps of Personhood questions can help you identify where you are today and create a plan going forward. I suggest that you start wherever you are, then ask yourself the same questions again, periodically. To keep things simple, you might want to develop a monthly or quarterly or annual practice of reexamining them, reviewing them on the same day of the month, quarter, or year. The sooner you start to ask these questions, the sooner you will be able to make the adjustments that allow you to live on your terms, discover who you were created to be, and experience the joy and satisfaction that come from becoming your true self.

As you reflect on the questions in each principle, I suggest that you write your observations in a journal. Pay attention to the conclusions you come to, the ideas that seem important, and additional issues that may arise, like:

+ What kinds of things do I feel passionate about?

+ What in this world do I really feel called to do?

+ Who will engage in my passions with me?

+ What will torment me if I don't get it done during my life?

+ What can I live with not accomplishing at all?

As you engage with questions like these, allow yourself to let go of the superficial things in life and distractions you don't really care about. Releasing them will free you to home in on your true self. So I dare you—no, I double-dare you—right now to carve out a few minutes of time to start thinking about who you are and what kinds of things are important to you. All you have to do is grab a pen and a piece of paper and take down some notes. Just write about whatever comes to your mind, no matter how uncertain or unclear your thoughts are, or how unlikely you think your dream is. Your thoughts will get sharper over time. Eventually you will cut straight to the chase.

I suggest that you start to ask questions like these no matter what stage of life you're in. The younger you are when you start exploring them, the earlier in life you are likely to figure out which of the many possible moves you can make will satisfy you most. That, in turn, will tell you how to focus your time and energy during the first two quarters of your life. Middle-aged guys and men on the back end of life should consider the same set of questions from their vantage point further down life's trail. The questions remain the same; however, the angle a man approaches them from changes. In other words, as he thinks about his Purpose a young man may ask: "What do I want to be in my life?" A middle-aged fellow considering that same question might approach it from the standpoint "What am I doing with my life?" While a mature man might ask, "What have I done with my life?" In that sense, both Millennials and Baby Boomers can be working on the same set of questions, but from their respective positions at the front and back end of life. The question "What will I be?" transforms to "What did I do?" or "Why did I do it?" as a man journeys across his life cycle. Wrestling with the answers not only helps the righteous man follow his spiritual path, it also positions him to course correct by focusing him in on the most important factors in life. The questions also create opportunities for men—from Millennials to Baby Boomers—to connect with each other. They are great questions for fathers to share with their sons, grandfathers with grandsons, mentors with mentees, and so on.

Conversely, guys who don't engage in this type of introspection—or who ignore the answers—will likely run headlong into heartbreak and frustration, as their actions (or lack of them) come back to haunt them. How do I know? Because I have experienced this with my regrets about quitting wrestling. The same type of frustration is likely to occur when we make career and relationship choices for the wrong reasons. Both can lead to heartbreak and dissatisfaction down the line. I can't tell you how many mature men who have not engaged with these types of questions find themselves wondering "What does joy feel like?" or "How can I change careers so I can experience fulfillment?" or "How can I get out of this marriage so I can just be happy?" The clarity you will create just by reflecting upon these questions can lead you to experience life very abundantly.

Just as a canteen, iodine, a fire-starter, and a machete are all we needed to survive in the wild, simple questions such as those we've been asking will help you lay the foundation for a powerful and purposeful life.

Distinguish Important from Interesting

Learn to tell the difference between things that are essential,
important, interesting, and distracting, so you can channel
your energy into things that matter, identify and categorize
risks quickly, and deal with challenges appropriately.

ONE YEAR DURING the middle of April, I stood in the infield of the track at Delaware State University with a few of the fellas. As our first foray back into getting in shape, we'd decided that we would run a 4x100 Master's race at the Penn Relays, the world's largest track-and-field event. We'd been training with a gentleman who attends our church who had been preparing to run in the 1980 Summer Olympics, which the United States boycotted to protest the Soviet invasion of Afghanistan. In order to participate in the meet, we had to run a qualifying time in an open track event, so we'd signed up for a meet at Delaware State.

There was no one on our team under the age of forty. And we'd assumed that our heat would require us to compete against other men. It wasn't until we walked out onto the track that we realized that all the lanes were filled with adolescents. The only men out there were the age of our children. All of them were wearing their college colors. They had the latest shoes with laces that matched their fresh gear. Suddenly realizing what we were up against and what was likely to happen to us, we took our marks, got set, and then the starter's gun went off. The kids took off out of the blocks like rabbits. It looked like we were running in slow motion; I think I might actually have run backwards. We were the tortoise and they were the hare. At the end of our heat, the kids turned in times somewhere around forty-two seconds. We ran around a forty-eight. A six-second differential is a lifetime in track. In short, they'd smoked us!

But at the end of the race, while we were doubled over catching our breath and wondering if anyone was going to have to call 911 for us, the referees began to confer with each other. Then a surprising thing happened. Apparently, the young men had committed all sorts of violations— some had strayed out of their lane, one team had dropped the baton during a handoff, another had passed the stick outside of the changeover box. Suddenly, we were declared the winner! Needless to say, we were in shock. We were not declared the winner because of our times, mind you; we had come in dead last. Our team was declared the winner because we had run the race right. Intentionally or not, the kids had cut corners.

Once all the dust had settled, we could see that we had taken better care of what mattered—in this case, things like passing the stick in the allowed zone and staying in our lane. So though we might not have looked the part, we'd beaten the young whippersnappers.

Our heat reminded us about how important it is to focus your attention on the things that matter, handle first things first, and prioritize the immediate threats that face you.

Important vs. Interesting

Life can be very demanding and unfold in unexpected ways. As a well-known passage of scripture instructs us: The fastest runner doesn't always win every race, the strongest man isn't always victorious in battle, smart people can find themselves hungry and living without, and the most educated people don't always lead successful lives or become wealthy. Time and chance happen to everyone,* as we experienced during our race.

---

*Ecclesiastes 9:11.

So, with many unexpected things bound to happen, in order for a man to get what he wants out of life, it's important that he has a method for deciding what's essential—a technique to help him prioritize what he *must* accomplish over what would be *nice* to do. A man needs a systematic way to consider his options so the results he gets in his life are running in the same direction as his desires. A way to distinguish between the importance of practicing strong handoffs versus going to the mall so he can sport sweet sneakers. To do that a righteous warrior must focus.

Whenever you weigh the significance of an object or situation—whether decisions at work or which event to attend: one child's soccer practice or the other's school play—I urge you to take the time to reflect upon four things. Ask yourself:

+ Is this essential to my life?

+ Is it important to me?

+ Is it just interesting?

+ Is it merely a distraction?

Distinguishing between these four levels of an item or activity's significance will help you determine how to prioritize and bring order to your life.

But how do you determine something's significance? My father always told me to handle first things first. In other words, take care of the essential stuff before you turn your attention to anything else. You know whether to label something essential when, if you don't do it, something else will fall apart. Things like getting to work on time or even early, paying your taxes, staying current on your rent or mortgage, keeping your car tuned up, and so on—these are examples of essential activities.

Label an item important if meaningful consequences would come of your actions (or inaction), though your world won't come to an end. If it needs to get done, and is in your important box, you may not have to be the person who has to do it. You might delegate to a subordinate at work, or ask your partner, children, or another family member, for instance. The lawn needs to get cut, but you might give your teenage son the responsibility of mowing it.

Put an item in the interesting box if it captures your attention, is nice to know, or adds to your body of knowledge without measurably improving your life. Interesting things tend not to be closely connected to your Purpose and you have to watch out for them because they may cause you to stray out of your lane. (We'll dig more deeply into Purpose in Principle 3.) In fact, you won't miss them if they're not there, and if you don't do them, life will still go on. Unless you are a professional working in these industries, the latest movie, TV show, fashion, or model of car is probably nowhere as important as marketers want you to believe.

Distracting things? Well, these can range from items or activities that waste your time, such as comparing your life to other people's lives on social media or spending weekend after weekend in your man cave. They can also include things that are detrimental to your well-being, like comparing your life to anyone else's or binge-watching TV every weekend. A man on a mission doesn't have time to involve himself in them at all.

One of the most important reasons that it's so important to prioritize is because in a society designed to sidetrack you, it's all too easy to get wrapped up in interesting or even distracting things when the essential and important issues beg your attention. One essential area I witness many men neglecting is taking care of their health. From going to the doctor, to eating healthy foods, to exercising regularly, caring for your well-being should always fall in the "essential" category. I mention this because some of the more toxic aspects of masculine culture—from garden-variety activities like eating thirty-two-ounce steaks, to drinking and drugging at college frat parties, to the dangers involved in extreme sports—put a man's well-being at risk. Each of us has only one body and it's really important that we treat it well. Pretty much everything you have been put here to do has to happen with it and through it. You will also need lots of energy to travel your life's journey and will only be able to make it physically as far as your body will take you. Treating it well by getting six to eight hours of sleep, eating healthy foods, exercising for half an hour or more most days a week, having a relationship with a doctor and receiving regular medical check-ups, and other healthful practices will help.

So even though we live in a culture that makes self-care challenging, no matter your age, I suggest that you start to make choices that will support your body to run life's race with as little illness and physical discomfort as possible. Plus, I want you to know that joy is your birthright. And whether you're eating too much fried food, engaging in too much couch-sitting, or ignoring your doctor's orders, a man's body can only put up with being mistreated for so long. If your health goes, everything you've done to secure your future and that of your family and children is in jeopardy. That's why I encourage you to treat your health as though it is essential.

As someone who has taken charge of his own well-being, I have found it particularly exciting to witness Jerome make major moves to gain control over his well-being.

"I was too heavy, like 370 pounds. I also had a lot of health issues: high blood pressure, high cholesterol, knee problems, arthritis, those kinds of things," he says. "I knew I'd really need to fight to improve my health. I wanted to open up a new chapter in my life, so I reached out to Leroy and Vernell to help me get in shape. A few months earlier, my older brother had passed away. I knew I really needed to get busy, so I started coming to boot camp every Saturday morning and doing everything they told me to do: the push-ups, sit-ups, rolling tires, carrying heavy bags. All of these physical challenges took me out of my comfort zone—because just look at them and look at me: They are Level 8, 9, 10 on the warrior scale; I was nowhere near that.

"At some point, Alyn convinced me to sign up for the Tough Mudder with them, a thirteen-mile-long obstacle course and endurance test where you have to do crazy things like crawl through mud and submerge yourself in a dumpster filled with ice. Some of the guys had done the Tough Mudder before. They encouraged me to do it in my brother's honor and to help me take charge of my health. Those guys look for physical challenges, but up until that point, I had been like, 'Hey, I ain't looking for none.' But they helped me, made room for me, and encouraged me. When I protested, they said, 'You may not work out as much as we do, but you are still part of our crew. You're our brother.' I was grateful that they'd even invited me, knowing that, physically, I'd be the weak link."

With this huge step, Jerome began what would be a years-long process of committing himself to take charge of this essential area of his life.

The principle of taking care of the most pressing matter first also applies to the martial arts. Martial artists are taught to look at a situation, determine what's most important, prioritize, and then deal with the big stuff up front. For instance, if two people were coming at me and one had a stick and the other had a knife, I would deal with the one with the knife first. If one had a knife and the other had a gun, I would disarm the gun, which is the greater threat, even though I know that I would get sliced. Back in the era of the fair fight—in other words, before so many men were walking around with guns and feeling so afraid and quick to use them—if you were being bullied you were taught that the only way to end it was to take on the biggest, baddest bully. You'd gain nothing from fighting the little one in the crew, even if you beat him. But if you fought back against the "big dog," you could lose the fight yet still come out being respected—all you had to do was land at least one solid punch. Now, just to be clear: This is not a strategy I recommend, especially since people no longer fight fair and they sometimes pull out or come back with a gun. I share it only to make a point: In life, as in a fight, some things fall in place or even go away after the big thing has been handled. And with the big stuff out of the way, the small stuff is often manageable.

Indeed, righteous manhood involves having the ability to distinguish between what's essential, important, interesting, and distracting or foolish. One way to distinguish between essential and foolish things is to explore the questions in the Schreck and 5P models. Let's start with the first question in each rubric: "Who am I?" and "What is the source of my Power?"

Who Am I?

If you ask the average guy to tell you about himself, chances are he'll rattle off his job title, tell you where he works and maybe even where he lives—basically, he'll feed you a bunch of data. The more conversations I have with men, the more deeply I understand how many of us believe that things like the family we were born into, the neighborhood we grew up in, the college we attended, or what organizations we've joined are what make us important. Others think we are significant because of how much money we have or the kind of car we drive. Still others believe we are relevant because of how good we look, how much we can lift, or the size of our pecs. But while all of this may be interesting, none of it tells us anything essential about the Identity of any man, for a righteous man's existence is about more than his looks, what's on his business card, or how he makes a living. Indeed, it is entirely possible to have a meaningful life, whether a man has any of these things or not.

I'd like you to consider that a man's spiritual Identity forms the foundation of a productive, fulfilling, and joyful life. What do I mean by spiritual Identity? Just as you have a physical identity—a name, an appearance, a gender, a race, a family that you're from, a community—you have an Identity spiritually as well. Everything that we can see in the physical world started out as something invisible. For instance, where did you come from? Your parents, for sure. Before that you were a sperm and an egg, but even then, each of them only contained half of you. And if we peel back another layer, what were you before that? Spirit, which is invisible. The physical book or iPad or Kindle you're reading these pages on started out as an idea first, before anyone ever put pen to paper. So did the chair you're sitting on, the building you live in, the job you go to, the schools you attended. You name the thing, and if you trace it back far enough, I guarantee you it started invisibly. Some scientists believe that everything begins with quarks; other researchers have reached the same conclusion that I have: that everything ultimately starts with God. Indeed, I believe that quarks are just part of how God works. Just as God breathed into Adam, God breathed this Spirit into quarks and into you. God's Spirit is the source of your Power. And no matter your name or what people you're from, you are first a child of God. That is your spiritual Identity. Even if you don't think of yourself as religious or Christian, I'd like you to consider this Identity. One of the reasons that it's really important is because a man who thinks of himself as God's child might imagine himself as having a more important reason for being than he might if he thinks of himself as merely being the product of two imperfect parents or a fallible family or community.

Now, what you believe about God may differ from what I believe about God. But all of us were created by a force greater than ourselves. I believe that we were all created in the spiritual image of God. That means our highest qualities are God's qualities: love, joy, light, peace, power, and so on. At your best, this is who you are. So no matter your circumstance or mistakes, you are divinely made. If we could look at you on a spiritual level, we'd see God's fingerprints all over you. So no matter what the media tells you about yourself, your beauty is not defined by the six-pack you'll see on the cover of *Men's Health* or the cool you'll uncover in *GQ*. Your worth is not found in your bank account. Your significance is not connected to your family name, where you grew up, or what fraternity or social/civic organization you're in. Every human being deserves love and respect, though not because we have done something to earn it but merely because all of us are divine creations. It's also important to me that you know that, as God's child, you have been endowed with great possibilities. Even if your daddy and mama messed up or messed you up, you don't have to go through your parents to access your destiny.

All these wonderful things are true about you; however, each of us also was born with some sort of imperfection, or "brokenness." Some babies arrive with obvious physical problems or deformities. Perhaps they were born prematurely or with a hole in their heart or spina bifida. Others of us arrive with a genetic predisposition toward things like anxiety, a hot temper, fearfulness, depression, shyness, heart disease, diabetes, prostate cancer—the list is endless. Many of these things are invisible and only reveal themselves over time. Yet they, too, are part of who you are. The human genome project has helped me understand that I was born with a gene that predisposes me to alcoholism. The neurotransmitter dopamine in my brain doesn't release in the same way it does in others' bodies. But back when I was drinking, when I would put alcohol into my system, I'd go from introverted (and sometimes even scared and withdrawn) to talkative, playful, fun, and extroverted. When the buzz was over, my body would tell me to get more—and to not stop. Other people can drink and they can stop. That gene is part of my brokenness.

Unfortunately, and to our great detriment, we live in a world that separates us from having a spiritual understanding of ourselves, which is why I feel so strongly that learning who you are spiritually is a particularly important part of a righteous man's life. Indeed, a man's quest for spiritual understanding will give him tremendous Power. Understanding your spiritual Identity requires having the courage and discipline to look within oneself. Though lots of guys demonstrate discipline at work, in their financial life, at the gym, and in other traditionally masculine areas, most of us aren't good at dealing with touchy-feely things, our emotions and spirituality among them. Not enough of us have seen other men be a role model to a man's spiritual walk, especially in a conventionally masculine way. As a result, lots of us mistakenly believe that spiritual things are for women. We feel weird when someone asks us to talk about our feelings or our spirituality. But limiting ourselves in those areas deprives us from fully understanding ourselves, accessing our best lives, and enjoying and displaying our greatest strengths.

Now, if you were fortunate enough to have attended college, you may remember Psychology 101, that class that had five hundred people in it. In Psych 101 one of the most important things discussed was the nature versus nurture debate. Psychologists can't figure out how much of who we are is predetermined by nature and how much is determined by what happens to us during our life. That's because we are all a composite of the stuff that we arrived here preloaded with, the good stuff that we experience in life, and the battles with our brokenness. To use a martial arts analogy, all of these factors affect who you are and generate the Power, or the fist, with which you hit the world.

For example, I am a product of factors that include the natural gifts of a wonderful singing voice and natural affinity toward instruments and music, as well as the parenting of my mother and father, my fight with alcoholism, and the challenges and victories I've experienced during my life and my ministry. All of these inform who I am as a pastor, up to and including how I preach each weekend. And while I am a loving, giving, and intelligent person, it is also true that my alcoholism can create narcissism, selfishness, and manipulativeness and cause me to be overly emotional. Good and bad, right and wrong, these are some things that I know to be true about me. Not all of them honor God or reflect my best self, but if I'm honest I have to admit they do inform who I am. At this point in my life, I am able to acknowledge these things. (Trust me when I tell you that I wasn't always able to.) In other words, all of us are a combination of some good stuff and some bad stuff, some dust and some Divine, and they come together to make us who we are.

Since every man has an invisible spiritual self, I believe that his relationship to this world should begin with taking care of that part of himself. Because your spiritual side is the source of your Power, it's important to take care of it first, even though you can't see it. I'd like you to think of the idea of spiritual self-care as being a lot like when you're on an airplane and the flight attendant tells you that in case of an emergency, you should put your own oxygen mask on first. This so-called airplane rule helps make sure that you're alive and in good enough shape to support the people who depend on you.

Locked and Loaded

Your life is not an accident; your existence is not happenstance. I believe there is an intelligent design to the universe and a moral underpinning to that design.

Why do the planets circle the sun and the tides rise and fall? The forces that make these and other miracles of the cosmos and nature take place are so great that no man can explain them. In similar fashion, a Creator much greater than any human being called you into existence. You needed your parents' DNA and to be born on a certain date and time and into a particular social situation that would inform your walk on this earth. But it doesn't matter what your mother and father or your circumstances in life are like—whether you are rich or poor, Black or White, religious or not. You were born right on time, even if your parents weren't expecting you.

Although your mother and your father conceived and gave birth to you, spiritually, both the seeds of your destiny and the characteristics you will need to carry it out had been invisibly planted inside of you long before you were born. You will learn new information and build additional skills as you move forward though life, but some of your traits arrived locked and loaded, previously installed as part of your package. These are all parts of your Power. A portion of your spiritual journey involves learning about this Power you've been given to work with and exactly what you should do with it.

Experts as wide-ranging as geneticists, neurologists, and theologians debate exactly which traits came already preloaded in you. For starters, there's your personality, which helps determine the type of person you are and your experience of and in the world. You may be an introvert—a person who recharges by being alone and going within—or an extrovert—who gains energy as he interacts with others. You may rely more on your left brain—the side many people associate with creativity—or your right brain—where logic and intellect reside. You may talk in order to think or you may think before you talk. Some of these attributes are designed right into you.

You have also been endowed with certain passions. Some of those passions are apparent early on and will stay with you throughout your entire life. Indeed, many of the things that excite me today are the same things that excited me when I was a little boy. Back then, I used to get hyped about my dad's work as a minister and I really had fun going to church. The first album I bought was that of a preacher. I would set up my bedroom like a church and preach to my teddy bears. Then my G.I. Joe with the kung-fu grip would come forward after my sermon to get saved. So that's me, but my point is that certain traits are in us from the very beginning. Sometimes life or the people who raise and influence us push us away from them; sometimes life makes us afraid of them. But the sooner and more closely you can connect with them, the more enjoyable your time on earth will be.

Whether you write poetry, hip-hop rhymes, or computer code, you also have certain talents. When I use the word "talent" I'm talking about a natural skill or ability that you possess that others don't and that has been handed down to you genetically through your parents. For instance, you may not carve wood as well as your grandfather, but somehow genetically a baton was passed to you and you have an ability and inclination to work with your hands in a way that other folks cannot. Every man is different and every man unique. But though we are unequal in ability, we are equal in value. And within the gifts that God has given you, your potential is endless. The question is: How much will you explore and develop it?

You also exist within a context. By context I mean the circumstances, conditions, and situation you are born into and will conduct your life's journey within. In other words, the lane you will run in in life, or your world. Your context can include things like your family, where you live, your socioeconomic status, your race, your gender, the traits that are passed down to you—whether your looks, your attitude, or your genetic predisposition to addiction or prostate cancer. Many of us expend a lot of time, resources, and energy buying into the world's norms. But when you accept the world's standards, you spend a lot of time trying to look like or be like another man. This dilutes your natural Power as a unique human being. If the world needed an additional version of that guy, he would have been born an identical twin. So let him be himself and you do you.

Stay in Your Lane

A spiritual journey will unfold in parallel to your physical journey across your life span. In fact, it began when you were born and will end when you die. Consider anything related to your destiny to be essential and or important; most everything else is either merely interesting or a distraction.

This journey is your destiny, the unique assignment every human being has that they and only they can fulfill on earth. Destiny is very different from fate. The word "fate" implies that everything that happens is beyond your control, that your journey is just a coincidence, that your trajectory is mere happenstance. Fate means whatever happens, happens. *Que sera, sera!* What will be, will be. On the other hand, destiny acknowledges the existence of a higher power and a higher plan for your life, a spiritual assignment much bigger than you, but that you are perfect for because you were born to accomplish it. As the old saying goes, destiny means "what God has for me is for me." Your destiny is for you and you alone. It is a full-employment opportunity that you can dedicate your life to. No one can hold you back from completing it. You cannot be laid off, nor will it be automated or sent overseas.

Your spiritual mission will unfold during your journey through life. The further your spiritual trek, the more of it will open itself up to you. Engaging it will make you feel more like yourself than you ever have before. Your destiny also comes with batteries included and whatever else you need to accomplish it. Indeed, you are born with enough Power to carry out your entire life plan; however, it's up to you not to deplete it and it is only allocated one day at a time. So put one foot in front of the other and move forward day by day. However, you only get to experience your destiny if you are aware that it exists. Even then, you have a choice about whether and when and how far to follow it. Sadly, many men live their entire lives searching for meaning and purpose because they do not know that they are born with them, or about the choice they must make in order to engage it fully. Others choose not to follow it at all.

Unfortunately, in our consumer-oriented society, advertising, marketing, and public relations target every man's psyche in the effort to make him feel that he is inadequate so various companies can persuade him to purchase their products. As a result of these forces, many of us don't know the difference between what we truly *need* and what we merely *want*. No wonder we get confused between what is essential and what is important, what is interesting, and what's a distraction. No wonder we fail to prioritize the big stuff so we don't get thrown off track. With a society that presents us with so many distractions, far too many of us never figure out that we were created for and are called to accomplish something significant. Other voices, distractions, temptations, and problems keep us from fulfilling our destiny. And particularly with the existence of social media, other people's accomplishments look so enticing that they, too, can seduce us off our chosen path. However, no man has been given enough Power to follow anyone else's destiny but his own. Indeed, deviating from your spiritual path will drain your battery and diminish your potential. Staying in your lane has tremendous Power, as the fellas and I experienced as we ran our race. It's particularly important not to waste energy on distractions, for they will siphon off your strength.

Rich got drawn off track early on by the fast life, as he explains.

"I came from a very good family, very well off. My parents were stone staunch Christians, married fifty, sixty years. My sisters all went to college and became very successful professionals. I could've gone to any college in the United States, but the street life caught my attention at an early age, and I chose to hang out with hustlers. The big cars, women, the diamonds, and the clothes—they just grabbed ahold of me. Even to this day, I can't figure out why. The guys I grew up with all went on to college, but for some reason I got distracted," he says.

"So I took that path and got introduced to drugs at an early age. I began to use cocaine and marijuana at the age of fourteen, fifteen. It was the early seventies; weed was everywhere. Before long, I got introduced to guys who committed robberies. I wound up robbing banks in different states. By the time I was eighteen, the authorities were looking for me. I was sitting on my parents' front steps when I got caught. The helicopters and police came from everywhere and they snatched me off the street and locked me up."

Although he was sentenced to more than forty years, Rich was blessed to end up serving about thirteen. Still, he lost a significant portion of his life and much of his youth wasting away behind bars.

So while your destiny is sitting there for the taking, God will not lay your destiny in your lap. Not only do you have to choose to step onto your destiny's path, you also have to go out and fulfill it yourself. Whether in your home, your community on the other side of the world, or at the businesses, organizations, institutions, systems, and causes that exist along your way, no society functions on its own. Every society needs righteous people to roll up their sleeves and make the world better by making the unique contribution that only they can. One of the most tragic things I see is that, while every man has a destiny, not every man goes after it. In fact, it is totally possible to miss your destiny altogether. I can't tell you how many fellas I meet who are living beneath their promise. Sadly, far too many men die before they ever started living, as almost happened to Rich.

I find that many men have well-developed gifts but put no spiritual Power behind them; some have become connected spiritually but have been too fearful to develop and share their gifts. Either scenario is a recipe for a lack of productivity and too little joy. Nothing of value in any man's life comes easy. To go after your destiny, you will need to harness all of your Power.

What Motivates You?

If you really want to develop your spiritual Power, I suggest that you get in touch with your spiritual gifts. Though during much of this book I will be spiritual, I am approaching this part of the conversation from an unapologetically Christian standpoint, understanding that for people of other beliefs, this topic may be a subject for debate. Equally likely, you may understand exactly what I'm talking about but just talk about it using different language.

I believe that at their foundation, every human being is endowed with what Christians call a *motivational gift*, or an ability that was given to you by God and that energizes you. You can tap into this gift at any time no matter your religion or belief system. To give you an example, I have always had the ability to stand up in front of a crowd and fire them up to do something and to understand that no matter what they're going through, everything will ultimately be all right. In Christianity, this is known as the spiritual gift of exhortation, a fancy word that means I am good at encouraging people. I believe that gift is best used in ministry; however, during my college days, I also used the same gift in the context of singing and musicality in the blues band I led. In that context, I would "make you want to shout"; however, I'd also tie that gift up with a bunch of alcohol-laden debauchery.

When you operate within your motivational gifts, life is more joyful and easy because you are not only being who you are but also the best of who you are. When you are at your best, you are also your most attractive, inside and out. So you don't have to go get it, life is naturally drawn to you. In fact, when you are operating within your gifts, you embody beauty in the Afrocentric sense of the word—you are beautiful not because you look good, but because you *are* good. The members of a healthy family or community demonstrate a variety of gifts, since human beings are not the same. Consequently, you cannot have a community if everyone has the same gift or is coerced, forced, or manipulated into behaving in the same way. We should be interdependent but not the same person. There are seven motivational gifts: prophecy, serving, teaching, giving, organizing, mercy, and exhorting. You can google them to learn more about them.

God also endows us with *miraculous gifts*; however, we only receive them in the moment that we need them. Our miraculous gifts appear in the instant another person needs them from us. Let me give you a sense of what I'm talking about. Once, a man came up to me after I led a Bible study. "I have been thinking about committing suicide," he told me. "I came to Bible study every Tuesday for one year with the thought in my mind that you needed to give me a reason to not kill myself that week. For one solid year, on Tuesdays, you gave me a reason to live one more week. You gave me what I needed to keep living."

Now, I was stunned when he told me that. I didn't even know the man, much less that he was counting on something I said to give him a reason to stay alive. Though I hadn't known what was going on, what happened week to week was miraculous. That is an example of a miraculous gift. On a different occasion, a woman in Bible study shared that her baby had been diagnosed with a hole in its heart. We laid our hands on the child—a spiritual hands-on healing practice—and prayed. When the woman took her child to the hospital, the child no longer had a hole in his heart. That was a miracle also. Sadly, miracles don't often repeat themselves. When my two-and-a-half-year-old nephew, Quinn, developed meningitis, I asked, "God, the same way you raised up the other child, please raise up Quinn." We laid our hands upon Quinn and prayed. Nothing happened. Tragically, Quinn passed away. Though for a brief moment, he brightened our lives, when Quinn went on home we were heartbroken. Understanding, exploring, and using your gifts will give you tremendous Power. Exploring them can also help you get comfortable with what your gifts are not, allowing you to gain clarity around both who you are and who you're not and what's essential or important versus interesting or a distraction in your life.

Though many people seem to take their gifts and talents for granted, I can't impress upon you enough how important it is to take care of them. I've seen many people who have amazing abilities neglect to safeguard or develop them; I've watched others allow them to weaken. I will not name any names, but we can all think of plenty of public figures who have squandered their abilities or ruined them by living recklessly. Think of your gifts and talents as being a lot like your muscles: As you practice using them, they become stronger; if you don't use them, over time they will atrophy and you may even lose them. World systems, including capitalism— whose primary concern is transforming people into consumers—will attempt to strip you of your gifts in an effort to rob you of your innate spiritual identity. In its place, a company will attempt to convince you that you need to purchase their product and create a false identity as defined by them. This attempt to rob you of your innate identity goes down a lot like what happens in football. On the gridiron, the player everyone wants to tackle or strip is the one who is holding the ball. In other words, the one who possesses something valuable. Beyond that, what the defender really wants is not the runner but the ball. In similar fashion, the world—from marketers to employers—is trying to strip you of your understanding that you are priceless and possess gifts that are valuable. The hope is that you will, instead, think that you need a particular title, money, cars, women, electronics, cologne, hair gel, and so on in order to be whole.

In football, a runner is taught to make five points of contact with the ball: at the chest, the fingertips, the palm, the bicep, and the forearm. A player who makes contact at all five points is far less likely to fumble than one who holds the ball more loosely. Similarly, I believe that five points of contact will help you develop your spirituality deeply enough that you will be able to survive life's hits and society's attempted "strips" so that you can push through to fulfill your destiny. They are:

1. Prayer—being in conversation with God, or a power greater than yourself every day

2. Praise—giving thanks for and celebrating the good things God does for you

3. Fellowship—developing relationships with other spiritual people

4. Worship—honoring and paying homage to God

5. Service—helping other people.

Finally, as you develop your gifts, it is important to evolve your character simultaneously. Dictionary.com defines character as the mental and moral qualities that are distinctive to you. Your gifts can carry you to wonderful and amazing places; however, a strong character is necessary to keep you there. The righteous man develops both aspects of himself—his gifts and his character—hand in hand.

Getting in touch with your personality, your passion, your talent, your context, and your spiritual gift will not only help you understand who you are, but will also provide the strength you need to walk in your destiny.

Not Your Father's Faith

A man's Power doesn't come from yohimbe, his money, how long he can last sexually, new clothing, or his ability to generate an energy shield out of a video-game enemy's soul. A man generates true Power by developing a rich spiritual life. Getting clear about yourself spiritually is far more important than anything else you can do.

Make no mistake: Strengthening yourself spiritually is the key to accessing your goals and dreams. There's no doubt about it, getting to know God for yourself falls into the essential category. By this I mean that you, first, accept and understand that there is a Power much greater than all of us. Second, you begin the quest to learn everything that you can about it and understand how that Power, which I call God, speaks, uniquely, to you. Finally, you place your life in God's hands. By that I mean you listen to that Power, or whatever you choose to call it, and do what it tells you to do. In order to experience your full Power, place your spiritual relationship before your relationship with anyone else. Neither your mom, your dad, your partner, nor your child should come between you and God. Taking care of your spiritual self will breathe life into you in ways that will make you better when you interact with each and every one of them. It's also important to have faith in something greater, even if the people around you don't.

You'll need to have your own reasons for prioritizing your spirituality—no one can do that for you. In his book *Stages of Faith: The Psychology of Human Development and the Quest for Meaning*, James Fowler talks about the development of a person's faith. Fowler says that we first operate from the faith that we borrowed from our parents—assuming that our parents practiced a faith at all (many people also inherit their parents' lack of a spiritual belief system). We use it until we reach a point where the situation we face is greater than our faith. At this point, we experience what Fowler calls a "crisis of faith," where our trust in God must grow in order to encompass the new situation. For instance, I received my theology from my father, but I've reshaped it to fit my form of pastoring. As a minister, my father wore a suit and tie to work every day. For him, the suit reflected his respect for God, his ministry, and his congregation. I wear a suit to work several days a week and usually when I preach. Other days I may wear just a shirt and tie, or a sweater, dashiki, or even a T-shirt (although typically not in the pulpit). My father would have a fit if he could see me at church wearing a T-shirt and dungarees, but my faith makes room for me to be comfortable. It's more scandalous to me that I have a bald spot, my hair is turning gray, and if I let it grow too long someone might mistake me for Don King! All jokes aside, every righteous man must develop a personal relationship with God that has nothing to do with the world or his parents. It's also important that your spirituality doesn't depend upon your partner. I can't tell you how many men I watch get dragged to service by their wife or their girlfriend.

For a man to experience his full Power, he needs to have a relationship with his spirituality that doesn't depend on any other person. In other words, a spiritual relationship that he's not only invested in but that he's also driving. Men who draft behind the strength of their women's spirituality limit their own Power and effectiveness. Furthermore, one of the wonderful ways in which God works is that God will always respond to your level of faith. If you want God to do something really big in your life, you have to do something really big for God. The question is never whether God can do it, the question is always: Do you have enough faith? So if you want big things, strengthen your faith.

In addition to helping you access goals and dreams, your faith will protect you from life's trials and tribulations. To use a metaphor from nature, both sunshine and rain are necessary for your growth. Beyond that, difficulty will take place both when you walk along destiny's path as well as when you wander away from it. It's a fact that both trouble and evil have their place in your development. Fortunately, life's struggles get resolved as God works them out for us and with us. When you turn control of your life over to a higher power, you are free just to enjoy the journey however it goes; there's no longer a need to force fit your life into previously determined outcomes that for one reason or another you've already decided upon.

Plug in to Your Power

As every man travels toward his destiny, he will grapple with two themes: the external pressure he feels from the outside world and his internal brokenness.

Each guy will tangle with enemies and difficulties that come at him from the world—the temptation to overspend on the latest flat-screen or to chase skirts, the financial pressures of helping your children go to college, the people who don't believe in your goals and dreams or "haters" who try to undermine them, and so forth. We also have personal problems, issues, and innate imperfections, as our brokenness manifests in myriad ways. At some point, every man will also experience external conflict, attacks, and even warfare directed toward his spirit and intellect. Spiritually, these attacks seek to knock us off kilter, throw us off balance, and cause us to lose focus. A man who is clear about who he is spiritually will deal with these strikes and attacks differently and more effectively than a man who doesn't know who he is. I talk to many men who feel alone, as though they only have themselves to rely upon. When they consider their future as they encounter serious problems, they often tell me that they feel like they are powerless, and just staring into a deep abyss. The righteous warrior has a relationship with the source of his Power and he knows that difficulty comes with the territory. Fortunately, as Grandma used to say, "Trouble don't last always." Even in the face of your greatest challenges, you can use the tools of your faith to develop yourself. As you grow, you will come to understand that with God on your side, it doesn't matter who or what opposition you face.

But how do you ensure that you're on your spiritual path and following your destiny? That is where prayer comes in.

When Leroy's wife, Felicia, was pregnant with their second child, he knew that life's ante was being upped and so he had to step up.

"Look, God, I'm an ass and I'm scared. I need help because these folks are depending on me—that was a prayer verbatim for me," Leroy says of that phase of his life. "It was early in the marriage, early in my faith. I would get up in the morning, while my wife, Felicia, was asleep, and come down to the living room and lay out crying before God on the floor. I had been an athlete growing up. Captain of the football team, track, a decathlete—I was that guy. I was also an ass.

"Felicia was very pregnant. Having a family was expanding my obligations, and I was afraid. I was really trying to be a better man and just be a better husband, a father; I was really striving hard. So I prayed, 'Lord, I wanna trust you more. I wanna have a deeper relationship with you.' And over time I became more spiritual, stronger."

If you don't have a prayer life yet, I want you to know that praying merely means having a conversation with God. It is all about taking the time to align your human will, personality, and priorities with your spiritual image—in other words, to make your priorities God's priorities. Once you do that everything else will eventually fall into place. You don't need to use big words or ones from antiquity like "thus" and "thou." When you pray, speak in the same way you'd talk to a friend; better yet, to your father or father figure. It's okay to talk to God using words like "Daddy," "Father," and "Pop." The model for praying is very simple: "You cry out, God hears, God answers, you and God talk." (As we will discuss in Principle 7, this is also the model for communicating in a healthy relationship.)

You will experience greater Power in the physical realm if you handle things in the spiritual realm by putting your own "mask" on first. You can pray at any time and in any place. God is present everywhere and will listen to you. If you don't already do so, find a quiet place in nature or set aside a sacred place in your home where you can commune with God. The space can be as humble as a candle you place on a windowsill or as ornate as a room that you dedicate for devotional purposes. You can also pray while you're on a walk or at lunch or sitting in your truck. Sadly, lots of guys wait until they're desperate and need divine intervention; then they wonder why they struggle to summon Power in the moment. Prayer, however, is not about getting something you want from God; it's about aligning yourself with your higher power. It works best when it is an ongoing spiritual practice. And though God often does intervene to solve problems, don't just tell your God about your problems; remember to tell your problems about your powerful God.

"I had to pray my way through the Tough Mudder. It was the most strenuous, demanding thing I'd ever done," Jerome says. "Because I was the weakest link, once the race started, the other guys ran off and left me. I basically ended up doing the course by myself.

"When they finally circled back to get me, I was on the last third of the course and ready to quit. 'I'm done,' I told them. 'I have nothing in me; I can't go on anymore.' They said, 'No, no, no, we're almost done.' Jerry found me a stick and Leroy said, 'Lean on us, we're gonna carry you through.' With their encouragement, I kept going. The guys literally carried me across the finish line. That was a significant moment in my life. I was still very overweight but had reached a new level of fitness. I'd also honored my older brother by starting to take charge of my health and dedicating the event to him. The guys dragged me across, but we crossed over together. God had given me brothers after the loss of my brother."

Most people get up and go about their business after they finish praying, but I'd encourage you to sit still and silent for a while. Staying still makes it easier to hear any response that you get in that moment. God speaks to every person subjectively; everyone's personal experience is unique. I have experienced situations where I have heard a voice, loud and clear, that I believe was God talking to me. Other people see visions. Still others feel a sacred presence. So be present and listen to the gentle nudges of your spirit. How will you know the difference between your spirit's whispers and your personal desires, you ask? One of the first signs is that you'll experience internal peace. Also keep your eyes peeled for messages from at least two more sources confirming that you are on the right path. The bigger your life gets, the more important setting time aside for prayer will be. Praying is your direct hotline to God's Power. In fact, there is a saying that goes: Much prayer, much power; little prayer, little power; no prayer, no power.

"Later, Felicia would tell me that she had gotten up to go to the bathroom a couple of times while I had been down on the floor in the middle of the night in the living room, praying," Leroy says. "She had come downstairs and seen me crying before God in a very private moment. She had heard my prayers, but never said anything about it."

Knowing that Leroy was praying and trying to be a better man, husband, and father created an atmosphere in their relationship and home where Felicia would not only strengthen their marriage, but a situation would later arise where she literally had to trust Leroy with her life.

Finding My Lane

I'd like to show you how several of these themes came together in my life.

When I was in college, I studied music and the music business; however, I was a very marginal student. I should have fought for my education, which was essential to my well-being, but the truth of the matter is, I didn't. Most of my energy was spent singing and playing keyboards for Bluesimus Maximus, our blues band that performed at colleges throughout the region. I wore my hair processed, a diamond earring in my right ear, a hanging cross in my left ear, and a piano bandanna on backwards around my neck. Though I had a gift around music, and that was important and perhaps even essential, much of the rest of my musical activity was a distraction at best. I was making $200 to $300 a weekend plus free beer. My lifestyle was pretty wild and I engaged in a lot of drunken foolishness. Little did I know back then that, for me, drinking was a big risk to my health and well-being. I got away with it for a while; I would pay later.

During this time my oldest brother, Alfred, who was seventeen years older than me and had followed my father's footsteps into the ministry, would call to check in on me.

"You know the Lord has more for you than this," he'd say.

"Alfred, I love you," I'd tell him. "But you be Dad's preacher; I'm gonna do music." Alfred had attended Columbia University. I thought he was way smarter than me and I looked up to him more than I did almost anyone else in the world. One of the reasons that I was resisting the ministry was because for all my life people had been saying, "God told me to tell you that you are going to be a preacher." It would make me angry when people would project their expectations upon me. Let Daddy be Daddy and Alfred be Alfred; I was gonna do me!

I wanted to be like my friends Gerald and Sean Levert, who had their own singing group, LeVert, which was experiencing great commercial success. I used to sing with them way back in high school. However, I began to feel called to do something deeper, maybe even preach. On the inside I started wrestling with whether I should continue playing the blues. I had started listening to contemporary gospel artists like BeBe Winans, Donnie McClurkin, and Keith Hunter and began to imagine being like them. Between my own restless spirit and my brother's weekly appeals to my sanity, in my prayer life I started to try to bargain with God about what was essential for me.

"Okay, I'll quit playing the blues and just do contemporary gospel and positive secular music," I'd promise. I figured that was way better than my weekly on-stage debauchery. In the meantime, the voice in my head began to call me to preach. Mad Dog, a cheap wine, helped me to silence it.

One day during the spring of my senior year of college, a young man walked up to me and handed me the catalog for the Southern Baptist Theological Seminary in Louisville, Kentucky. For some reason, I said, "Okay, I'll take it." Right after that, my then-girlfriend (now-wife) Ellyn showed up. "You need to call home," she told me. I walked back to her apartment and called my mom. This was back in the day of the landline and before cell phones.

"Your brother Alfred is dead," my mother told me. "You need to come home."

It was just two days before my birthday and my brother had been only thirty-seven years old. Later, I'd learn that he'd had diabetes but had tried to ignore his loss of vision and failing kidneys rather than get help. After I got off the phone, I cried. Then I went out and got drunk. When I went home the next day the Lord started shouting at me: "IT'S TIME FOR YOU TO PREACH." I heard a literal, audible voice. This was how God was speaking uniquely to me; other people experience God in other ways. I tried to drink the voice into silence.

On the night before Alfred's burial, I was sharing a hotel room with my father, laying in the same bed with my back to him, unable to sleep, wrestling with the voice in my head. My father tapped me on my head.

"Here he is, Lord, here he is," he said.

Will you leave me alone?!

I rolled over, but my dad was fast asleep. What had just happened?

We buried my brother later that morning. By nightfall, I had grown so sick of hearing God's voice yelling inside of me that I finally said, "I'll do it; I'll preach." The following morning, I told my father what I had decided. "I already knew," he told me. "I was waiting for you to catch up to it."

When I returned to campus, I remembered the seminary catalog the stranger had given me. I applied even though my 2.3 GPA was barely high enough to graduate, which I did. Somehow, not only did I get in, I received a scholarship and a summer job in the admissions office. That fall in 1987, I started Southern Baptist Theological Seminary feeling a new-found sense of purpose. At Southern, I stopped underperforming academically and for the first time connected with the scholarly part of myself and fought for my education in ministry. For the first time in my life I started to win academically as I focused on what was essential in my life: educating myself and preparing to excel in the discipline God had called me to pursue. As I plugged into my Power, I began handling first things first and tending to what mattered. I found myself feeling less interested in activities that were merely interesting or distractions. For the first time in my life, my grades were fantastic. I had found my lane in life and had stopped running from my destiny.

Tell the Truth

Anchor yourself in enduring truths rather than in pop culture or fads,
then stand on those principles even through difficult times, so you
can experience meaning, joy, and success in all circumstances.

IT WASN'T UNTIL we'd circled the island twice that we realized we were lost.

It was dark. We were on night ops in a black rubber boat, one of six on the Chesapeake River in Virginia, taking part in a Navy SEAL extreme adventure. We'd been sent on a mission to rescue some hostages our "enemy" was holding captive. Our faces were painted with green, brown, and black camouflage paint. We were to travel by river to a drop-off point, cross over some land, encounter the enemy, and get the prisoners out. I had been charged with leading two boats.

But things weren't going as we'd planned. We'd identified the North Star to orient ourselves, or so we'd thought. Now we were reading a compass and map in the dark using a small military light a lot like the kind of flashlight you'd carry on your keychain, except that it emitted green light. It was important to be stealthy and move quietly. We'd be traveling through communities, people's actual neighborhoods. So we whispered to each other and used hand signs to communicate between boats.

At one point, the river split and we passed a tree-covered island. Then we faced a series of choices where we chose to stay left. But the trip seemed to be taking too long. A lot too long. The landscape seemed increasingly familiar.

After a while someone whispered, "We've seen this before."

"Wait, that's the same island!" another guy responded.

In the pitch dark, we hadn't realized it, but if you keep turning left at every choice, eventually you go in a circle. We'd actually gone around the island a couple of times. After the initial embarrassment, it was actually kind of funny, though I felt kind of stupid—especially because *ABC Nightline* had been filming at the SEAL complex during the time we were at the camp. I'd be embarrassed if that were caught on tape. Finally, we picked out a beacon pulsating from a factory or airport. We realized we needed to be near that light, so we hugged the tree line and headed toward it.

Of course, *Nightline* had, in fact, been reporting on this part of the adventure. When the episode aired, they closed the segment with the line, "Pastor Waller's boat returned considerably later." The fellas still haven't let me live that down.

When we conducted our postmortem of the boat trip, we realized that we got lost because we had not prepared properly to point in the right direction. Before we headed out, we should have read the map, identified some landscape markers, and created a plan. Instead, all we'd done was look for the North Star. Even then, we didn't orient ourselves well enough to tell where we were by what we saw in the sky. We also hadn't practiced reading a map by limited light. All of our shortcomings—our struggles to follow the North Star, read the compass, row the boat straight, and communicate with hand signals—contributed in getting us lost.

Getting lost on the river that night reminded us of how important it is to build your life upon the Truth and all the work it takes to make that happen.

Your Feet Are Your Truth

Psychologist M. Scott Peck opened his famous book *The Road Less Traveled* with the words "life is hard." Peck is right. Life is definitely hard. But the fact that life is hard isn't negative. A person can find tremendous purpose even in the midst of the greatest difficulty—and even *because of* that difficulty. Indeed, any man can find massive meaning in hardship. But to do that he must build his life upon Truth. A righteous warrior is truthful.

There is a difference between things that are true and things that are True. I distinguish between them with the use of the initial capital letter.

Something that is True is true everywhere. It's True no matter your race, your gender, your ethnicity, your sexual orientation, how you look, or where you live. For instance, on earth, gravity is True. So are the other principles of physics—the laws of aerodynamics that allow airplanes to fly, the laws of motion, conservation of mass, thermodynamics, and so on—unless you create some sort of laboratory experiment or technology specifically created to defy them. On a compass, True North is the North Pole, the fixed point that travelers use to orient themselves on a planet that's spinning at a thousand miles per hour as it hurtles through space. God's undying love for you is True. No matter your religious background—or even whether you consider yourself religious at all—I believe that you were created in the spiritual image and likeness of the Almighty. So you are not an accident; you are not a mistake; you cannot lose God's love for you no matter what you do.

Something that's True endures over time. Consistent with this, so does telling the Truth. When we tell the Truth, the version or story we tell will last. A truthful character persists as well. That's one reason a righteous guy can take pride in telling his Truth. Whether or not people like or agree with what he tells them isn't the issue; the important thing is that he is honest. At times it may cost him some friends; it may cost some opportunities. But whether people like him or not, they respect a man who stands by his words and thinks enough of them not to deceive them. More importantly, he respects himself. Indeed, a righteous man tells his Truth regardless of the consequences he may face. He also needs at least one person in his life who is willing to tell their Truth to him.

In self-defense, we discuss tactics as being either "true" or "false." In this context we don't mean morally right or wrong, but physically and bio-mechanically proper or improper. When I use the term "biomechanical," I'm referring to the mechanical laws that affect living beings. When you're fighting, a True stance is a fighting stance balanced over your center of gravity. Your feet are slightly more than shoulder-width apart, your knees are bent, your weight is slightly forward on the balls of your feet, and your upper body is relaxed with your hands out in front of the chest. A fighter whose stance is True has found his center of gravity. He is at his most stable and it isn't easy to throw him off balance. He can launch both attacks and defenses when he has centered his weight. Even if you're not a martial arts fighter, you may already be familiar with this posture. In many sports this stance that we know is True is often called the "ready position."

When a fighter's stance and his footwork are True, he can hit harder by throwing his body weight while simultaneously maintaining his balance. The strength of the punch comes not from the arms, but from the stability of the man's stance. When he launches a kick, what makes that kick a kick is how the fighter moves his feet and adjusts his hips. A stance that is too closed will make a man wobble. A stance that's too wide will make him too slow. (We all know what happens to a man in the ring who moves a step too slow.) There's a perfect stance that makes a fighter strong, agile, and stable. Any adjustments to that stance will impact his abilities. False footwork will cause a fighter to lose his balance, make it difficult to launch an attack, and make him struggle to defend himself. He may even fall.

Somewhat different from what I am calling True, things that are true with a lowercase "t" are subjective—they change depending upon the perspective from which they are viewed. As a result, they tend not to endure. The difference between things that are true and things that are True is the difference between things that are temporary and things that will last. A group of people can witness a car accident and tell entirely different stories about what happened. None of them intends to lie or deceive, yet their stories are different. Indeed, things that are true are not permanent, so they don't endure the test of time. In the martial arts, footwork that is not True leaves the fighter a little bit off balance. This won't necessarily make him a sorry fighter, but it will definitely make him less effective and leave him more vulnerable to getting hurt.

Stunning Discoveries

During his life, every man will have to fight, so it is essential to build a True foundation.

If a man's foundational postures in life are True, he is far more likely to ride out the challenges and experience an amazing life. However, if a man's foundational postures are off center or weak—for instance, if he doesn't have sufficient support from his loved ones, his education has fallen short, or he is low on resources—he will struggle at least somewhat and may even stumble and fall. But no matter how much support or resources he has, he is even more likely to flounder if he builds his life upon lies, whether lies he tells to others or lies or half-truths he tells himself. When we performed our postmortem on our not-so-peak Chesapeake experience, we discovered that we'd told ourselves a number of half-truths. Though we'd believed at the time that we were following the North Star, we later found out that we weren't. In one way or another, most of us had intentionally or unintentionally cut corners (making other assumptions, looking at other things on the horizon, and not being disciplined enough about what we knew to do). This turned out to be the equivalent of lying to ourselves, since it made us believe we were prepared when we were not. Our individual errors compounded themselves when we laid them on top of each other.

One area of life where I find men deceive themselves is in the area of their health. In the years before he got his wake-up call and started to take better care of himself, Jerome had been a yo-yo dieter who wasn't yet serious about his well-being.

"On Monday I'd tell myself, 'I'm gonna change and start this diet and I'm gonna really work out, I'm gonna do all this stuff.' By Wednesday I'd say, 'Oh, I worked out two times this week so I can celebrate by having a cheesesteak.' I always went back and forth."

At church, we had a very sobering experience of how men deceive themselves about their well-being. Leroy and I had been reading a national report about the disparities between the health of Black and White American men. For a whole host of reasons—from the unconscious racism that has been documented in medicine to the fact that we are more likely to live in communities with more pollution and less fresh foods—the health of African-American men is generally much worse than that of White men. This shows up in Black men's higher rates of illness and shorter life spans. The report listed issues like not having a doctor, lacking insurance, probe-a-phobia, and fear of hearing bad news among those things that kept men from going to the doctor.

"We can overcome eighty percent of these barriers," we thought. So we teamed our church up with a local hospital to organize a men's health event. The idea was to create a man-cave experience, where guys would feel comfortable to hang out for three or four hours, get a haircut, watch the game, play cards, ask the docs questions, and take diagnostic tests: height, weight, blood pressure, blood sugar, cholesterol, HIV, and the PSA test with the digital rectal exam. (A lot of the guys had been avoiding that one.) Aside from medical staff, no women would be allowed. Breakfast, lunch, and dinner would be provided and any man who wanted to was welcome to come.

More than twelve hundred men of all races, religions, and backgrounds—members of our church and nonmembers, as well—came to what we called our "Know Your Numbers" event. We were surprised that a handful of guys' test results were so abnormal that nurses walked them straight to an ambulance and sent them to the hospital. In fact, the docs didn't know how some of them were still standing. We sent another three hundred guys to be triaged onsite because their numbers were so far out of balance. Many immediately scheduled a doctor's appointment. We learned that a lot of guys had high blood pressure but hadn't been taking their medication. They'd been deceiving themselves that their health wasn't too bad—boy, that sounded awfully familiar to me. My father was known for adjusting his diabetes medication based on whether he was preaching that day. In hindsight, he was probably trying to control the medicine's side effects. But when we don't tell our healthcare providers what we're doing, they can't give us the appropriate advice or assistance.

Two weeks after Know Your Numbers, the endocrinologist shared the data from the entire event.

"Everybody's a walking heart attack, stroke, pre-diabetic, or obese being," he told us.

We weren't exactly shocked. Every year one of our ministers preaches a funeral for some forty-seven-year-old Black man who's had a heart attack.

"You gotta get them moving," the doctor told us.

The issue became personal and part of our Purpose. Leroy and I had both lost brothers and fathers to health problems. We didn't want to lose anyone else.

Many men lie to themselves about their health; however, lots of us also deceive people on purpose. Intentional lies fall in an entirely different category than self-deception, misread situations, and mistakes.

Many philosophies and religions have thoughts about the destructive nature of intentional lies. For instance, because we believe that Jesus was God in the flesh and that God and God's word are the same, Christians believe that lying is the most anti-Christ thing that anyone can do. When we are being Christlike, we are in alignment with our words and our words are True. As a result, they endure and pave the path to greater freedom in everything we do. In order to access our very best life, it's important to build upon a firm and True foundation. Indeed, Truth not only gives strength to our words but also to the quality of our life. What's more, our ability to tell and deal with the Truth shows our true colors and reveals who we are.

Lies, on the other hand, are a destabilizing force. When we tell intentional lies, we should expect negative things to arise and knock us off course, both from the energy the fabrication sets in motion and because of how off-balance telling them makes us. Conversely, when your word is intentionally not True, that's the most anti-Christ thing you can do. That's why Christians call Satan "the father of lies." Building your life upon falsehoods is the equivalent of a martial artist demonstrating poor foot posture. Rich's youth provides a perfect example of this. By ignoring the sound moral instruction he had received from his parents and becoming involved in a life of crime, Rich started his life out on poor footing. It was merely a matter of time before he would fall.

One of the biggest challenges that every man faces is that he must figure out his own Truth—his personal True North, his North Star, his destiny in a constantly changing world that's trying to distract him onto society's agenda. We live in a world where people—whether family members, bosses and coworkers, or friends—will attempt to pull us in different directions in order to get their needs met. This doesn't mean they are necessarily evil or even bad; most often they're just being human. It's also important to understand that businesses can make a fortune off of you if they can make you believe that you need the things they sell, many of which tend just to be interesting or a distraction. So taking the time to discover your Truth will provide you with a way both to center and defend yourself in a constantly changing world where marketers always vie for your attention.

But just like any explorer does, you must embark upon a personal quest to discover your Truth. No one can do this work but you. I highly recommend that you do it. There is great beauty in the discovery process, and the rewards are many. Among them, you will find that organizing your life around Truth and telling the Truth will not only free you from many mundane human experiences but will also allow you to transcend them.

Don't Drop the Rock

The second P of Personhood involves identifying and occupying your spiritual Place.

Every human being gains Power when life is breathed into him. He is also endowed with the innate ability to align himself with a unique spiritual position that no one else in the history of humankind has ever occupied or ever will. That position is his spiritual Place. Your Place is within God's will for your life. God's will for my life is as a pastor seeking to preach Christ and break down stereotypes and walls of partition that divide the human family. Just as four rivers flowed through the Garden of Eden, when a man aligns with this higher position, he won't have to hustle and scrape; life will flow to him.

A man's Place is not a static physical location. Though it may include a particular place, it moves forward across space and time as he embarks upon the journey toward his destiny. This is his spiritual journey or path. Now, I'll be the first to admit that this concept can be hard to grasp, particularly because, one, our traditional masculine manhood socialization devalues a man's inner emotional and spiritual life; and two, we live in a physical world that overflows with interesting and distracting experiences and items. Depending upon who you are, you may have to work hard to find your Place. Then again, this may come easy to you.

So if a man's Place is in the invisible world, how is a man supposed to know when he occupies it, or when he's on his path and when he's not? I'm so glad you asked. There are a number of telltale signs. For one, when you're on the right track, you experience inner peace no matter what's going on around you. Conversely, whenever you wander off your path, you tend to feel stressed out and frustrated. Indeed, when you're totally lost and circling a dark island in the Chesapeake, you tend to lose your peace completely. Second, consider the extent to which life's blessings are flowing to you. Things that could be more difficult tend to happen more easily than is logical. For example, as soon as I shifted into my spiritual Place by accepting my call to become a minister, I received the scholarship to seminary despite my poor grades. This inexplicable and illogical type of stuff tends to happen as life begins to flow toward you.

It's also important to know that even when he's in the flow, a man's blessings don't necessarily flow to him directly. They flow to the spiritual Place where he's supposed to be. It's a lot like when Tom Brady or Russell Wilson throws the perfect spiral pass. They don't throw it to where the receiver is, they lob it to the location where the receiver is going to be. Whether the receiver catches the pass depends upon whether they are in that position. The same holds true for you. God throws the "pass" but you can only receive it if you're in position. Since, unlike Wilson and Brady, God doesn't throw a bad pass, the spiritual placement and timing are always accurate. It's merely a matter of whether you'll be there. So, learning how your spirit speaks to you becomes one of the most important activities along your spiritual journey.

To help you geolocate yourself within your spiritual Place, it's important to set aside regular time to listen to yourself. Go to the park, sit in your car, or find a place in your home where you can be still and ask, "Am I on the path to my destiny?" Then be still and listen. If you're like me and many other men, you will have to resist the urge to get up and go on about your day. Instead, pay attention to the still, small voice inside of you and the gentle nudges that come from your spirit. In the beginning, these may be hard to feel. What I'm asking you to do may seem stupid. You may wonder if you're imagining things or even making them up. You may think you sense something or you may be unsure. Sometimes you may feel certain; other times unclear; still other times, you may be moving so fast that you don't hear it at all. Get still and trust that God or something greater than yourself is real. I promise you that if you commit to having this conversation, you will begin to learn what your inner voice sounds like as it speaks to you. Sometimes I hear a voice speak to me clearly and loudly, as I experienced after my brother passed away. Other times, that voice is merely a whisper. I may just feel a sense of the most wonderful peace. Once you discover how your spirit speaks to you, you will begin to develop the confidence to move through your life based on that information, no matter what appears to be happening around you. When this occurs, you will sense that you are firmly in your Place.

Your Place is spiritual and therefore invisible, but it can also involve physical locations. For instance, during this season of my experience my spiritual Place not only involves being a preacher but also carrying out my call at the Enon Church in Philadelphia. It may be easiest to imagine me being in my spiritual Place at my church, preaching and otherwise serving my congregation, but my Place is not limited to my physical church. I was also occupying my Place at the Navy SEALs training, where we were the only Black participants and my peaceful presence challenged negative and limiting stereotypes about Black men who come from urban settings (as well as what ministers do and do not do), and as I ministered to and encouraged the White men who led and also attended the program as we trained and shared meals. I occupy my Place, as well, when I attend meetings in Philadelphia that require me to speak truth to power to our political, civic, and religious leaders. Recently, I've been learning that my Place even extends around the world as I've been called into leadership roles that challenge me to provide more imaginative solutions to human problems in other countries. That said, I don't always get my Place right. Even though God has told me that I'm not supposed to be a professional musician, I am constantly trying to identify the line between expressing the gifts that God has given me and not allowing my ego to pull me out of my Place and into the music industry.

As much as I love it, I am also clear that becoming a gospel recording artist is not part of my spiritual path.

Part of the Power of engaging in your spiritual journey and making sure you're in the right Place is that it puts you along the path to your destiny. The path between where you find yourself in your life today and your destiny is rich with meaningful experiences, contexts in which you can grow, and engaging opportunities. You don't have to get to the end of it today or be perfect at every step of the process; it's a journey and you should enjoy it. While you are on your spiritual path, life will come to you, but when you drift off of that path, you are likely to find that the pickings will be slim. If the pickings are slim in your life right now, consider making some adjustments spiritually. If you stray outside your Place for a while, doing so will undermine your productivity and sense of purpose. Stay outside of God's Place for too long and it will kill your spirit.

It's Not About You

Once you've figured out your Place, it's time to figure out your Purpose, the overarching and passionate pull that people experience that helps you understand both yourself as well as the meaning of life.

Every human being was placed on earth for a reason. The reason that you are alive is connected with the same reason that every other human being was born. This reason—this Purpose—that connects all of humanity is so great that human beings cannot comprehend it. Every human being has free will, or the freedom to choose to do whatever we want. We can be good and even exceptional people, we can commit grievous errors or do anything in between; the choice is ours. Though every human being will experience difficulty in life, when we strive to find our Place and our spiritual path as well as to be the best person we can be, we possess the Power to overcome our troubles, large and small, as well as the rewards that come with fulfilling our potential and destiny.

Human beings aren't the only living things created with a Purpose. Everything in nature was created with a Purpose. In fact, if you want to understand better how God works, just spend some time outdoors and observe what's going on in the natural world. In nature, not only is everything purposeful, it is also interconnected. Whether human beings or trees, everything natural fits into the larger ecosystem of life. For instance, consider this simple example: The rain waters the tree, the tree transforms carbon dioxide into oxygen, the oxygen supports human life, and so on and so on. A living thing's Purpose can often be found in its fruit or its seed—whether the acorn that grows the mighty oak or the sperm that germinates humanity. So like the seed, which grows into the food or fruit that feeds insects, animals, and people, everything in the natural world exists for something greater than itself, and so do you.

Indeed, every human being is born with a spiritual Purpose. Every human being has been designed to bear fruit—and I'm not just talking about having children. Innate within every one of us is both the ability to make a difference in the world and the desire to do good. And because every human being is interconnected, in the invisible realm we are like puzzle pieces that fit into each other. One of the most important goals of life is to identify and develop the fruitful aspects of yourself to the greatest extent possible, so you can connect with others and share your seed in humanity's fertile soil. Between now and the time you take your last breath, you want to complete the things you were put on earth to accomplish. When human beings line up with their Purpose, they experience an incredible sense of meaning, as well as peace and joy. When we fail to fulfill our Purpose, life can feel painful, meaningless, and irrelevant. As I speak with men these days, I am growing to understand that far too many people are feeling lost. I get it—there have been times when I've felt lost! But when you haven't yet found your Purpose, life tends to frustrate you far more than it does when you're living for something much greater than yourself. But even if you're down right now, I really urge you not to give up. Because you haven't really started living yet, you haven't discovered the thing you were born to do.

Lots of guys have a sense of what their Purpose is even if they're not pursuing it. Your Purpose may scare you, just as my Purpose scared (and still sometimes scares) me. You may not have all the answers. You may be afraid of making a mistake and making moves that cause other people to think you're crazy. You may even need to remove mental blocks or develop yourself. But far more guys than you might expect have a sense of the direction in which they should be heading—whether or not they are making any moves or are fearful about pursuing it.

In the same way that Purpose plays out in nature, where among a tree's many Purposes is to create oxygen for other living beings to breathe, your spiritual Purpose is not about you. There were things going on in your family, in your community, and in the world long before you got here. You are part of a much larger narrative. Your Purpose is connected to that. Your Purpose exists to support and even bless other people. So if it's just about you and yours, your vision is too small and that's not your Purpose. You will have to make sacrifices to accomplish it: time, money, relationships, and so on. But what you give up will be replaced by things that are even better.

In order to figure out what your Purpose is, I'd like to invite you to spend some time reflecting upon your gifts, your talents, the things that bother or even burden you in the world, and the areas of life where you've been disappointed, or hurt, or even traumatized, or otherwise "broken." Make a list of these. I encourage you not to be ashamed, afraid, or worried about the things that are "wrong" with you. Indeed, every character in the Bible is imperfect. And the world is full of stories of folks who have done amazing things against all odds or with something wrong with them. From Barack Obama, who felt lost because he'd never known his father; to basketball player Kevin Love, who shared his mental health struggles; to actor James Earl Jones, who struggles to speak without stuttering, but can recite his lines from a script stutter free and selects parts that allow him to use his voice to fight for Black people's rights.

One of the amazing things about exploring and following your Purpose is that you will address the thing that troubles you in the world at the same time you heal the thing that is hurt, scarred, broken, or "wrong" within you. Because when you hook up with your Purpose, you will find meaning and strength in the areas where you are broken. And I don't mean *in spite of* your brokenness, I mean *because of* your brokenness. As you embrace your brokenness, it will give you power, as Leroy's and my brokenness empowered us.

Also ask yourself questions like:

+ What do I do well?

+ What do people value in me?

+ What do I like to do?

Once you've examined all those areas, create a Venn diagram of overlapping circles that depict the places where what you do well, what other people value in you, and what you like to do come together. Your sweet spot is where they all intersect.

Leroy and I felt a sense of Purpose about the health of the men in our church community. We are leaders at our church. Between the two of us we have spiritual gifts around teaching, leading, and encouraging others. We felt burdened by the health of the men who attended Know Your Numbers and our hearts had been broken by the loss of our dads and brothers earlier in our lives. We are also good at sticking our necks out and taking the lead. Our church has grown immensely during my tenure. People tend to value my ability to break down the Bible and make it plain. They value Leroy's compassion and concern for other people. He is a people person and will give you whatever he has to help you.

In fact, we both have a heart for other people. The situation was ripe for our leadership.

"Not on our watch," we said to each other. "We're not going out like that."

We wanted to demonstrate leadership and to use our considerable platform to address this issue that was so much bigger than us. So with a doctor's recommendation, we decided that we needed to create a boot camp. That's where Leroy's and my Purpose intersected with Vernell's. I'd known Vernell because he'd been coming to Master Robinson's martial arts training. One day, he also came to my rescue when I needed a haircut. Eventually he became my barber. And not only did I like Vernell, we are about the same height, unlike the other fellas, who are taller than me.

"I was a scrawny dude who got picked on when I was growing up," Vernell recalls about his difficulties earlier in life. "I began boxing when I was thirteen and during my late teens started training so I could put a little weight on my frame and take better care of myself. Eventually, I got into personal training. At one gym, I got to train the clients and in exchange come to the gym for free."

One day, I picked up the phone to call Vernell, but as I tried to dial, he was already on the line. Turns out he was calling me.

"I had a revelation—I want to run a boot camp at church," he told me.

I kid you not; this is what he said to me.

"I don't know what it's gonna cost. I don't know how it's gonna play out. I'm just telling you I've got a very good idea," he told me.

That's the perfect example of the kind of thing that happens when you're in your right Place and following your Purpose. I invited Vernell to put his plan on paper and submit it. When he turned his proposal in, he had already created workouts. But his workouts were not only for men; they were also for women, children, people who had never exercised before, people with back problems. In other words, he had already created exactly what we had been envisioning.

So beginning in 2011 and until this day, Vernell shows up every Saturday morning and leads the physical activity at our church. And as Vernell has stepped into his destiny by showing up week after week to train church members without fail, he has attracted like-minded people and developed deep relationships with other men, which has helped fill the hole he faced from losing his dad and being an only child. To take this even further, shortly thereafter Vernell's Purpose overlapped with Jerry's.

"I still wanted to stay fit because that's what that lifestyle called for," says Jerry, a thirty-three-year military veteran, of the time right after he retired and when he joined our church. He met Leroy and started coming to boot camp. "That led to 'What else do you guys do?' That's when I found out about the Tough Mudders and other activities. That's when I became part of the group. At first, we called ourselves the Philly Four: Alyn, Leroy, Vernell, and I, then the other guys joined in."

Seek Your Purpose

In the event you haven't already had the experience yet, at some point in your life, something will begin to pester you and the burden won't go away. When I use the word "burden" in this context, I mean thematic burdens, or the issues in the world that trouble you. I'm talking about things that disturb you in a way they don't seem to bother other people. Issues that lay heavy on your heart, problems in the world that attract your attention, worries that cause you distress and even haunt you. Maybe you see certain things, but other people can't, don't, or won't. For instance, the level of disorganization and lack of leadership in your department may work your last nerve, or unfair systems that cause working people to lose their homes may infuriate you, or the corruption at the heart of the opioid epidemic may get under your skin.

The reason this jacked-up situation attracts your attention isn't the only thing bothering you. A large part of why you're attracted to the issue in the first place is because your gifts are absent from the situation and your spirit is disturbed by that reality. The reason that you have the burden is because you also have the gift. People who don't have the gift don't feel the burden. Applying your gift to the situation would improve it. This is related to your Purpose; follow it.

Even seeking your Purpose is part of your Purpose. So commit yourself to figuring it out. This is particularly important because, if you don't know what your Purpose is, other people will try to tell you what it is. But the direction in which they will point you will serve their ends, not yours—and it definitely won't lead to your destiny. Doing things that are in line with your Purpose, and doing them right and with excellence, opens the door to opportunity, even in circumstances where there appears to be none.

Another way to think about your Purpose is when your talents line up with your spiritual gifts in the Place where you're supposed to be, doing the things you and only you were made to do. That said, it's possible to have some things right and other things wrong. You can be in the right ZIP code but in the wrong neighborhood. In the right church, but the wrong ministry. The right organization, but the wrong city. The right city, but doing the wrong thing, et cetera. It's not uncommon to have to make some adjustments across the course of your life.

One of the reasons a righteous man pays attention to his inner spiritual life is so he can learn to become sensitive to the gentle nudges from the spiritual realm. When you're doing what you're supposed to be doing, when you're supposed to be doing it, in the Place you're supposed to be doing it—you will have found the sweet spot of life. Part of how you locate it is by listening.

Get Uncomfortable

When I first accepted my call to ministry, the path seemed very daunting to me. If you can relate, don't worry; that's natural. Your Purpose will fall somewhere between your ability and your anxiety. To fulfill it, you have to work hard and stretch out of your comfort zone. As a matter of fact, one way to know whether you're on track is by whether it both calls you and scares you. If you're on the right track, looking further down the path is going to scare you because what you are supposed to do is so much bigger than who you are today. If you don't feel scared about the thing, it's probably not your destiny. Life will help you grow so you can get there.

When I was a young preacher, I asked my father about a problem that I continue to have: being very nervous every single time I preach. "When the nerves stop, you stop," my father told me. He said I should always feel like my calling is daunting. Similarly, in the beginning, preparing for and leading the boot camps was a big stretch for Vernell. Over time, however, he grew into the role and his leadership came naturally.

The fact of the matter is the journey to your destiny requires you to be spiritually, mentally, and emotionally strong. You have to be willing "to boldly go where no man has gone before," as William Shatner, who played Captain Kirk in the original *Star Trek*, would say. You'll need to overcome your fear and work hard to do your part. This includes doing things like sharing your gifts. So don't wait until you are in high places before you practice using them. I strongly suggest that you develop your gifts one step at a time as you go. By the time you hit the big stage—whatever the big stage is for you—you will be strong enough to stand up to the pressure. In fact, if you want to be ready on game day, practice using your gifts when you're in the basement of your life. Trust that life will take care of everything else. If you are along the path to your destiny, the world can't stop your destiny from unfolding, but if you're living outside your spiritual Truth, whatever you're doing will stop itself.

Another way to get a feel for your Purpose is that it gives you joy and a consistent sense of meaning and fulfillment. It feels very oppressive to live outside of your Purpose. In fact, it feels a lot less like fun and a lot more like work. You are also at your most attractive when you're following your Purpose. Not only do you attract every resource you need—in part because you have found your right spiritual Place—but you look your best, you sound your best, and you have a smile on your face. Living in a capitalist system, we're told that marketing is essential; however, a person pursuing their Purpose doesn't have to promote himself. In fact, if you do have to promote yourself to make it work, there's a good chance that what you're doing isn't "it." It may be true, but it's probably not True. Similarly, if you have to tell someone who you are, you probably aren't. I watch too many people chase after things they see other people do, or follow in other people's footsteps instead of hooking up with their unique Purpose.

When you're expressing your gifts, pursuing your calling, and being "it"—the person God called you to be—people will naturally be drawn to you. In fact, you won't even need to tell other people who you are; people will start telling you. Mark my words: You will attract partners of all kinds—from business to romantic—because people will be able to see who you really are and what you have to offer. I was attracted to Vernell's work ethic, hustling and running from job to job. I saw how committed and disciplined he was. I had no doubt he could run our boot camp.

Now, while prospective romantic partners will be attracted to you, just know you're not ready yet to find your ideal Partner, because you haven't figured out your Parameters yet. However, you're getting close. Because once you figure out your Purpose, you know where you fit in the world. Your Purpose gives you Power, peace, and attracts the right people into your life. How significant you become in your life depends upon your ability to hook up with your Purpose.

That being said, following your Purpose is going to cost you something. Just as Jesus gave up his life on the cross, you will have to sacrifice yourself to achieve it. Your hands will get dirty along the way and you will have to learn to live in the dissonance of life.

From Good to Great

Now, even though I live in Philadelphia, I'm originally from Cleveland, Ohio. Yes, the 216, the CLE, the North Coast, *Believeland*, the Rock and Roll Capital of the World. That's us! And as a native of Cleveland, I'm a Cavaliers fan. Unbeknownst to him, LeBron and I had a tough moment when he took his talents to Miami. But once he came back home, we were good again. I'm fine with him heading to Los Angeles.

When people think about guys who have found their Purpose, they often think about great men like Martin Luther King Jr. But you can see a great example of a modern-day man who's living his Purpose in LeBron. No, I don't mean because he's a basketball legend, though he's clearly that. I'm talking about how he's living his life.

Since I grew up in Cleveland, I watched a young LeBron grow up playing basketball in his hometown of Akron, located about forty miles south of Cleveland. Even back then, people knew that LeBron would be great. The residents of Northeast Ohio hoped the Cavs would draft him after he graduated and that he'd turn the team's longtime losing fortunes around, bringing the city of Cleveland the sports championship that had eluded its fans for decades. Our hopes rose when he first came to the Cavs; however, he didn't have the right players—and some would say the management—around him that he needed to lead the team to the championships.

When he took his talents to Miami, he followed his dream because, like any professional ballplayer, he reached a point where he wanted to win. But he never lost sight of Cleveland and Akron. In 2014, when LeBron wrote his *Sports Illustrated* letter stating he'd be returning home in hopes of helping to bring Cleveland a championship, he knew that he would be the team's "old head" and mentor, responsible for helping to cultivate younger players. He also knew he'd be collaborating with Tyronn Lue, who back then was the new head coach.

I cannot tell you how greatly I admire that righteous decision. But

LeBron had been leveraging basketball and his celebrity to change the economic tides for the residents and the city of Akron long before he returned home: from building his house in Akron, to renovating the Boys & Girls Club there (and nationwide), to starting schools, to helping to educate and then hire the friends he grew up with—guys who have become major forces in their own right rather than the usual hangers-on—to starting a foundation that emphasizes education, physical fitness, and a healthy lifestyle. Even while he was playing in Miami, LeBron still did for his hometown.

Many guys like to argue about whether LeBron is the greatest basketball player of all time. See him as a basketball star if you will. I see a man who has found his Purpose—a humanitarian who is using his celebrity and basketball to save lives in the community he comes from. He's used his ability to play basketball to be a blessing.

Yes, when people think about guys who have found their Purpose, they often think about great men of the past like Martin Luther King Jr. and not of contemporary men or even themselves. But I wonder if King knew who and what he would become. Dr. Lawrence Carter, professor of religion at Morehouse College in Atlanta, and the first dean of the Martin Luther King Jr. International Chapel there, says that in reality Martin Luther King was a very normal and ordinary guy. He didn't get great grades when he attended Morehouse, but he always had a great passion for what was right and equality.

Ordinary guys can become heroic men when they follow God's guidance and seek their Purpose. Don't ever underestimate yourself. Your greatness, too, is just waiting for you.

Find Your Why

The German philosopher Friedrich Nietzsche once said: "He who has a why to live for can bear almost any how." In other words, a man who is clear about and committed to what he's been put here to do can deal with most anything that happens as he gets the job done.

Consistent with this, the second question in Peter Schreck's rubric asks "Why am I here?" The question covers similar ground as the 5Ps question about Purpose; however, Schreck's "Why" question deals with a man's productivity and industriousness, or what he calls Industry.

In order to live the life you deserve, you need a cause that you feel excited about. Indeed, every man needs to feel that he is wanted and needed. He also needs to feel that he is effective at whatever he does. Because a man's existence is not about what station in life he occupies now. It's about whether he has a dream that causes him to jump out of bed in the morning so he can reach toward the vision in his mind's eye—or whether, on the other hand, he allows himself to become what my grandmother used to call "breath in britches"—lacking meaning so not contributing.

Every man needs to have a why and every man needs a dream. Now, I'm not talking about dreams (plural) that run you ragged and stretch you thin, I'm talking about a single vision that you can focus upon for the duration of your life. I believe that every man needs to connect with a cause that he can fight for and is perhaps even ready to die for. And when I say "die" I don't mean physical violence—unless you are in the military, law enforcement, or some other frontline protector experience or are protecting your loved ones, children, or other innocent people. When I say "die," I mean that you're willing to give life everything you've got. You are willing to lay everything on the line and leave it on the field or on the floor. You are all in and willing to sacrifice everything you've got. In fact, I find that a man isn't really living until he finds something he is willing to give his all for. When he was in the military, Jerry gave his all, as he supported men on the battlefield.

Now how do you figure out your why? All human beings have a vision within themselves—and this vision comes with a plan. But unlike the toys you assemble at home, this plan requires you to read and follow the instructions. All too often a man looks for a woman to give his life meaning, but Eve cannot give a man either a dream or his sense of purpose. Adam needs a dream first, and then Eve can encourage him as he goes after it. But let's put a pin in this topic for now. We'll dial back to Eve's role later. Achieving your destiny becomes your mission, if you choose to accept it. Achieving that vision will become your why. Your why will wake you in the morning and make you get up instead of hitting the snooze button. It will motivate you to do what you have to do and compel you to continue when the going gets tough and the tough part of you has to develop or get going.

Each man's vision appears first within his mind's eye, but as he embarks along his spiritual journey and his life unfolds, that vision will slowly begin to play out in his world.

Trust the Process

Every righteous warrior will face challenges related to his vision.

First, there will be times when your next steps may not be clear. You may experience weeks, months, or years when you grapple with the meaning of life and perhaps even the existence of God. You may also wrestle with your vision. When this happens (and it's likely to happen) continue to stay engaged; this is part of your spiritual growth process. Don't be surprised if you experience fear or other emotions about your vision. Many guys feel intimidated by how enormous it is. Because it can seem so daunting, a lot of dudes choose not to do it. In fact, many men feel the pull or spiritual call to follow this path, but relatively few will answer it. Even among guys who do respond, many pursue part but not all of their destiny. As someone who has run from his calling at various points in my life, I include myself on this list. Most guys neither start it nor finish it.

Once you start to get clear about your vision, don't be surprised if it takes years, decades, or maybe even your entire life for it to come all the way to fruition. You may even experience a gap in time between the moment you begin to envision it and when it begins to manifest. Expect to experience an interval—maybe even a long stretch—where what you imagine does not match your external reality. During this time, you will be the only person who is able to see your dream. Because it is part of your spiritual journey, no one but you will ever be able to see all of it. In fact, the people you share your dream with—even, and sometimes especially, the people who know you and love you the most—may express doubt, uncertainty, questioning, skepticism, negativity, and/or even downright "hateration." I'm sad to say it, but don't be surprised when that happens.

It's important to learn to have faith in your spiritual path. Or as the motto of the Philadelphia 76ers once stated: "Trust the process." Remember, the vision and the ability to achieve it were given to you, not others. Spiritually, when you are given a vision, the provisions—the resources you need in order to get it done—will arrive along with it. Other people have their own vision (though they may not be aware of it or are pursuing it). They can't see your vision and you can't see theirs. So just stick to your own and pursue it.

As you wait for the ultimate vision to unfold, keep taking steps in that direction. Just imagine that you are the wide receiver heading downfield to make the game-winning catch. Keep moving forward toward your dream, and over time it will land in your outstretched hands. Though he couldn't always see where it was heading, Vernell continued to train one-on-one with Master Robinson even as he juggled all his jobs. He also learned more about the security field. Over time, he began to feel called to safeguard others. Today, he provides protection to some of our city's leaders.

Life is calling you to your next level, but you have to do your part to get there. By that I mean don't just say your goal is to graduate from high school, demonstrate your faith and make plans to enroll in college. Don't just say you're going to have a business one day, have faith and take steps to start it. So even though all the pieces may not be in position, I encourage you to pursue the degree you need to do the work; obtain the professional certification; apply for that job that will teach you the skills; start stacking your loot; place your down payment on the equipment you'll need; build relationships with people who can help you. These are the steps that men who are serious about their dreams take in order to slowly move themselves into Place. I meet a lot of men who talk about what they're going to do, but never get started. If you dream of being an entrepreneur, stretch yourself and take steps toward starting your own business. Don't just talk about it, be about it.

But even when I ask men about the steps they're taking to follow their dream, all too often I hear "I'm waiting on God" or "I'm waiting until the time is right." Usually this means that they're waiting for the perfect conditions or for their dream to just land in their lap. In other words, they're being passive and aren't really doing their part. You must go out to get your dream; Santa isn't going to leave it under the Christmas tree. As long as you are on your spiritual path, life will give you everything you need, but you have to get there yourself. You have to trust the process. In the meantime, during the period after you step into your vision and before you begin to see it unfold, I strongly encourage you to pray. Ask questions like: Is this really what I'm supposed to be doing? How can I encourage myself? How can I use my own resources to make the vision manifest? What resources are already available to me that I haven't used or seen?

Work It

I will never forget back when I was ten years old and I overheard my father say, "A real man always sweats when he works." Of course, I wanted to be a real man, so the next morning, I put on my little white sleeveless undershirt and went outside and pushed the manual lawn mower until I perspired. I didn't mow the lawn to help my father; I mowed the lawn so he could see me sweat. Working hard was a rite of passage I believed would transform me overnight into a man.

You may not wear an undershirt to work, but to carry out your Purpose you are going to have to work hard. Because no matter how much you may want to win the lottery, most of us have to earn our keep. But for some reason I don't understand, the idea of hard work today turns some people off. (Sadly, some folks seem to be turned off by the thought of working at all.) But you are a part of the fabric of humanity, so it's essential that you contribute your gifts and talents to society. The good news is that work is an inherently humanizing experience. It feels good to contribute to something bigger than yourself and participate in the greater good. There is something intrinsic to a man's makeup that helps him be at his best when he's being responsible, taking care of something or someone, and knows that others respect him. And most guys feel satisfied by and enjoy the fruits of their own labor. So whether you have a full-time job, a part-time job, or you do volunteer work, it's important to have someplace to go and something meaningful to do.

Doing something productive just feels good, whether that involves laying cable, hitting your sales plan, changing the oil in your car, coaching the local soccer team, mowing your elderly neighbor's lawn, volunteering at the area Boys' Club, or helping out at a store in the neighborhood while you look for a job that pays. Even—and perhaps especially—if you're unemployed, it's essential to get up and out of bed and out of the house every day so you can contribute to the world. Life is not easy and it's not always fun. Nobody wants to sit on the bench. Even if you've lost your job, have been out on disability, or have been unable to find a job for a long time, try to figure out a way to turn your unemployment into an opportunity to learn, grow, and develop in some way. For example, consider helping the little old lady down the street get to the doctor, or go get her groceries, clean out her basement, or weed her garden when she's not home. Volunteer at your local house of worship, sports organization, or a business or nonprofit in your community. Take another young man under your wing; teach him how to read, or tie a tie, or fix a flat; talk to the young boys hanging out on the corner. Because the truth of the matter is, at some point over the course of their life most guys will experience some economic uncertainty and a good number will lose a job for some amount of time. For this reason, if for no other, it's important not to center your self-worth in your job title or even the type of work you do.

But not only does working make men feel industrious and give us a sense of meaning, it's important to take pride in your work, whether it's digging a ditch, building a house on a construction site, or bolstering a young man so he can rise up and become a leader. Do your job well because you respect yourself and are proud of who you are.

After seeing him bagging groceries at Trader Joe's, a woman job-shamed Geoffrey Owens, formerly an actor on *The Cosby Show*. After experiencing the initial devastation of being humiliated for making the honorable choice to both provide for himself and his family *and* remain committed to his calling as an actor, Owens told People.com that he hopes the conversation sparked by his experience will reshape "what it means to work, the honor of the working person, [and] the dignity of work."

"There is no job that's better than another job," he said. "It might pay better, it might have better benefits, it might look better on a résumé and on paper. But actually, it's not better. Every job is worthwhile and valuable."

Take pride no matter what type of work you do, how big your paycheck is, or what anyone else thinks of you. I want you to feel good about yourself even if, for you, going to work means volunteering or doing pickup work that doesn't pay. There is dignity in that fight. Unfortunately, some people think of work as just a necessary evil or believe that life should come easy and you just reach out and grab its riches. But if you want to experience life's riches, you have to put in the time.

One way you can learn more about work is to spend some time enjoying and studying nature. Everything in nature that is healthy is fruitful.

Every healthy tree will produce fruit in its season. So set your sights on fig-uring out how you can be fruitful with the gifts you have to offer in the spiritual Place where God wants to plant you. If you don't have the type of job you want yet, wherever you can find work, it's important to show up. Every job teaches some type of skill—whether high-level technical skills or the discipline of showing up and giving your best effort when things are unenjoyable. Building those muscles will pay off when you need them in other aspects of life. Unfortunately, the work ethic is diminishing in American culture. Too many men no longer take pride in their work. Other guys think certain jobs are beneath them. Don't think any job is be-neath you. There are times when you may have to live beneath your pay grade; that's okay. But no matter what kind of job you have, be the best you can be and give it your all. Don't work hard because somebody's watching you; work hard because you respect yourself. Even if you do not like your job, the discipline and suffering that you are engaged in can be a proving ground to grow and develop the skills that will help you reach the next level.

Significance over Success

This brings us to the subject of success. In our capitalist system, the main-stream definition of success revolves around possessing material things. Titles and wealth may make you a success in society, but wealth isn't the same as significance. He who dies with the most money still dies; even if you have the most toys at the end, it's still game over for you. A man can be wealthy yet insignificant; he can also be poor yet significant. No matter how much material wealth he has, a righteous warrior strives to be signif-icant.

Significance is not about what you have, it's about what you do for someone else. You become significant when the part of the world you touch is better because you're there. A man can be significant while having little or modest financial means. People like Martin Luther King Jr. and Mahatma Gandhi, both of whom are dead, are far more significant than many living people who are very rich and have lots of social media followers. Though they are no longer with us, their names are regularly upon our lips. As they and many other memorable men did, a righteous guy dies having made a positive impact upon humanity.

No matter how spiritual you are, for at least part of your life you're likely to have a job that is not your actual Purpose. Some people's work is actually their Purpose or calling; other people's work funds their Purpose or calling. Leroy was an insurance broker before he became a minister. As he began to change his career, the income he earned from his insurance business paid for him to return to college to prepare for the ministry. Everyone's work provides an environment where they can grow and develop, in the process preparing them for their next season of life.

So even if the job that's available to you is lower than your pay grade, just get in where you fit in, do the best that you can. As Vernell's story of struggling and taking odd jobs for years demonstrates, if you work with the right spirit, over time things will work themselves out. When we are faithful in how we handle things that are small or even seem to be beneath us, we build the skills and prepare ourselves to assume responsibility for bigger things.

That said, I believe our society has a moral obligation to provide opportunities for people to be employed. In our capitalistic democracy, our political and business leaders are responsible for creating an Eden where everyone can work. If it's a moral responsibility for everyone to work, it's also a moral responsibility for our leaders to create a context in which work can take place. For far too long and for far too many people, that contract has been broken. Stepping into your Purpose to help fix this breach would be a powerful way to demonstrate significance.

Economic prosperity is one of the signs of good political leadership. A sign of righteousness among business leaders, middle and upper managers, politicians, government officials, and other leaders in our communities and society is the understanding that they have a moral obligation to create jobs, not just profits. Such a mind-set runs counter to our current business and political culture, so it will likely take you outside your comfort zone. Indeed, the idea of standing up for what's righteous may both appeal to you and scare you. But wherever you lead, you can find great meaning if you make it part of your Purpose to help create just outcomes. In turn, the members of our society have a moral obligation to pressure leaders to provide jobs that pay adults a living wage, not force them to do work originally intended for kids, and employ people at home, not just overseas— and to support those leaders who do. Indeed, jobs can't leave our nation unless business titans and political leaders allow that, and jobs will come back here if leaders commit themselves to bringing them home.

Righteous leaders take responsibility for the long-term well-being of the human beings they shepherd, rather than merely their own short-term success or profits. Yes, there are times when being righteous will cost you, but great Purpose can be found in the fight. And your choices will not only serve and sustain humanity, they will withstand the test of time and the critique of later generations who will look back and ask what you did with your power and resources.

Deal with Life on Life's Terms

To thrive in the middle of a challenge and to change, take life as it comes, accept both the truth of the situation and your limitations, and handle whatever circumstances life serves you, rather than fantasizing about or ruminating over what could or should have been.

YOUR FIRST NIGHT in the Amazon is a frightening thing. First of all, everything is scarier because you aren't used to that kind of darkness, so your eyes haven't adapted and you can't see three feet in front of your face. Then they scare you by taking you out on the river, pointing out the various animals that inhabit the forest: boa constrictors, various monkeys, jaguars, wolves, river rats, bats—all sorts of creatures. Of course, they show you this then they take you back to your tent. It's part of creating the atmosphere. Then you're sleeping only about a foot off the ground. We must have cut down half the forest to make sure we had enough wood so our fire didn't go out.

At some point in the middle of one night, Mark shouted out *"Oh!"*

"Oh, what?!" I yelled back.

"Something touched me," he shouted.

Now, Mark had once played professional football. He was the biggest and strongest of all of us. I wanted to cry. We never did figure out what it was that touched him, but we all stayed awake until the sun came up. Another time in the middle of the night, a bunch of frogs came hopping through. We just sat there, "Oh God, please don't touch us!" Apparently, we had built our hut in the middle of a frog crossing. If you ask me, about a hundred toads came through; in reality, it was probably about five or six. We stayed awake that night, too. We talked and whistled a lot. Sometimes we could hear movement around us. We were definitely out of our element.

But after a couple of days I started to settle down. Our guides had been teaching us that if you respect nature, nature will respect you and give you what you need to take care of yourself. Our primary challenge was to learn how to live on its terms, face the facts and deal with them appropriately. If something looks like an animal hole, it is an animal hole—don't mess with it! If it looks slippery, it is slippery. Don't wish it to be something different, try to make it something different. If it's going to be dark in an hour, you can't change that. You're going to need a fire, so nothing else matters. If you're caught without a fire, the odds that you're going to die go way up. Don't wish things to be different or try to make them into something different. When you start pretending or wishing for other things, that's when you're going to get hurt. You face the facts and you handle them. There's no time to be afraid.

Though we've all been taught to fear wild animals, we learned that most animals become dangerous for the same reasons humans do. If someone jumped on you, you would probably fight them back. If someone threatened your children, you would probably do something to them. If someone came into your house, you would probably fight them. You might also attack if someone messed with your food source. Same with an animal. If you don't bother a wild animal, the animal won't bother with you. If you don't get in between them and their children, you're cool. If you don't walk in their front yard, they won't come chase you out. And just like you're not walking around hungry eating every hamburger you see, they're not walking around just waiting to eat you. That said, if you run into one of those big cats at lunchtime and happen to mess with their food source, you may learn an interesting lesson or two. But other than that, we learned you should be okay. We learned the feeding times of the different animals, how to identify their tracks, what their homes look like so we could stay out of them, the difference between feces that are fresh and feces that are a few days old.

In other words, we learned the rules of the rain forest and what to look out for. If you pay attention and deal with what's in front of you, you can survive. We realized it wasn't so different from our experiences in life.

The Combat Mind-set

Even though there were many times in the Amazon when the fellas and I almost jumped out of our skin, most of the things people worry about are things they are going to survive.

A righteous warrior faces life's facts and prepares to deal with reality. Instead of wasting his time and energy resisting, complaining, or personalizing things that are not personal, accepting the facts frees him up to focus his efforts on the circumstances. There's no need to lie to yourself (or others), fantasize about things being different, or try to avoid or sugarcoat things. Expect that life will challenge you, know that trials can happen at any time, and always be mentally prepared for difficulty. Over time, you may even shift into a state of mind where life's complications actually excite you! There is Purpose in life's struggle and God will always lead you through—even when you find yourself in a predicament.

One of the best ways to thrive during a struggle is to develop a mind-set that prepares you to play whatever cards life deals. When I use the word "mind-set," I mean a set of beliefs that frame how you approach a situation. It's important to learn what in Commando Krav Maga is known as a combat mind-set. A combat mind-set means that when you've readied yourself in the ways you're supposed to, you can face life knowing that you're well prepared for whatever you encounter and that circumstances cannot defeat you. In CKM you do the push-ups, run the miles, practice your moves so often that the responses become second nature. At one point in my training, I had to repeat every technique a thousand times.

When you first start, it's extremely hard, even overwhelming. Even when you've practiced, it can be mind-numbing. But day-to-day life can be mind-numbing, too; every day is not exciting. When you do this, you can step onto the mat knowing you're more prepared than the other guy. And when you look at him, he will know it.

Leroy intentionally practices this mind-set. In fact, he believes in making himself uncomfortable on purpose. Once, to train for a Tough Mudder, he made us literally break the ice and jump in the Schuylkill River, which runs through the center of Philadelphia, during the middle of the winter. Please don't try anything like this at home—I'm warning you that the man is nuts!

"The more you sweat in practice, the less you bleed in battle," he says. In fact, when we practice, Leroy will fight you like he's in an actual fight. The first time he got in the ring to spar with Vernell, he clocked him in the head.

"He hit me so hard that it knocked my headgear so far around my head that I was looking through the earpiece," he says.

Mind you, Vernell had no idea this was about to happen. He's also about eight inches shorter and fifty pounds lighter than Leroy.

"I was upset because I didn't think he would hit me that hard," Vernell says. "The next minute he pulled me close, prayed for me, pushed me back, and we started fighting again. But now I knew what to expect."

"We really go at each other very hard because we don't want anyone to have a false sense of who they are," Leroy says. "When we're around other people, they can't do anything to us that we haven't already done to ourselves."

A martial artist knows how to defend against whatever his attacker does. After Leroy hit him, Vernell knew it was "on" and raised his fight to a higher level.

Gauging risks accurately is essential to a combat mind-set. In Naphtali, we teach students how to see, how to accurately perceive and then deal with each threat. In fact, the threat itself is not the problem; the only problem is not understanding what the real problem is. Commando Krav Maga teaches students to defend themselves by using the same fundamental skill set from any position—whether they are sitting, standing, being attacked by a group, or disarming a lone guy with a gun. The whole point of Jeet Kune Do, the martial art form Bruce Lee adapted from Wing Chun, is not to have choreographed movements, called forms or katas, at all. Instead, Lee taught fighters not to be so committed to a form that they can't address what's coming at them. These principles are also true in life, where it's essential to tell yourself the truth and accurately assess what's going on so you can remain flexible and deal with it in a disciplined manner and strategically.

A righteous warrior rolls with the punches.

Be Water

Every man's life will bring a level of pain and hardship. Though your hardship may hurt, it's not personal, so don't be surprised when life challenges you and you face opposition and it's hard.

You may notice that I wrote "when," not "if," life is hard. Opposition and hardships occur within every man's life. And as much as we may wish things to be different, struggles, trials, and tribulations play an essential role in our maturation process. Once we accept this fact, we are open to understanding that life's drama and difficulties are intended to grow us. Even evil can play a role in our development. When you adopt this mindset, rather than taking it personally, avoiding or even running from hard times, you can center yourself in your fighter's stance and practice using your skills as you battle back. Now that he's emerging from all his years of grinding and struggling to do the right things for his family, Vernell can see how they strengthened and positioned him for his next season.

No matter the difficulty we encounter—whether the rough patches that seem to show up out of nowhere or the consequences of our own mistakes—if we practice a combat mind-set, hardships can grow us and help us make progress. Because if you're anything like I am, you, too, may prefer sunny days and blue skies; however, sunshine can only get us so far. Just as too much sun can kill a plant, too much ease can weaken a human being. Clouds and rain, too, help a plant to grow. Similarly, struggle can strengthen you for the next level, since difficulty develops you differently. And when we engage our struggles with a combat mind-set, we increase our confidence that everything that happens takes place for our good, whether or not it's easy or unfolds within our time frame. We also adopt a mental outlook that life isn't only about our personal good. A Power greater than us is working for the good of all humanity. In other words, life won't be easy for anyone all or even most of the time. Even though our society constantly sells us on living the high life, ease and affluence are no man's birthright. Accepting these facts and dealing with this Truth frees you to roll with the punches no matter what happens—whether peak experiences or times you must grind. So I strongly suggest that you neither deceive yourself about difficult things nor run away from potentially life-changing challenges.

When I look back upon Jerome's experience, it couldn't have been easy for him to face the facts about his health, attempt to get fit with us, or participate in the Tough Mudder.

"I was carrying a lot of weight and I hadn't been working out," he says. "I knew I couldn't compete. Yet it was a challenge for me that was totally outside of my comfort zone, and so I went for it." Even though Jerome's progress occurred in fits and starts, all of us grew to admire his tenacity. Eventually we would come to see that his challenges were about something much greater than himself, but at the time he still had to struggle.

Standing and fighting, as Jerome often did, helps you develop the ability to thrive in the midst of challenge and change. Over time, you will grow to see how taking life as it comes and learning to navigate all of it—good and bad, easy and difficult—strengthens you. That said, it's important to accept your limitations. Learn what you can handle and when you need to seek support—whether from your partner, your friends and family, your spiritual adviser, a coach, a doctor, a therapist, a lawyer, and so on. During the final three miles of the Tough Mudder race, Jerome hit the wall. It was all he could do to keep from quitting.

"I had nothing left, and when a couple of guys I didn't know asked 'Are you all right?' I said, 'No,' " Jerome says. "They told me, 'Well, you can walk with us.' And they walked alongside me until my brothers circled back and got me."

Even then, Jerome literally leaned on the stronger fellas as they helped him cross the finish line. No matter where you are in your process, there's no need to run, hide, or avoid difficult things or areas of weakness. Instead, be introspective about the challenges you face. As you do this, avoid wallowing in defeat or wasting your time ruminating over what might have been. Whining and spinning your wheels wondering "Why me?" won't help. Instead, during both good times and tough times, I recommend that you ask a far more useful question: "What is to become of this?" Act upon the answers. Jerome realized that he needed to hunker down and increase his level of commitment.

One way to manage yourself through hard times is, no matter how much you may hope for or desire certain outcomes, try not to need any particular thing to happen in your life. Approach each situation with the mind-set that you don't need to experience any specific result. In other words, try not to live an outcome-based life. Instead, always try to be ready for anything. For this dimension of the combat mind-set to work, you cannot be willful. In other words, "got to haves"—I've got to get that woman, I've got to have that car, I've got to have that job—can cause a man to get into trouble. Learn to let life come as it comes, let a situation be what it is. In the meantime, try not to allow yourself to become overly anxious no matter what happens.

One of my favorite lines from the movie *The Untouchables* captures the essence of the righteous warrior's mind-set. Sean Connery, who has to be one of the coolest actors who ever lived, was playing police officer Jim Malone. Officer Malone knew that a shipment of liquor from the gangster Al Capone was about to arrive. He told his colleague: "Don't wait for it to happen. Don't even want it to happen. Just watch what does happen." In fact, if you are a hunter or sportsman, you may recognize that this mind-set closely mirrors how you've been trained to shoot. Hunters set themselves, aim, then slowly increase the pressure on the trigger so that the gun "shoots itself." In fact, when the gun goes off it almost surprises them. Bruce Lee described this state of mind when he advised, "Be water, my friend." You go with the punches and accept what life allows. You learn to live your life as it comes: on its terms. And come what may, you handle it. A righteous warrior must adapt.

Secure the Parameters

After you've identified the source of your Power and are learning more about your Place and your Purpose, it's essential to define your Parameters. By that I mean boundaries, borders, and limits.

Just as God told Adam in the Garden of Eden, you can touch this, but you can't touch the tree of the knowledge of good and evil, a man must figure out who and what he is called to "touch," or impact, by applying his gifts, talents, and abilities to them. It is equally essential that he create, understand, and honor boundaries that mark what's off limits for him. In other words, he needs to develop his own internal and external rules and limits.

Having high standards, principles, yardsticks, benchmarks, and measures of righteousness and quality not only protect a man, they help establish guiding ideas that focus his energy and call him up to a higher level of his humanity and potential. In the process, they help open the door to a man's best life.

One way to think of Parameters is that they are like the sidelines, end zones, and rules in sports. These boundaries help us understand what game we're playing, and how to stay on the field score. When we define clear Parameters and stay inside them, their focusing power will help strengthen us. Say, for example, you set a standard for yourself that you will practice a skill for fifteen minutes each day to develop yourself. Over time, your focus will turn a new area of knowledge into a strength. In this respect Parameters help focus our efforts.

Parameters also assist us by helping us figure out who we are and who we're not and what we will and will not do. Say you're working your way through school and your money is tight. You have to decide whether you can go out every Friday night. Though you'd love to hang out and have fun, you decide to stay home and study as you build your future life.

A man's Parameters can help him differentiate between his field of play and that of others. For instance, if you own a restaurant you may decide that you want to specialize in a take-out rather than a sit-down menu. In other words, it helps you stay in your lane. Parameters also set a man apart and help to brand him. For instance, some celebrities are known for living life in the fast lane, but others live quiet and private lives. These Parameters become part of their reputation and brand.

A righteous man knows that he can't have everything, nor does he even want that. It's important to create mental, emotional, physical, and spiritual boundaries. For instance, creating mental boundaries helps us focus our mind and attention so that we get the results we want. Getting our mind right about where we're heading and where we're not can help us home in on what's important in our life. This also means that we need to let some things go. Emotionally, we need Parameters around factors like how much of other people's issues we are going to take on, or what we will and will not allow other people to say to us. Many of us also demonstrate limits about who we confide in about our hopes and dreams. We may share openly with people who believe in us but draw a line around sharing our aspirations with people we find discouraging. Physically, we may require a certain amount of personal space around us or have standards around whether, who, when, how, and under what conditions we will allow other people to touch us. Many guys also have standards that relate to their spiritual life. Some men end their day by spending time with God or in some type of spiritual study; others won't let their children leave home without praying over them.

Having strong Parameters also helps a man protect himself from threats to his time, treasure, talents, job, family, and even his freedom. Of course, it's essential to safeguard ourselves and our loved ones—whether from the consequences of bad choices, danger, temptations, ill will, and even evil. We must set boundaries and limits around things like where we will and will not go and what we will and will not do—and to know why. Parameters also help us know what to turn our attention away from. All of us need a deeply held belief, or even a theology, that tells us when we should stop and when we need to say "enough." We need to know when to stop wasting our time, stop spending our money, stop sleeping, eating, flirting, and so on. Indeed, Parameters also become part of our internal governance system that can help us to choose between right and wrong. Rich lost many years of productive life because he did not observe the moral Parameters his family had taught him. Without their protection, he found himself addicted to drugs and leading a life of crime.

How can you establish your Parameters? The process is different for every man. You have to take responsibility for setting boundaries around yourself; no one else can set them for you. Some men intentionally draw a line around certain topics or behaviors and then take ten steps back from it for safekeeping. For instance, some married men won't have dinner or drinks with a woman who's not their wife. Other guys create rules like what they will and will not say or do to women; for instance, they don't cuss in front of a woman. Others adopt rules to self-govern, like prohibiting themselves from dating anyone they work with—a rule that can protect them from misunderstandings, workplace breakups, and allegations of sexual harassment. Each of us knows our own personal proclivities. Whether over-spending or pornography, consider setting limitations based on things that tempt you. Some things also need to be taboo—lines you never cross. For example, no man should ever look with lust at any child.

Just as practicing martial arts moves thousands of times causes those moves to become second nature, men who live by clear Parameters when life is going well will find that those Parameters provide structure, comfort, and support when difficulties hit. Indeed, the same ground rules, guidelines, and limits that help when the sailing is smooth become even more helpful once the sea of life gets choppy. When you have already been practicing a structured and principled approach to life, you can just continue to do what you've already been doing and you won't flounder morally or need to start a new lifestyle.

Not Gonna Be Able to Do

Parameters also help clarify what we will and will not agree to do.

Whether you are laughing at a joke, shaking hands on a new job, or cosigning on your son's new car loan, it's important to be clear what you are and are not giving your approval to, whether written or implied. Whenever you agree (or cosign) with someone, you're saying outright or implying, "I am with you." When you agree with the right person in the right situation, the positive upside implications are tremendous. Agreements can open doors, start new businesses, create new possibilities, kick-start partnerships, and add new people to your life—including your life partner; marriage is the ultimate agreement. When people agree to come together, doing so compounds their abilities.

But it's important not to say yes all the time. A righteous man has to be able to say no. He has to say "I don't like that," "that's not good," "I disagree," "that's out of bounds," "you can't do that," "I'm out!," and even "I'm gonna call the police!"

In other words, every man has to both define and hold the line on his righteousness. Your standards not only strengthen you, but your ability to stand by them will make other men respect, look up to, and even want to follow you. Lowered standards open us up to people disrespecting and even hurting us. Beyond that, if everyone can always count on you to be a "yes man," can anyone trust you to tell the truth? And if you always think the same thing and agree all the time, your predictability may render you useless.

That said, there are different ways a man needs to learn how to say no.

Agree to disagree. First, every man needs to be able to say, "I disagree with you on this, but I am still connected to you." That is to say, you can disagree with someone or have a different perspective, yet still believe in and respect them overall. There's no need to separate yourself from, give up on, or speak poorly about another man just because you see things differently. You can even strongly disagree with someone and stay in a relationship with them.

Cut them loose. However, there may be times when you disagree with someone enough—or about something so important to you—that you need to part ways, whether temporarily or even permanently. Marriages can heal from affairs and lots of them do. But the key component in doing that is that communication with the third party has to cease. You and your spouse can rebound or bounce back, but it cannot happen until the outside person is no longer part of the conversation. There is no other way to do it.

It's likely that your dreams involve going to college, or hitting a deadline, or obtaining a certification so you can progress to the next level. If your friends want you to hang out too late on game day, you have to set boundaries and limits. Every man needs to learn to say things like: "No thanks—I want to study for class"; "I'm leaving, I need to be on time for work"; "I'm working my plan, so I want you to stop distracting me"; "No thanks, I'm good"; or "Nah, I'm out!" You can catch them another time.

Sometimes holding on to your standards means choosing to go your

own way permanently. Every man will face turning points where uphold-
ing his ideals or achieving his dreams requires letting select people go. You
may have to call folks on their stuff and tell them, "Listen, I cannot ride
with you on this because the direction in which you're heading is not only
bad for you, it's also bad for me!" You have to develop the ability to say
things like, "I love you, but this is not worth it." You have to be willing to
tell people, "I'm heading to my next level and if you're not ready or willing
to adjust, I'll have to leave you here!"

Once Rich was released from prison, he didn't want to go back, so he
established extremely strong boundaries around himself.

"When I came out, I had no trust in nobody. I didn't want to deal
with anyone. Because that's how I wound up in prison—by trusting the
wrong people," he says. "Most times, in the world I was living in, if people
did something for me, they wanted something back."

Rich established a strong perimeter around himself and maintained it
until he got clean and began to trust himself and demonstrate better judgment.

"As time went on, I found friends first, then we became brothers and I
learned that I could trust again," he says. "I grew up with sisters; it took
me sixty years to finally get some brothers. Now I'm clingy!"

Break the bro code. A righteous warrior must also know when it's important not to demonstrate a misguided loyalty to other men's immature,
dishonorable, and even toxic behavior and expressions of masculinity.
There are times when we may bite our tongue because we don't want to
say anything harmful or out of order—or something genuinely isn't our
business. But it's a whole 'nother thing to know that something wrong is
going on, yet to be cynical, selfish, or so fearful to stand up and say no
that you turn a blind eye toward what you see. For instance, only men can
break the bad behavior that perpetuates the inhumanity and inequality of
racism, sexism, misogyny, homophobia, Islamophobia, hatred of immi-
grants, and other similarly despicable behavior. Whether racist or sexist

jokes, emails, or memes, the bullying of someone vulnerable, sexual harassment, intimate-partner violence, sex trafficking, school or police shootings or gun violence toward or between civilians, and even terrorism, far too often guys witness things they know are wrong yet say nothing out of a misguided loyalty to a type of manhood that is harmful to everyone. Just as we experienced in the Amazon, if it looks like an animal hole, it is. If it looks slippery, it is. Face the facts.

Whether we're the ringleader or unexpectedly find ourselves in situations like these, our silence constitutes our assent and agreement. From a moral standpoint, not saying something is the same as doing it. Not only will going along to get along weaken you as a man, because you have not separated yourself, you will face the same consequences as those who are acting out—whether in the realm of spiritual law or in the material world. When a man actively or implicitly agrees with things, he either reaps the benefit of them or suffers the punishment associated with them. Men who are silent when they should dissent can find themselves in a storm that was not of their own creation and catching hell for someone else's stuff.

No means no. In addition to learning to say "no" himself, a man with good Parameters is able to hear and handle "no" when it is said to him. Indeed, a man is in trouble if he doesn't know how to handle "no," deal with things that don't go his way, or distinguish between something that's not resolved and something that's not to his liking. Men who don't know how not to internalize a "no" so they don't feel like a failure will eventually find themselves in deep trouble.

Hearing "no" when you have poor Parameters can trigger needless confrontations, abuse, broken trust, rape, and worse. You certainly aren't ready for the fifth P of Personhood—your Partner—because a man who cannot live within Parameters isn't ready to be a Partner. Though many women beat their heads against the wall trying, his Partner cannot give a man his Parameters—and whether in a romantic relationship or otherwise, a man who doesn't have Parameters cannot be trusted.

A Man's Stand

That said, disagreeing without being disagreeable and telling people difficult things without sounding judgmental is an essential skill. Guys need a productive way to express differences, which is particularly important since most of our disagreements will be with people we love and respect.

Loving someone does not require us to close our eyes and cover our ears when we believe they are doing something wrong. Love involves standing up for what is right and being the standard when our loved ones stray. The fact that you love someone should not mean, "I will change my values for you." Sometimes the most powerful thing a man can do is hold the line on his Parameters and say, "This is not good for you, and it is because I love you that I will not help you do it."

A man must also be willing to walk away. You can do this in a firm but respectful way: "I disagree—and even if we must part company and go separate ways on this issue, I will remain in relationship with you." This African-centered approach emphasizes relatedness, not exclusion or expulsion, in the face of human difference. We also need to distinguish between people who have a blind spot or weakness or whose struggles we have contributed to (and so we should assist) versus someone who is willful and hell-bent on doing their thing and whom we should let hit rock bottom, forgiving him only after he apologizes and changes his way.

It's important whenever you correct or discipline someone you love that you also give them a way to come back into your life. The truth of the matter is that none of us are perfect. We all deserve another chance. So even when someone in his life does something wrong or even immoral, a righteous warrior gives them the chance to repent, meaning "change directions." People make mistakes, have human weaknesses, and exercise bad judgment occasionally. A firm but loving conversation about your differences can allow both of you to go to the next level, perhaps even together.

But if I'm going to be perfectly honest, standing on principle can be uncomfortable. It's no easy thing to tell someone you care for that "I disagree with you strongly" or "I can't roll like this anymore." The truth of the matter is, there are times when holding your values will require you to take a position that people who matter to you do not want you to take. There are times, when you stand up for what is right, that people will look at you like you've got two heads.

In my life as a public figure today, I'm wrestling with how to call out systemic evil and racism—which are important, real, and well documented—while at the same time raising issues of personal accountability. It's not always easy for me to talk to Black people about the ways we can be complicit in our own demise. I'd imagine that the same is true for a White pastor talking to his congregation about White privilege and unconscious racial bias. These are difficult issues; I know that I don't have all the answers. But my theology says that people can break through unfair systems, so I also can't settle for the belief that racist systems have the power to keep us entrapped forever. But sometimes the places where I draw the line make other Black people uncomfortable.

As I often experience, you should expect times when, because of your stand, you will no longer be invited, permitted to participate, or be part of the "in" crew precisely because you stand firmly upon your standards. A righteous warrior risks losing friends, having some folks not understand him and others talk about him behind his back. It hurts when people we love don't understand us or can't accompany us to the next level—or when we can no longer be with them. It can be very painful to have others who matter to us exclude, reject, and even cut us off. Though your standards may make you unpopular in the short term, Parameters give you a strength and clarity that give you power. Your stand will not only clarify who you are, it will attract strong people with similar morals and values.

The Tough Get Growing

All living things change. In fact, things that don't change eventually die out. But change can be challenging—and we may not have chosen it. For instance, our world may be turned upside down when our father passes away, our daughter develops an addiction, or our wife wants a divorce. Every man will be faced with facts such as these throughout his life. I was devastated after my brother died, and even though I knew that my father was ill and about to pass away, knowing that in advance didn't make it any less heartbreaking when it happened.

While most guys want to experience the fruits of our growth, lots of guys don't like experiencing growth itself. We like to talk about where we are today, but if we look back at the process, our growing pains probably got pretty uncomfortable. During periods of challenge and change, we all experience situations where nobody else can help us, people just don't understand, or folks whom we never expected to envy or "hate" us. In other words, while change may be good *for* you, it doesn't always feel good *to* you.

In the weeks leading up to our Amazon adventure, a member of Bear Grylls's team sent out an email asking for more information about the members of our crew.

"We had to provide our physical description, height, and weight," Jerome remembers. "At the time I was 330, 340—somewhere in that range. The guy emailed back questioning my ability to even participate. That became motivation for me. I was like, 'You don't know me, dude! Who the hell do you think you are telling me what I can and cannot do?!' "

The truth of the matter was that Jerome copped an attitude as a defense mechanism because he wasn't well prepared. During the months prior to the trip, "Sometimes I'd be like, 'I'm gonna hang out with Leroy and work out,' but other times I'd say, 'No, I'll catch ya later.' I'd go back and forth, back and forth," he admits.

The hike out into the jungle turned out to be much more demanding than he had expected.

"The terrain, the steepness, and not being in great shape made it difficult. We carried backpacks that weighed forty or fifty pounds. At one point, Vernell ended up carrying my backpack. He had to carry mine and his own," Jerome remembers. "Even with no backpack, I reached a point where I could hardly breathe. The camp was right there, but I was like, 'Oh my god, I can't breathe!' It was a very humbling experience. I ended up having to admit that the guy was right."

That night around the campfire, we had a meeting.

"We said, look, man, you can't keep doing this," says Leroy. "Nobody was actually cussing, but we kind of cussed him out, since the rest of us had had to share his pack. We said, 'You have to make some decisions.' We were trying to build him up, but what we were really saying was, 'You have to do some stuff differently.' "

Indeed, change signifies that something is over—whether a season, a place, or a relationship. It's not unusual for it to hurt; that's why so many of us run back to familiar people, places, and things whenever our life becomes uncomfortable. Sometimes things get worse first.

"Listening to my brothers was hard, but it was motivation to say, 'You gotta get it together. You can't continue to live your life overweight and out of shape. You're a heart attack waiting to happen,'" says Jerome.

Some medicine tastes bad going down—you may even feel lousy after that first dose, then it starts working and begins to make you better.

"You could call it a midlife crisis," Jerome says. "But it was like, okay, if you're gonna be in this, you can't go half ass. If you're really going to be serious about changing your life and changing your mentality and really looking at your life differently, you can't have one foot in and one foot out—you have to be all in."

There are also times when change feels so difficult because you're not moving from good or even okay to bad, or even from bad to good, you're going from good to great. In fact, it can be hard to identify or even ac-knowledge that the wonderful life or good part of your life that you've been enjoying is no longer for you or no longer good for you. No matter the nature of the shift, change requires adjustment. At first, the new cir-cumstances may not feel or fit right. You'll need to adapt, and that is a process. To get to the next level, you may have to let go of old hurts, old ambitions, and old accomplishments. You can't keep talking about the things you used to do, that season is over. You have to let the old you go so you can become the new you.

"I was sick and tired of being sick and tired, of being heavy, of being out of breath, and my arthritis, my knees hurt, my back hurt," Jerome says. "You get sick and tired of 'I'm gonna change and on Monday I'm gonna start this diet and I'm gonna really work out, I'm gonna do all this stuff.'"

When we returned home to Philly, Jerome went to his doctor.

"Of course, my doctor had been beating me up about losing weight," Jerome says. Fortunately, this time Jerome really wanted help. His physi-cian enrolled him in a two-year weight-loss study.

"Basically, it was counting calories, which wasn't ideal, but it was what I had to do," Jerome says. "They also taught skills about what to eat, when to eat, when to recognize when you are hungry and when you're not hungry, and so forth like that—and just making smarter choices. I learned that when I had to check in every week and get on that scale, I wanted to be held accountable to somebody. I didn't like the feeling of 'Oh man, I know I gained a couple pounds, this ain't gonna be good.' I liked hearing 'You did a great job!' and it motivated me. Eventually, I got down to 299 pounds!"

Change requires us to stretch. We must push past some of the old parts of our selves in order to bring the new parts to life. We may need to renegotiate old agreements, ways of being, and relationships to make room. Sometimes this can be very exciting; however, this isn't always the case. Growth can also be difficult and even cause heartache and pain. Some growth seasons feel very dark and lonely. Folks may not see what you envision or understand what you're doing. The promise of your idea may not yet be visible to others. You might even struggle to explain it to the people that matter. These are the times when you have to encourage yourself and when prayer and a spiritual community become particularly important. This is a Truth of the human condition.

I witness many guys struggle to deal with their Truth—whether they need to develop themselves more in order to get a promotion, or stop spending so much money, or accept that their relationship or marriage is over. I don't count myself out; I, too, wrestle with it, particularly in the areas that have fueled my addiction. Indeed, alcoholism and addiction tend to be such a part of men's stories because so many of us haven't developed the ability to live on life's terms. Learning to handle life however it comes is one of the keys to breaking free from your drug of choice, whether food, overworking, shopping, or gambling; otherwise, for those of us who are addicts, rather than dealing with change and challenge, we run off into our addiction. While most people are able to enjoy a glass of wine with dinner, I need to establish Parameters around what I drink; I usually stick with water.

The recovery process teaches us to stay where we are and deal with facts, rather than lying or using our addictive substances or processes to escape them. The goal isn't to white-knuckle our way through challenges, but to become a person whose body, soul, and spirit line up. When we achieve this, we have integrity—meaning not that we are a good person but that we are a whole and complete person. In other words, our mind says do it and our body and soul can make it happen. From this place, we can not only control ourselves, but also demonstrate a healthy form of leadership, whether at home, in our workplace, in our community, or in the world.

Check the Expiration Date

In nature, seasons have a beginning, middle, and end, then they transition gracefully to the next season. As much as we may want spring and summer to stick around, April rains turn into May flowers, and beach season draws to a close and it's time to go back to school. Even good things end and you have to go through the door to the next season.

Everyone's life is full of beginnings and endings; we all experience both gains and losses. Over the course of your life you will meet new people and embark upon new adventures, master them, seek new ones, and eventually experience the thrill of the hunt again. The circle of life requires us occasionally to say good-bye to familiar people, places, and things. In order to start something new, you need to stop—or at least cut back on—something else. You may have habits to break and routines to outgrow. You may need to transition out of one job or career and into another—you may even lose your mate, or job, or home as part of that transition. Increasingly men are discovering that the career path they have prepared themselves for is shifting or even drying up. This is not personal; it's part of life. Even disruptive activities like returning to school, letting go of your home (or moving back home), or relocating to a different city can be part of a man's growth.

Just as the clock may run out on certain activities, it may also wind down on some relationships. You may have to let go of old friends, as Rich did, or spend less time with them. You may experience a tense period during your marriage, a separation, or, if you're not paired with the right partner, divorce. You may experience tense moments or seasons with your children, particularly during their adolescence, or if your family breaks up. As Vernell, Jerome, Leroy, and I experienced, some of your loved ones will eventually die. If you become injured or as you age, you may lose some or all of your health. Eventually, all of us will lose our life and hopefully go to heaven.

Loss, too, can be a context for development, when looked at with the combat mind-set.

No living thing produces in the same way forever. Sometimes in order to stay productive or become even more productive, a plant must be rotated into different soil or pruned. Pruning cuts off dead parts of the plant to allow the nutrients, energy, and resources to be redirected. Activities in some areas of your life may need to be cut back to redeploy your energy more productively. You have to know when the current "soil" has dried up and it's time to move to the next place. Though, in the short term, pruning and repotting shock the plant, ultimately it will bounce back and become bigger and healthier than before the dead limbs were cut off.

Some men aren't as productive as they could be because they refuse to submit to life's natural pruning and purging process. We aren't supposed to stay in any level of development forever. All seasons have the equivalent of a sell-by date. If you get stuck in one season, your life will "curdle" and the "pickings" in that environment will get slim. There are also times when there is no next step—when it's important to develop wherever you are. Because sometimes life just is what it is, you can't fix or improve it in that moment or phase. Wishing for what doesn't exist won't make it come true. You must face the facts and let go of the fantasy. You cannot get to your dream until you deal with reality. You have to catch up on your rent, pay your back taxes, pay down your credit card, develop professionally in place. And since wherever you go you take yourself with you, if you want your life to change, you first need to change yourself. Sometimes that happens exactly where you are. Your spiritual practice can help you find meaning and purpose however things are. Growth often hurts, but it's worth it.

At a New Level, a New Devil

When I was a child, my father would give me chores to complete in his garden. That's where I learned that threats to growth come with the territory and are part of each season.

Opposition can threaten your development. Like it or not that's just a fact of life. This is another area where your Parameters come in. There are two categories of obstacles that I think you need to watch out for: the internal obstacles that can be found within yourself and external factors. Every difficulty isn't outside of us; sometimes *we* are the challenge. We may need to do healing work to clear belief systems or trauma that limit us. But even if we haven't been traumatized, we may need to engage in positive self-talk to encourage ourselves as we face challenges. Indeed, many of us stay stuck because of the way we speak to ourselves, not because other people discourage us. We all need to engage in self-criticism, but we should not let it debilitate us. We all have to learn to fight through any negative voices and tapes that family members, other people, and our society have created for us. It's important to affirm yourself in the process. Sometimes this requires the help of a counselor, therapist, minister, or spiritual adviser.

In addition to his own self-talk, every man also faces opposition from the world. If you're a gardener or enjoy working in your yard, even cute animals like chipmunks, rabbits, and deer can consume months of your labor, seemingly overnight. Then, too much sun and too much rain—both of which are necessary for life—can also threaten a plant's well-being. Just as I refer to them in the garden, I call these threats to a man's growth "critters." Whether credit cards, women, electronics, cars, grown family members who don't stand on their own feet, or other distractions, it's important for a righteous warrior to identify what critters jeopardize his "crop," or the goals and dreams he's going after, and what steps he needs to take to protect his harvest. Remember, if it looks slippery, it is slippery. Particularly in a society designed to separate you from your money, materialism can distract or even derail you from your destiny. The opposition you'll face changes at each new level of development. Difficulties, nuisances, obstacles, and anxieties unique to each stage of or place in life exist. Just as a new burst of opposition suddenly arises in a video game right before you reach the door to the next level, expect the same thing to happen in real life. God doesn't show you a door unless you can walk through it, but you have to fight through opposition. The good news is no matter what challenges you, you must always remember that the doorknob is on your side.

In life, nothing of value ever comes easy. The presence of opposition af-

firms that what's on the other side of the door is worthwhile. It also con-
firms that what you have to offer is valuable. Think of your opposition as
helping you. Similar to the opposition in a video game, life's challenges prepare you to handle the next level. Whether the assignment is an aspect of the
"weed-out" class, which exists on many jobs to distinguish the halfhearted
from the resolute, it's important to face the facts, recognize what you're dealing with, and not to take it personally. Once you make it over that hurdle,
you can feel confident that you are prepared for what is to follow.

But let me be the first person to tell you: Fighting through opposition
can be very lonely. There are some things that every man has to go through
by himself. Yet, when you're clear about your Power, Place, and Purpose
and live within your Parameters, neither this loneliness nor your haters can
thwart your ambition. In fact, your haters can even become your "eleva-
tors," propelling you upward as you walk the righteous path toward your
destiny. Pushing past such fear and obstacles will allow you to access more
of your destiny, because each man must reach beyond where he's been in
order to become the man he is capable of being. Every season comes to an
end, and as a creek flows into the river, be like water and follow the river
of life. No matter what is happening during any one particular phase, by
the time your life is wrapping up, you will look back and see how it all
made sense.

In the meantime, there's no need to fixate on any particular outcome
in any particular moment. As we experienced in the rain forest, face the
facts and respond accordingly. Whatever happens in your life, be good
with it.

Conserve Your Resources

Identify and protect your assets so you can invest in your goals and protect yourself from society's seductive attempts to part you from your money and pull you into narrow definitions of manhood that can limit you and keep you from fulfilling your dreams.

AFTER NINE DAYS in the Amazon with the fellas, the time had come to attempt to live on our own. The rubber was hitting the road.

"Tomorrow morning, we're going to put what you've learned to the test and see what you know," Craddock said.

I was excited and felt like I was up to the challenge, but I wouldn't be fully honest if I didn't admit that my heart started racing.

"Everything you've learned during the past nine days you will need to apply in a thirty-six-hour experience," he said. "We will drop you off at eight in the morning and you will need to survive until eleven the following morning."

Rather than being dropped off individually, we decided to partner up. Vernell and I ended up together. We had to find water, build our hut, identify food, and start our fire. In order to do this we had to manage our time. Time was of the essence because it would eventually get dark. We also had to create a plan, identify and manage our resources, and work our plan. At this point in our excursion, a mistake could cause one of us to get hurt; a big mistake could even be deadly.

Step one was to figure out where we would build our hut and where to find the wood. This was important not only because we needed a place to stay, but also because when the sun goes down the one thing you do not want to have happen is for your fire to go out. A fire not only keeps you warm, it also helps to keep the animals away, so finding our wood was of the utmost importance.

We knew from our dress rehearsals that finding the right trees, gathering and chopping wood, and building the hut would take about four hours. We needed to find four smallish trees with Y-shaped branches above our heads that could serve as the corners of our hut's roof as well as four Y-shaped branches down low that could form the corners of our beds. The trees also needed to be in a rectangular relationship to each other and not in the middle of any animal's stuff. In addition to that, we had to find two long pieces of wood that could form two sides of our roof and four long pieces of wood that would form the sides of our beds. We planned to do these tasks, leaving some margin just in case something didn't go as planned or took longer than we'd expected.

So we paid attention and applied what we'd learned, asking questions like: "Are we in an animal's front yard?" and "Are we messing with something's food source?" We studied the ground looking for signs of animal life and steered clear of them. We spent the entire morning chopping enough wood to build our hut and burn. I joke that we probably chopped down half of the Amazon—we *did not* want that fire to go out at night! But we were also very aware of the importance of this natural resource.

We then located a big "papa crit" tree, whose bark can be used as rope, and began to shave its bark off. We tied each rope off at the ends to secure our hut's framework. We then identified a different tree with very big leaves. We used those leaves to create our roof; some other leaves formed the back wall. We secured much of our structure with *capidula* vine. Once that was done, we identified the trees we could use as medicine and the trees that would provide the cotton we'd ignite to start our fire.

After that, we located the Amazon River, which would be the source of our water. Standing along the riverside left me awestruck by its size and power. Looking up and down the river at all of the trees from ground level—and being able to see how massive they are—gave me a deeper appreciation for why the Amazon rain forest is called the Lungs of the Planet. Amazonia produces more than twenty percent of the world's oxygen. It was awesome to stand virtually alone in the midst of it.

Then we turned to food. We'd already been taught to identify what bugs we could and could not eat. We located a tree that grew a particular nut that contained a larva, a little worm, inside it. We could eat the larva because it contained a lot of protein, but that same grub was also good for catching piranha and other fish. As we gathered these nuts, we had to make a decision: How many were we going to eat right away and how many were we going to use to catch a piranha? Because while one grub might stave off our hunger in this particular moment, a piranha would be much more satisfying and would nourish us for a longer period of time. Should we eat the larva now or use it as bait to catch something bigger later? We'd been practicing this trade-off all week. Now the time had come to decide on our own. Since we only had to make it through thirty hours, we chose to conserve our energy by eating the nuts and living on vegetation rather than hunting or even fishing.

When we weren't chopping down wood, searching for materials and food, or building our hut, we stayed pretty still, trying not to expend energy. We were nervous and wanted to keep our knife sharp, so we spent a lot of time sharpening our machete. We were forced to conserve stuff, save and take care of what we had far better than we ever did at home. The entire time we kept our eyes on the clock.

A couple of hours before nightfall, we turned our attention toward making our fire. We separated the wood that burned fast to start the fire from the wood that burned slow to maintain it overnight. Then we took the flint and the cotton and started our fire. Once night fell, things got a little scary. Vernell and I just sat there and whistled and talked. We figured that if we whistled the animals would know we were there and leave us alone. It was one thing to be in the Amazon with people who knew what they were doing; it was an entirely different thing to be in Amazonia by ourselves. Our eyes still hadn't adjusted enough for us to see beyond our hands in front of our faces. Vernell and I talked about everything that night. Eventually we felt safe enough to sleep in twenty-minute shifts. One would nap while the other stayed awake.

In the Amazon, understanding your resources and managing them well can be the difference between life and death. Once we got back home, the experience had helped us understand that conserving resources can mean the difference between an inspiring life where you live into your destiny and one filled with disappointment, regret, and unfulfilled wishes.

Mass Consumption

The Amazon contains everything you need to survive, but you have to know what's in the environment and how to use it. You have to keep your eye on your most important resource—time—as well as how you're going to apportion your day. While the clock ticked, we had to do things like start our fire, distinguish between the bark that makes strong ropes and the bark we could cook for medicine, figure out which nuts contained edible larva, and whether we should eat it or use it as bait. We had to decide when and whether to exchange the short-term pleasure of eating bugs now for the promise of something better and longer lasting, such as catching a piranha—or whether you even want to waste your limited time and energy fishing at all.

Similarly, a righteous warrior must protect his assets and be aware of how he allocates them—his time and his money, in particular. In other words, a righteous warrior must be resourceful. The world is full of distractions designed to pull him off course, so a man needs a long-term vision for what he wants to accomplish, a passion that pulls him into that future, and a strategy for managing his resources if he wants to fulfill his destiny. He has to consider things like what quarter of his life he is playing in, where he's positioned on life's field, and what game plan he needs to execute in order to advance toward his goals. He has to decide how much of every dollar he's going to spend on himself or his family today versus how much he's going to save and invest in things like his children's future or seeding his own dreams. He also needs to set some money aside to protect himself and his loved ones from financial disruptions, which occur as part of the natural economic cycles of life—whether a parent passes away and he has to pay for the family's flights back home, or his wife's health scare requires her to take time off from work, or his career path goes poof when he turns fifty-five. Along his journey, a righteous warrior considers the risks and rewards and the trade-offs and costs inherent in his choices.

But thinking about responsibilities like conserving our time and resources, taking care of our possessions, and saving and investing for the future runs counter to popular culture, which promotes consumption and the short term over the permanent and enduring. From coffee pods, to plastic grocery bags, to disposable plastic water bottles, our society is so addicted to throwaway items that they threaten our rivers, clog the oceans, and endanger the planet. Even expensive goods like cars and electronics are designed to become obsolete. This mentality pervades our lives so deeply that many of us even spend time judging potential life partners as "hot" or "not," swiping through people's pictures as though the human heart is expendable. Some people even plan to have starter marriages, assuming that the first one is just for practice rather than for permanence.

By definition, a consumer society conditions us to acquire and consume goods and services in ever-increasing amounts—and entices us to come back for more. Indeed, I have watched many a man get himself in trouble trying to be a "baller," "shot caller," or otherwise trying to fit into someone else's image of manhood, which often involves living beyond his means. I often watch young men try to "live large" before they have laid down a solid foundation consisting of the education, training, and personal development they need in order to build their life on rock rather than sand.

In a society set up to separate a man from his money even before he has the chance to plant his feet in adulthood, every guy has to learn to distinguish what he wants from what he needs, what society wants him to want from what's best for his future and that of his family. Because while it isn't bad for you to have things, it is essential to ensure that things don't "have" you.

Know Your Niche

Many men believe that they have dominion over others. The concept of dominion comes from the Bible, which states that man has dominion over the other creatures of the earth. I interpret the use of the word "man" to mean human beings, though some people interpret it literally to mean only men. Whether or not you're Christian or even spiritual at all, dominion is an important concept to understand. Our nation's Founding Fathers were Christian and many powerful men in American society were raised in the Judeo-Christian tradition. Consequently, the idea is prevalent throughout American culture, though often invisibly; it's rarely explicitly discussed except in church. But even within religious circles there is more than one definition of "dominion." So it's important that we ask ourselves: What does "dominion" actually mean—and what ways and under what circumstances should a man exercise it?

One definition of "dominion" denotes "taking over." In other words, human beings—and men in particular—were created to be in charge of everyone and everything. Consistent with this, throughout most of American history, men have exercised either the right or their ability to dominate women and children; the most powerful dominate those who are less powerful, and human beings use people and creatures for their own purposes, in general. Men who live according to this definition of "dominion" tend to believe to one level or another that they have the right to be in charge of, take advantage of, exploit, or otherwise do whatever they want to other people, animals, and things. At its most extreme, it plays out as a zero-sum, winner-take-all, survival-of-the-fittest, dog-eat-dog approach to life. We see it when guys attempt to control and even dominate women, make business decisions that exploit natural resources yet destroy the environment, and in the tremendous pay gaps between CEOs and workers as the gap between the haves and the have-nots grows wider.

A different definition of "dominion" carries the idea of "taking care of." It acknowledges that everyone and everything has a life and Purpose of its own as well as a Place within life's ecosystem. Men who live according to this definition do not seek to dominate others but to help to create and contribute to an environment in which everyone can fulfill their Purpose. We witnessed this idea of interconnectivity in the Amazon, as all kinds of wildlife—from river otters, to jaguars and cougars, to bats, to tarantulas—coexisted with one another. Consistent with what occurs in the natural world, a man's Purpose, then, is to find his Place, inhabit it fully, and participate in the connection that exists between all living creatures.

A righteous man lives according to this second definition of "dominion."

A man can deepen this commitment by practicing good stewardship. When I use the word "stewardship," I mean planning, managing, and caretaking of your resources. A man who practices good stewardship empowers himself to shift the focus of his life away from how much he makes and what he owns. Instead he develops a deeper understanding of the resources he has and focuses on what he does with them no matter how much (or how little) that is, because a man's resources are not limited to money. Even though for much of his life his financial resources have been tight, Vernell takes great care of his word and his reputation.

"One of my grandfather's biggest rules was that you need to be on time, do what you say you're going to do, and do what you need to do as a man—what is required of you," says Vernell. "If I say I'm gonna do some-thing, I'm gonna do it. That kind of consistency becomes a point of pride. I have people counting on me. Who am I to let them down?"

In fact, a man who understands good stewardship can break free from his dependence upon money. People see that he's extremely disci-plined, trustworthy, and reliable; as a result, he gets offered wonderful opportunities.

Because a righteous warrior knows that uncovering his Purpose, be-coming excellent at it, and making good use of whatever resources he has, financial or otherwise, is priceless. Indeed, wealth is about more than hav-ing a big paycheck or how much cold hard cash you can hoard or sock away. While it's definitely important to use your money wisely, far too many men miss out on the riches that result from things like training and educating themselves, taking good care of their health, sharing their gifts and talents with others, caring for their children and creating a rewarding family life, educating and developing themselves to their fullest, exploring their dreams, and so on. These and other nonfinancial assets can be put to good use. And as someone who has sat at the bedside of many men who have lost their health or are dying, they're not thinking about their car or their bank account. It's much more common for men to regret that they missed their children's childhood or to be tormented about lost time. Said another way, though there's nothing wrong with aspiring to do well finan-cially, that should not be the goal; that's the "gravy." A man who practices good stewardship not only gets the most mileage out of his money, he also experiences the riches of having a fulfilling life.

Even a man with a tremendous amount of money can be taken down by poor stewardship. We see a very dramatic example of this when ath-letes, entertainers, and people who win the lottery lose their fortunes. I don't bring this up to shame or blame them. Most haven't been educated about what it means to have that much money, or how to handle it. So be-tween taxes, agents, managers, their own consumption, caring for family and hangers-on, most of them end up broke within five years. Because they lack the support they need to be good stewards of their riches, many end up no better off than the man who earned a modest income but who managed his money well. The man who understands that his resources mean more than money and that he has the power over what he does with them can have a surprising amount of Power.

Pick Your Spots

The concept of conserving your resources is also essential in the martial arts. Every fighter knows that he has to hold on to his energy.

During a workout or fight, energy conservation actually has to do with the fighter's breathing. In fact, learning how to breathe is one of the keys to staying fresh and maintaining access to his power. A fighter will tire if, as a result of getting tense, he starts holding his breath, as most people do under those conditions. Not breathing zaps all your energy. So a fighter must take in enough breath, then exhale the tension and stress. You have probably heard a fighter manage his breathing in the loud *shh-shh* you hear each time he throws a punch. This oxygenates his limbs and keeps his energy in his body. And not only does a fighter need to keep breathing, he also needs to steady his breathing. He breathes in through the nose and out through the mouth. (In and out through the mouth tends to dry out the mouth and throat.) This circular pattern also helps to create a steady rhythm. If he disrupts this rhythm or stops breathing evenly, he will tense up and his energy will plummet. Being conscious of the breathing also helps a fighter focus.

It's also important that fighters keep moving. Indeed, fighting is like a dance; everything is in motion. Just like athletes in other sports want to play their own game, every fighter wants to move to the beat of his own drum, not to the beat of his opponent. Every fight or style of fighting should have its own cadence. One way a fighter can find his own rhythm is by listening to music. Master Robinson hears James Brown in his head. He sets up and moves into his positions to Brown's tunes. If you let him, he'll even draw you into his rhythm. When he successfully does that, he has you dancing his dance. In other words, you're moving to the rhythm of his resources. He breaks that rhythm whenever he wants to hit you.

A good fighter sticks to the style and skill set he knows well. In that way fighting is very simple. Your opponent has a right arm and left arm, a right leg and left leg, a head and a neck. In Naphtali, we have defensive moves to deal with each appendage. If he grabs at you with his right hand, you've trained so you know what to do with that. If he puts his head forward, you've trained so you know what to do with that. If he picks up his leg, you know what to do with that. In fact, the well-prepared fighter just waits for his opponent to do one of those things. When I'm fighting, I want you to put your left hand straight out. Because when you do that, I have prepared a series of moves and disciplines that will make me win. It's about preparing, keeping your breath, moving to your own rhythm, knowing what to do when an opportunity presents itself—then doing it.

That said, you don't have to get into every fight or exploit every opportunity. A smart fighter doesn't engage in a fight unless he is very sure he will be successful. He needs to ensure that the fight will be worth it. Even then, he wants to avoid engaging in any unnecessary tussles. A disciplined fighter picks his spots and avoids superfluous confrontations. Sometimes his opponent is playing the same game. He'll stick his foot out because he wants you to grab it, so he can then pull you into his rhythm. It's like a game of chess or cat and mouse: I know you want to grab it, so I'm not going to stick it out. So every fighter goes into his bout with a plan. He wants to get it over with quickly, but since he never knows when he'll have to go the distance, he prepares for that possibility. In the meantime, he has to manage his energy throughout the entire fight.

Grass or AstroTurf?

In addition to understanding the source of his Power, a righteous warrior also seeks to identify his Place. Because when he fully explores and inhabits the unique life he's been given and understands his resources, those resources begin to flow to him. In fact, many were already there; he was just unable to access them. In other words, when you occupy your Place, you don't always have to go out to chase money, you leverage the many forms of abundance you have, including money, and life comes to you. Just as the Amazon contains everything a man needs to survive, so does the path to his destiny.

In order to experience your most fulfilling life, it's important to remain open to the many ways that abundance can show up, whether in the form of opportunities, contacts, networks, gifts, opportunities for training and education, people's goodness and grace, coincidences, divine timing, and so on. For instance, when you've found your Place in life's ecosystem, the right people tend to show up when you need them and the things you've been searching for will often drop into your lap. When you free yourself from the belief that a man's wealth consists only of his money and possessions, you open yourself up to experience life more abundantly.

One of the powerful things about finding your Place is that it comes with the means to accomplish your Purpose. In other words, both the instructions to the game of life and the batteries for living it are included when you inhabit your lane. But you have to stay in your lane, as the Penn Relays taught us. That means you have to draw a boundary line between where you end and other folks begin—between your lane in life and another's. This is an area where many men struggle. It's easy to think the grass is greener on the other side of the fence. Sometimes what looks like green grass is actually AstroTurf. Or, your neighbor's lawn might be greener but your lawn can get green, too, if you water it. Uncover your own gifts, then work hard to develop them. Share them in the Place that exists only for you. Do this to the best of your ability and watch your blessings multiply.

Lots of guys get involved in things because someone told them to do it or because they see someone else doing it and they want their life, their possessions, or their results. In other words, we wander out of our lane, which doesn't usually get us the results we want. If there's anything I wish I could take back from my thirties, it would be the time I spent wishing I had some of my peers' gifts. I'm almost ashamed to admit that I envied one friend's oratory skills and another's ability to integrate hip-hop into his sermons. While I was coveting their gifts, I was overlooking my own very unique abilities. Enamored by my friends' skillfulness, I found myself on the cusp of being jealous. My envy got in the way of what could have been much richer friendships. You can't be your best in a relationship if you're jealous or keeping count of another person's abilities. As I matured and confronted the covetous mind-set I had toward their gifts, I realized I couldn't become my best self until I asked for their forgiveness.

Imitating another man's life won't re-create their results because we don't have their destiny and we don't have their needs. But even more painfully, placing our feet in other man's footsteps deprives us of the masculine journey that comes with forging our own journey.

But while our Place comes with batteries included, that doesn't mean that our life will be easy. A righteous man knows that he will always have to work hard, even when he knows the source of his Power is following his Purpose and his Place along his spiritual path. That said, when you are new in your journey and just developing your muscles you will likely experience a season where you will live above your pay grade, so to speak. This season will take place to encourage you. As you mature, you will graduate into seasons where you must use your resources thoughtfully and demonstrate increasing levels of stewardship. It will also be important that you contribute your part to the ecosystem of life by paying it forward, by becoming a blessing to others.

Even those of us who have found our path must remember that our society encourages us both to take more than we need and to accumulate things. Digital algorithms, big data, public relations, marketing, and commercials work on our psyches and spirits, making it difficult for us to distinguish between what we want and what we need. Lots of guys pray for what they want. Sometimes I count myself among them. However, the path to our destiny only comes with what we need. It's essential that we differentiate between the two. A need will be satisfied as soon as it is met. If you are thirsty, for instance, the solution is water. Once you drink enough water, you will no longer thirst. But the solution that appears to solve a want may not satisfy or resolve it. If you still hunger after the initial fix, it is a want you're dealing with.

Knowing your Place also helps protect you from the onslaught of marketing by helping you clarify your own vision and dreams. Your Place and Parameters complement each other, forming invisible boundaries that help protect your priorities and identify what falls outside of your Place. When you understand your Place, it's easier to protect your resources so you can direct them toward the goals and dreams that matter to you—whether a new "bun in the oven," a child's ballet or basketball camp, roof repairs, or stacking your loot for the business you plan to launch.

Discovering your Place doesn't mean that life will be easy or that you will (or won't) be wealthy according to the world's standards. To get there you will have to demonstrate faith. Indeed, the more faith and commitment you have, the more of your destiny you will achieve.

The Root of All Evil?

Though we are all spiritual beings having a human experience, life as spirituals beings includes material things. Therefore, all human beings require a medium of exchange. One hundred years ago, people often bartered with each other. Stores back then didn't always require money so banks existed but so did trading posts. My grandfather, a sharecropper in Rappahannock,

Virginia, didn't use money as much as he bartered eggs and flour. He would send my father to the store with three eggs and the instructions "Go get three eggs worth of" whatever he wanted.

Today, some people mistakenly believe that money is evil—often because they've been taught that by a religious Christian or at church. This is a misunderstanding of scripture. The Bible actually teaches that the love of money—in other words, *lusting* for money—not money itself, is the root of all evil. Indeed, craving money often lands us in trouble, as Rich discovered. His hunger for money, cars, diamonds, and women combined with the shortsightedness, risk-taking, and hardheadedness common to teenage males as well as older men made him a prime target of those who were eager to exploit him. As the only boy in a family of girls, he also longed for male friendship and companionship. But it was his lust for the symbols of material success that brought him down and caused him to be locked up for so many years. Of course, Rich is just an extreme example of what happens when you crave material things. More often this looks like an overextended credit card or buying things at Christmas that you can't really afford.

Indeed, commerce is central to human life, so money itself is merely a tool of the trade. Once you understand that your wealth is not limited to financial riches and your blessings are not restricted to material things, you increase your capacity to leverage all of your assets—whether your ideas, your networks, your training, or your physical strength. Money does not determine the quality of your life, but what you do with your money and other resources helps you create your life. Don't wait until all your loot is in place to start. Even before you have a knot in your wallet, begin to work your other assets. In fact, you can tell a lot about a person's spiritual life by looking at how they handle their money. Our faith plays itself out in our financial life. Do you have the faith to create the life of your dreams? Do you have the faith to step further and further into your destiny?

Most Americans are materialistic. We have way more than we need but feel we can't do without what we have. Life is easier when you don't own too much stuff. Spending consumes financial resources and having too much stuff can tie you down and undermine your ability to thrive. Plus, the world of money will periodically break down, as happens when the stock market melts down, when economic bubbles burst, and during economic slowdowns, recessions, depressions, and so forth. So, as you think about and interact with it, engage money in such a way that *when* it fails, not *if* it fails—that is, *when* you don't get the raise or bonus you'd hoped for, *when* interest rates climb, *when* the economy slows, *when* financial things don't go the way you want them to—you will still be all right. Because bumps occur in the economy and even the best-laid financial plan will occasionally go awry. One of your children will break their arm and you'll have an unexpected medical bill; you may need to travel to a funeral; you may need to return to school to retool. From time to time most of us will live with a sense of uncertainty about how we're going to make it.

Responsible financial stewardship opens up other ways to prosper. It also provides protection when the economy fails and opportunities to invest in yourself or others grow. You will have the peace of mind that comes when you're taking care of business. But to relate to money with a warrior mind-set, you may need to adjust some beliefs.

The Circle of Life

In the Amazon, it's easy to see that a Power exists that is much greater than ourselves. It was also easy for our elders to see the evidence of that force. For example, my grandfather sowed his seeds and then looked up to God and prayed for rain. The rains came, the crops came up, my father cultivated and sold them, then he gave thanks. Because God provided the sun and the rain, my grandfather could feed his family. If you go back 100 to 150 years, this is how most of our ancestors lived. The connection between what God gave them and what they had was clear. They were in tune with the sunrise and sunset, the stages of the moon, when to plant and when to harvest, the changing of seasons—the circle of life.

Between our grandparents' era and today, we've moved from a primarily agricultural society to one filled with cities with neighborhood stores that people could walk to, to one of suburbs with malls and big box stores, with big businesses and international organizations located everywhere. Today, you're more likely to work in a call center than plant your own seeds. The treasurer of your company likely signs your paycheck. But just as the sun and rain watered my grandfather's crops, the origins of your direct deposit began with God and passed through your employer's hands on its way to you.

Understanding and believing that God is your Source can give you the confidence both to provide for yourself and to be generous. Because when you believe that what you have came from God, not yourself, there's no need to be afraid to release what you have. It's hard not to be stingy when you believe that your survival is all on you, or that you have to replace anything you give away, or when things run out there won't be more. But when you understand that you're part of the larger pattern of circulation, you can feel interacting with the world more generously and unencumbered.

Give in Order to Live

Whether it's a tree that breathes in carbon dioxide and exhales oxygen, or rain that falls and waters plants, or human adults who bear and raise children, in nature nothing exists just for itself. Since everything's Purpose lies outside of itself, you can place yourself in the flow of life's resources by giving.

No wonder every major religion believes we should share our blessings with others. An African proverb sums this up well: "To whom much is given, much is required." You may also be familiar with this idea from the Bible. Spiritually, giving multiplies what you have, so the more you give away the more will come to you. A righteous man seeks to be a conduit of money rather than a reservoir. What I mean by that is a righteous man understands that money comes in and money goes out. The language "cash flow" and "currency" reflect that idea. He seeks to create a financial current. One of the best ways to create movement in your financial life is to share your time, your talent, and your treasure with others. Indeed, things come to you so you can pass them along to somebody else. If you need more, start giving more of yourself. Give without looking for a return and watch your needs get met.

You must have heard the saying "actions speak louder than words." A man becomes known by what he does, not by what's in his heart or what he says. When I talk about a man's heart, I'm not talking about his ticker; I mean how his mind, his will, and his emotions come together to be a force. A lot of guys talk a good game, but when the going gets tough, they can't walk that talk. They have no heart. We see athletes lose heart—or show tremendous heart—all the time. A man's actions in the world reflect his heart. We may hear what a man's saying but we see what he does.

Whether you achieve your destiny or buy a house, it doesn't happen with magic wands and fairy dust. To accomplish anything meaningful, you are going to have to work. Working is part of what makes us human. Not only does it provide a way to create inner meaning for yourself, it also gives you a context in which you can grow and develop. Don't try to keep up with the Joneses or be someone you're not. Take time to set your own vision, work your own program, and enjoy your spiritual journey.

A righteous warrior works hard; he isn't lazy. He has no problem jumping into a situation, rolling up his sleeves and leveraging his gifts and talents to help, whether by going the extra mile on the job or cutting the grass on the football field. But he doesn't jeopardize himself or his family by spending an inordinate amount of time away from home. Nor does he run himself and his health into the ground. It's important to rest and take care of yourself. In our entertainment-oriented society, we are socialized to believe that a life of leisure is the height of accomplishment. Though the

American societal norm is to work for five days and take two days off for R&R, I suggest working six days and taking one day off. You don't have to work at your job on the sixth day, but I believe you ought to be productive somewhere. Fix the faucet, mow your lawn, get the oil changed, volunteer at the youth center, teach your son how to throw a curveball, help your daughter or son with their homework, volunteer for the local political candidate. Also be sure to set aside time to work on your dream! Be productive on day six and take the seventh day entirely off. Eat a healthy breakfast, go to service as a family, go on a hike together, hold your wife's hand, watch the game with your daughter, take a nap, cook dinner, get ready for next week. Not only is this a smart restorative practice, it reminds you that God takes care of you rather than your job.

Create a Budget You Can Live By

To step into your destiny, you'll need to live by some financial standards.

I suggest that you follow management guru Stephen Covey's strategy and begin with the end in mind. Ask questions like: What are my dreams? Where do I want to be five years from now? What do I want to be doing when I'm fifty? What practical steps can I take to live that commitment? What will it take to get there financially? How much should I set aside to seed my dreams? Make your spending serve your dreams rather than keeping up with the Kardashians, so to speak.

I am not a financial adviser, but I do know that it's important to create a financial plan that reflects your vision and lines up with your destiny. I offer the following rubric for thinking about your financial life. You may need to tweak the numbers to fit your situation and lifestyle.

First, start by creating a budget. I suggest you begin with the 10:10:80 rule. When you get paid, I strongly believe that you should give ten percent off the top to the source of your spiritual development, such as your church, synagogue, mosque, or spiritual center. If you're not religious, give to charitable causes or things that inspire you. Try to save the next ten percent and live on the remaining eighty percent. In general, you should allocate your money according to the following guidelines. If you're not there yet, make adjustments over time until you come in line with them.

ten percent tithing or charitable giving

ten percent savings

nine percent investments

thirty-six percent housing

twelve percent transportation

nine percent food

six percent clothing

five percent debt reduction

three percent entertainment

If you live in a place where housing costs are high, consider a roommate or spending a little longer at home. Living at home needs to be a family conversation, where you lay out your second quarter goals for your family and live into them. Since only nine percent of your budget should cover food and three percent entertainment, you will have a very hard time making ends meet if you don't know how to cook or go to the club every Friday. There's not necessarily anything wrong with eating out or clubbing, but if you do it too much you'll find yourself in trouble.

The average American consumer is carrying more than $8,000 in credit card debt.* When you subtract from that the people who don't have

---

*Kathleen Elkins, "Here's How Much the Average US Family Has in Credit Card Debt," CNBC Make It, May 17, 2017. Accessed at https://www.cnbc.com/2017/05/17/how-much-the-average-us-family-has-in-credit-card-debt.html.

debt, the average amount of credit card debt totals almost $17,000.[*] The average person with a car loan is almost $30,000 in debt. And the average person with a student loan is roughly $50,000 in debt. To clear your debt, you have to make very hard choices to avoid what our economy is designed to make you do: spend more money than you have and create debt. This is another reason why your vision, not society's vision for you, needs to drive your spending. If you're paying back your student loans or other debts, adjust your budget so you can realistically achieve it and recalibrate over time.

Once you settle on a budget, it becomes part of the Parameters that guide what you will and will not spend your money on and why.

Save Your Money

As we did in the Amazon, it's important to ask: "How much do I spend now and how much do I use to get something bigger and more fulfilling later?"

Wealthy people develop a plan to get them where they want to be in one, two, five, ten, and twenty years. You should, too. Every human being also has seasonal needs we need to plan for. For instance, we need to be honest with ourselves. One day we each will reach an age where we have more sense than strength. So if you are in your thirties, forties, or fifties, you can't consume everything you earn. In America, the average millionaire lives in a $300,000 house. Yet people who have far less wealth live in $500,000 homes when they could have been saving the difference.

Avoid Debt

The righteous warrior protects his credit and avoids getting in debt. Though he lives in a world that sends him credit cards and advertises payday loans, he understands that debt will handcuff him.

---

[*]Erin El Issa, "2017 American Household Credit Card Debt Study," Nerdwallet. Accessed at https://www.nerdwallet.com/blog/average-credit-card-debt-household/.

As a general principle, avoid debt of all kinds. Of course, few people can purchase a home, or pay for college, or even buy a car without it. But we should strive not to take debt on as a rule of thumb. Debt is designed to be part of our economic system, so carrying consumer debt is a societal norm. It also undermines many families. The number-one reason for divorce is money, not infidelity. Be content with what you have so you don't live beyond your means.

But in a society that teaches us that we "deserve to have it all"—and to have it all now—we need to learn the difference between good and bad debt. Many of us need to learn to delay gratification. Delaying gratification does not mean that we can't have a thing, but it may mean sacrificing now so you can get it later. Everything is not for everyone, nor can anyone have everything all at once. Spiritually, life provides for us seasonally as our vision unfolds over the course of our lifetime.

Once a man borrows money, he's responsible for paying it back according to the terms he agreed to. But if you owe someone, you also need a strategy to get out of debt. You also need a strategy so you don't incur new debt to replace the old debt.

For most of his life, Vernell didn't have specific financial outcomes in mind for himself.

"When you don't have a goal or a plan, or you don't foresee more for yourself, then you don't expect more for yourself. When you don't expect any more for yourself, it doesn't matter what your credit score is," he says. He wrongly believed he was destined to live a life below the level he imagined for himself.

"My credit was crappy; I was making crappy money. My credit score was a 453," he says.

But once he began to envision a purposeful future, Vernell started to set some big-picture five-year goals. To be the man he imagined, he would need to improve his credit. He had $22,000 worth of debt, about $16,000 of which was for a car that had been written off in an accident. At first, he ignored the payment letters. But eventually he faced the fact that he had to pay up.

"At first, I set up a monthly payment of $85 a month," he says. "Later, I learned that if I did that I would be paying for ten years. When you don't understand the rules, you end up blindly paying for stuff."

So Vernell started doing credit repair. "I called the company and asked if they would settle the $16,000. They settled at $2,100, so I paid that off," he says. "Now when I get my income tax refund, I pick a bill and pay it off. It took two years to deal with my old debt. I had to sacrifice. A lot. If my minimum was $25, I paid $100. If my minimum was $75, I paid $150 so I was paying toward the principal instead of just interest. Taking on extra jobs has helped. I began to see how being consistent opened up a door to allow me to do more."

As Vernell began to learn more sophisticated money-management practices, he freed himself to live a more abundant life.

"Being consistent opened up a door to allow me to do more stuff," he says. In time, someone noticed his hard work and diligence and recommended him for a more prestigious job that came with health and vacation benefits he'd never had before.

"Now, I direct-deposit my check and automatically pay my bills. Already, I'm seeing the benefit of my discipline and sacrifice," he says. "Just a couple of years ago, I got declined for a line of credit trying to buy my son some sneakers. Two weeks ago, I bought a MacBook Pro for college within seconds. Now my credit score is over 700 and I'm still working on improving it."

That said, many people feel poor when they actually are not. What I mean is that a spirit of lack can make you feel that, no matter how much you have, it is never enough. A person can have a poverty spirit without being financially poor. As a matter of fact, many wealthy people have a poverty spirit, which is among the reasons why some rich people are greedy. So, strange as it seems, it is possible to be poor even if you have wealth. Greedy people often self-destruct because they will do anything for the next dollar.

Debt can also be relational. It's possible to become too indebted to others' help. All of us need people to help us, and sometimes we need help more than at other times—I'm not saying don't accept help. But as a matter of foundational principle, be careful not to allow your relationships to get out of balance. The giver will stop respecting you if you're always on the receiving end of the relationship. Even in personal relationships, the debtor is always "slave" to the lender. That is to say, if you always owe people—whether money, a favor, or whatever—the relationship will become uncomfortable because it's too far out of balance. In other words, they will "own" you.

"There was a time when I owed fifteen, twenty G's to the cocaine dealer," Rich says.

During his days of addiction and drugs, Rich was owned.

"Today, my bills are paid, my mortgage is paid, my finances are finally straightened out," Rich says. "I'm actually on top."

Be Content with What You Have

A righteous warrior lives with a sense of sufficiency for the season that he is currently in. He isn't materialistic or attached to physical things. He becomes increasingly content with having food, clothing, and shelter and stops letting himself become seduced by materialism and consumerism.

Not being caught up in things frees him to make choices that men who are burdened with debt or material possessions cannot make. His conservative approach to money protects him as seasons change, including financially. Most of us are in an uphill fight against a system that takes money from low-income and middle-class people and redirects it to the very affluent. It's important to acknowledge that this system exists. The best way to fight it is to implement these principles—and it is, indeed, a fight. Having nice things isn't a problem, but we must ask ourselves if we can live more simply.

Live Life with Margins

A medical doctor named Richard Swenson wrote a wonderful book called *Margin: Restoring Emotional, Physical, Financial, and Time Reserves to Overloaded Lives* about the fact that most of us don't give ourselves enough breathing room. We know that we live twenty minutes from work so we leave twenty minutes before work starts. We're all right as long as nobody drives too slow, but if we get stuck behind someone who obeys the speed limit, a school bus, or a garbage truck, we lean on the horn and have road rage. Leaving thirty-five minutes early is living with margin.

The same is true emotionally. Many of us are frustrated because we have no emotional margin. We have enough emotional energy for life to go well but lose it when something goes wrong. In financial terms, "margin" is another word for savings. A good financial steward lives his life with some margin. He has room in his life for somebody to make a mistake. He has financial room to cover an emergency. He has room for someone who needs to lean on him.

Use Your Economy to Help Others

Sometimes you experience blessings so you can pass them on to others. You're not supposed to hoard everything you have.

During ancient times, many landowners practiced a principle that allowed poor people to have dignity. For every hundred acres a landowner had, he farmed only ninety. He left the other ten acres for people who didn't own anything to glean. Gleaning gave people who didn't own land an opportunity to work for a living. The owner took responsibility for not consuming everything he owned. He created an economy for somebody else.

Every human with a little spare change can create an economy for someone else out of their economy. In other words, they can hire a housekeeper to help them keep their house clean, someone to cut their grass, a young person to shovel their snow and rake their leaves. You can create ways for other people to earn money. It is a sin to use everything you earn on yourself. Remember, sin doesn't necessarily mean that you're going to hell; all it means is that you're off the mark. Those who have money left over should use their economy to pay someone else.

No matter where he started, a righteous warrior takes control of his financial life. He takes stock of where he is and compares that to where he wants to be. He then conserves his resources and seeks out the information he's missing, so he can achieve his goals.

A righteous warrior understands that he has to keep his knife sharp. Not only does he have to conserve his resources, he has to get better at who he is and what he does and what he knows. That is part of what he must do during the earning season of life. He knows he cannot waste evening after evening and weekend after weekend in his man-cave watching other men pursue their dreams.

Expect the Unexpected and Be Consistent When Life Gets Chaordic

Remain focused on your goals and dreams, always doing what's right even during confusion and difficulty; refuse to allow yourself to become distracted. God will work things out over the long term.

"OH, LORD, I'M gonna go down in the middle of nowhere and the rescue teams will never be able to find me!"

That was the thought that took over my mind as snow plastered the windshield of the four-seat Cirrus SR20 I had rented an hour earlier.

I was about fifteen minutes into my first solo flight. After struggling for two years in flight lessons, I'd left Philly's Wings Airport thinking I was going to have an exciting thirty-eight-minute run up to the Cherry Ridge airport in Honesdale, Pennsylvania. In my mind's eye, it would be a triumph.

But just a few minutes after I'd flown north and hit the Pocono Mountains, I had run into snow flurries. Strange. It was late September. I was certain it was a fluke. But suddenly I saw these clouds roll in and it started snowing like crazy.

What?! Really! This is my first time!

During flight school I'd really struggled to nail my landings. For some reason, I just could not get it. I'd worried I might have to give up and accept that I just can't fly. That thought had been devastating to me. Part of the reason I'd wanted to become a pilot was to avenge one of my brother

Alfred's greatest losses. He'd lost his sight before he died of diabetes, which he'd denied and let go untreated. To honor him I had vowed to do the thing he could not do: become a pilot.

Now I feared that I might die, too. I was scared to death! Thoughts of my wife and daughters swirled around my mind. I thought of my wife's undying loyalty and love for our family. The way she'd helped me get my life on track during our twenties, when her pushing and prodding had helped me to stop drinking and living beneath my pay grade in life. The way that I'd lie across our bed with my head on her belly, when she was pregnant with each of our girls, even though we were so broke and I didn't know how I would provide for them. The devotion that she demonstrates each morning as she writes in her prayer journal. How she's stood by my side as the small church of 157 people I was called to pastor grew into a congregation a hundred times that size, and we went from believing we'd shepherd a small congregation to having one that at times overwhelmed us. The way that she's always loved me, though at times I've taken her for granted.

I was also sick with worry about my girls. What would their lives be like without me? Would they be safe? Would they find men who loved and respected them? Who would they turn to for protection? Who would walk them down the aisle and make sure their husbands treated them right? I flashed back on tossing them into the air behind Ellyn's back when they were babies. How amazed I was as I watched them morph from newborns, to infants, to toddlers, to teenagers who lost their minds from time to time when they were talking back to me! Going to recitals, daddy/daughter dances, and concerts together. And would my mother lose her only son?

Every possible nightmare scenario suddenly flashed through my mind. Would I go down in trees so thick that no one would ever find me? Would I experience excruciating pain or would it be over instantaneously? Would the plane blow up or catch on fire, so I'd be unrecognizable when they found me?

My own arrogance had put me in this situation. What had made me think that I could redeem my brother's legacy by learning how to fly—the thing he'd wanted to do more than anything before diabetes robbed him of his sight? Why hadn't I listened when Ellyn had asked me to stay on the ground? Now I worried that not only myself, but also my innocent family would pay the ultimate price.

The plane had started bouncing around so much that I began to feel sick. I had only flown in the summertime; I had no idea what to do in winter weather. All I could think about was getting ice on the wings. I knew that only God could get me out of this situation, so I confessed every sin I could think of and promised God I would never do them again. Then I prayed without ceasing.

I gained the presence of mind to call air traffic control. A voice told me to follow marginal VFR. VFR is short for visual flight rules. In other words, you are responsible for seeing other aircraft and not flying into them. I had to stay a thousand feet beneath the clouds, two hundred feet aboveground horizontally and be able to see the ground. But unlike on a clear day, when you may be able to see twenty miles, there was only three miles visibility, which isn't as far as it seems, especially when there are other airplanes in the air.

All I wanted to do was cry, but I knew that if I was going to make it, I'd have to calm down and remember all the things I'd practiced.

After what seemed like forever, I saw the airport, circled, and landed. *Hallelujah!*

Once on the ground, I learned that conditions weren't going to get any better. The flight was only thirty-four minutes; only part of the route would be in poor conditions. I figured I could manage that.

So I cleaned up the plane, got back in, then put the pedal to the metal and took off. The sky was very snowy and turbulent. As I flew I was so focused that I forgot to do the check-in I'd normally do with Allentown, Pennsylvania, as I passed through its airspace.

All I wanted to do was get to the other side of Mount Pocono. When I finally made it, the snow vanished as quickly as it had appeared. I breathed a big sigh of relief.

Then my radio went dead.

"Shoot!"

Even more disaster scenarios ran through my mind. Now I was sure I was gonna go down and no one would even know. But I stuck to the VFR and drew closer and closer to home.

It was my very first rental flight, but I was gonna have to land with no help from air traffic control. As I neared the airport, my hands were shaking so much that I couldn't even get into the pattern to circle the airport right. Not to mention, landings were not my strong point. Instead of circling the airport, I flew straight in.

I was *done*!

Once I brought the plane to a stop, I sat in the cockpit with my heart racing and hands shaking, thanking and praising God. I was grateful that I'd had the VFR to follow and that I'd had to fly so many hours before obtaining my license, as long and frustrating as my learning curve was.

The friendly skies are not the only place where life unfolds unexpectedly. A man's life often requires him to navigate chaos in a way that he can thrive and excel even when experiencing stress.

Play the Righteous Chaord

Every man will have to ride out bumps and bruises, challenges and difficulties, trials and tribulations, and even attacks. The question is not whether he will experience life's storms, but how he will let them affect him. A righteous warrior must remain steadfast.

It doesn't matter if you're really disciplined and organized, a man who goes with the flow of life's randomness and disorder, or one who experiences life as being totally out of control. Life does not transpire according to any man's blueprint. Indeed, some folks believe that life is what happens while you're working on your plans. (Nevertheless, I'm a big fan of planning.) But life is much bigger than you are, so even though life does not unfold in your perfect order, neither does a man's life have to be a mess.

Most of the time life unfolds somewhere between order and chaos. The founder and former CEO of Visa, Dee Hock, coined the term "chaordic" to describe this. "Systems, perhaps even life itself, are believed to arise and thrive on the edge of chaos with just enough order to give them pattern," he wrote.

From our personal perspective, life may look a bit crazy or sometimes even feel out of control. But if we could experience life from a higher perspective, it would be much easier for us to understand how everyone and everything connects to the other. One way to think about this is to consider our viewpoint when we're in an airplane. Rather than hyper-focusing on the disorder that is our teenager's bedroom, as so many of us do, we can not only see our entire house, we can also see the grid of the city streets or the pattern that our housing development is laid out in. Pull out even farther to outer space and nations and oceans that from the ground seem so separate all become part of one thing: planet Earth.

Now, imagine not only that you could see life from this higher perspective, but also that you could see it unfold over all of time. It would be much easier to see that life is designed intelligently. So what's happening at any particular place at any particular point in time, it turns out, is best for everyone and everything, as well as over time. From a spiritual standpoint, over the course of our lives everything does happen for our good; however, that doesn't mean that any particular event will be easy, or that it happens in our time frame or goes down the way we want it to. When we imagine life from this high-level perspective, it's easier to conceive of how its chaord could be good. It also implies that our life cannot always go the way we want. Viewed from this standpoint, nothing is personal. Not even the occasional storm, opposition, or attack.

But while we should expect life to be chaordic, it should not consistently be chaotic. Practicing the 5Ps and reflecting upon my former seminary professor Dr. Schreck's model will help you create enough structure and order that life's chaord does not cross over to chaos. Working consistently within this framework will free you to take life as it comes and allow it to flow off you. It allows you to trust, from a higher level, that everything is working out for everyone, including you—even if your good isn't present right away. This mind-set frees you to thrive no matter what's happening. Because no matter what comes, you know you can handle it.

Expect the Unexpected

Just as a righteous warrior knows that life unfolds in unexpected ways and that he will have to fight, a martial artist is trained to believe that the attacker is always right.

Whether you're having your feet swept out from under you or you're ducking a punch, you can't stop and tell the attacker to make a different move or pull back his blow either because you're not ready or you learned to defend against it differently—that just ain't how it works. No matter how much you prepare yourself, a fight never goes down in real life like it did in practice. Your attacker grabs you the way he grabs you; he punches you the way he punches you. (Or, as I experienced with one high school wrestler, your opponent may even be a she!) You have to defend against whatever the attacker does even though it gets crazy and messy.

Fighting is wild; fighting is unpredictable; fighting is all over the place. Sweat (or even blood) may drip into your eyes so that suddenly you have to defend yourself from blows you cannot see. Your opponent may clock you between the eyes, leaving you wobbly or barely conscious. To recover, you may have to cover up and absorb body blows as you lean against the ropes. That's why a fighter practices principles as he trains, so he can bring those abilities into the ring. First, we learn basic tools and techniques: stances, punches, kicks, blocks. We then practice those skills a mind-numbing number of times. We rehearse them until they become reflexive. In CKM or Naphtali, I may practice the same move a thousand times, until I do it automatically. Within each martial art, a single principle exists for blocking a blow, no matter where or how that blow comes. For instance, we follow the same principles to disarm an attacker, whether he's wielding his fist, a belt, a knife, or even a gun. The warrior mind-set requires us to practice these principles so many times that there is no doubt in our mind that we've out-practiced our competitor. Then we carry both our skills and our confidence into the ring.

In addition to practicing until they can go no more, fighters also visualize each fight before they engage in it. We never enter the ring without having a plan, so that in the heat of battle we are merely executing moves we've already rehearsed. No matter what our opponent comes at us with we do our best to fight the fight we prepared for rather than our competitor's fight. Instead, we try to force our opponent to fight our fight. When we have prepared to this extent, no matter how fast the fight comes to us, we maintain a calm and simplistic mind-set. In the process we discover that when we slow down and stay calm, rather than being headstrong or all over the place, everything else slows down as well. It's almost like in the movie *The Matrix* when Neo slows down reality so he can bend out of the way of oncoming bullets.

Seasons Change

Just as a martial artist literally rolls with the punches, in a chaordic world you must learn to thrive as things change. But change is not always comfortable. In fact, it can be very unsettling and at times even devastating. Change forces us to grow whether we're ready or not; however, resisting that growth is far more difficult.

The legendary guitarist and vocalist George Benson once sang, "Everything must change / nothing stays the same." He was right, and not only does everything change, but change is often cyclical, as seasons change but then return again. Not only do we experience spring, summer, winter, and fall as we travel forward in time from year to year, but people, places, and situations tend to come back around, giving us an opportunity to engage them again, either from a different perspective or with the benefit of hindsight and greater life experience. As you travel through your life, I strongly encourage you to remain committed to your growth—spiritually, mentally, physically, and emotionally. This is extremely important because developing yourself helps you to handle more of life's challenges. It also equips you to access more of your destiny. Your growth will bring challenges as well as discomfort, but that's okay. Because even if a man chooses not to change, he will discover that he cannot continue to do things in the same ways throughout his life and still get the same results.

For years Vernell was a cook at a hospital and was surrounded by people who were very unhappy. Needless to say, Vernell was unhappy, too. Even though he came to work on time each day and always did what he was supposed to, he reached a point where he began to run into unexpected difficulty.

"Even though I worked the same shift each week, every Friday my pay was different. I was supposed to get $800 but I might get $650, and it would take until the next payday to fix it. As a result, my money was always funny. I couldn't figure out what to do," he says. "I believed that a cook was all I was gonna be. I wasn't gonna be anything else, and that was just that."

Back then, it didn't occur to Vernell to consider that perhaps his situation was becoming uncomfortable because this season of his life was ending and it was time for him to move on.

"I didn't understand that God was trying to move me out of there," he says. "Instead, I was just getting upset with my life."

As a season of life begins to draw to a close, it's not uncommon to reach a point where you may feel at a loss, experience some chaos, or even sense that you've run into a brick wall. These are all signs that it's time to grow. Growth requires us to develop new skills and stretch outside of our comfort zone. During my adventures and as I travel, I speak with many men who want everything to remain the same. They seem to believe that a consistent and predictable life is their birthright, so they don't seem to be interested in changing or developing.

But the Truth of the matter is, when we are feeling stuck, one of the challenges we may be facing is around our ability to change. It is the nature of things to change, so if you remain rigid you set yourself up for pain. It's important that we begin to ask ourselves if we are willing to do things like a beginner again, to interact with unfamiliar people, to participate in unaccustomed activities, and to otherwise exist outside of our comfort zone. Indeed, I believe that one of the most important skills a righteous man must master is learning how to become comfortable being uncomfortable. Though we live in a society that stresses comfort and ease, developing the ability to be comfortable being uncomfortable will free you up to flow like water as difficulties arise, as well as to journey further along your life's path. Because no matter how much any of us may want things to unfold smoothly, life isn't easy nor is it linear. Just as happens in nature, seasons in life have a beginning, middle, and end. We must develop the ability to transition into new phases continuously.

In order to change seasons gracefully, a righteous warrior must learn to let go, say good-bye, and grieve the things he's releasing. Because, to put it quite simply, anytime you start something new, you have to stop something else. And though there may be times when you are excited about moving on, releasing an old way of life can also feel difficult or even uneasy. For example, it's not uncommon, as you wrap up a season, to find that you don't fit in the old place or with the old people anymore. You may find yourself becoming bored or feeling unsettled. Significant difficulty may even arise along the way.

Despite the paycheck irregularities he experienced, Vernell had finally saved enough money to take a vacation. But when he returned to work, the check that should have been waiting for him hadn't even been cut and the company played games with the money that was owed him.

"Suddenly I couldn't pay all the bills," he says. "I didn't know where I was gonna go. I wasn't gonna borrow it, but I was at a loss."

Unexpected problems will certainly arise but it's important not to take them personally. Oftentimes the opposition occurs because it's time for you to move to the next level. Instead of internalizing the issue as being either your fault or somebody else's, think of yourself as being like a baby bird breaking out of its shell. You have grown as much as you can within your current life. Staying inside it will eventually become toxic to you. The hard times that you must peck through constitute the gateway into your next season. So expect difficulty and some trouble to be part of your experience of pushing forward into each new level. Instead of focusing on the trouble, keep your eye on your next level.

As he experienced all of this difficulty, Vernell had begun to hang around the fellas. He grew particularly close to Mark.

"I told him, 'I just can't do this no more, but I don't know where to go,' " Vernell says.

Mark is an avid reader, as are many of the guys in our band of brothers. We would often read the same book. Mark's reading habit rubbed off on Vernell, so Vernell read what Mark read. At the time, Mark was reading *One Word That Will Change Your Life* by Dan Britton, Jimmy Page, and Jon Gordon. Vernell began to consider what one word inspired his "why" in life and made him who he is.

"I was trying to find things that would help me be a better person, a better follower of God, a better husband, a better father. I started asking myself: What is it about myself that I find unappealing? What is it about myself that I feel needs work? What is it that I think I can bring to the table where these gentlemen are concerned, where my life is concerned,"

Vernell says. "I realized that I was consistent with some things but that I lacked consistency in other areas. It was like a light went off. Boom! That's my word. I saw that it was already a part of me, but that my consistency could be a strength. Okay, let's start with that."

If we approach times of trouble with an open mind and spirit, our challenges can help us gain greater insight and our trials can help us develop perseverance, strength, and other characteristics we will need to succeed. Struggle also produces character. Vernell's introspection helped him to take his character, which was already strong, to an even higher level, which he would later learn would need to be rock solid for his next season in life.

A warrior develops his character even as he develops his natural gifts. While your gifts can take you to high places, it's your character that keeps you there. If a man's gifts outpace his character, he is likely to slide backwards or even fall because he is not morally strong enough to maintain the level.

But even though life doesn't unfold smoothly or easily, the Truth of life's hardship conflicts with common marketing messages that encourage us to aspire to a relaxing life. Many of us will, in fact, experience spells of relative ease or contentment; however, an easy life is no man's birthright nor are easy seasons permanent or even normal. Any period of comfort and order is likely to last only until a man's next season, whether a man actively pursues his destiny or sits back and takes whatever life dishes out to him. I strongly recommend that whenever you enjoy any period of tranquility, you consider it to be a staging time during which you plan and launch the next phase of your life. Indeed, use that platform to expand your vision, so you can see the promise of your next season from a higher vantage point than you previously could.

Practice the Principles

Knowing the source of your Power, as well as your Purpose, Place, and Parameters, will help sustain you through challenges and difficulties.

So will trying to do the right thing no matter the circumstance. Every human being is born with a built-in moral compass, although not everyone uses it, or uses it consistently. Though it may not seem expedient at the moment (and society doesn't always encourage it), doing the right thing is always the answer, in good times as well as bad. Moving from your moral center strengthens you, prepares you to overcome obstacles, and helps you deal with life's fights.

When you're being your best self, you can handle whatever life throws at you. But that's hard to do if you do not practice. Men who live in a principled and disciplined way under normal conditions develop the skills to behave more consistently when life gets confusing. Indeed, life as a righteous warrior requires us to consider our Power, Place, Purpose, and Parameters again and again. We consider and reconsider them in light of the person we've so far become and as we reflect upon the new person we aspire to become moving forward. These provide the framework that keep life stable as you take on life's difficulty, obstacles, and disorder.

Together, the principles transform chaos into chaord.

The questions of life change as you pass through the phases of your life. As you become more mature, your questions should grow and deepen alongside you. The young man (or any man just beginning his spiritual development) may ask himself questions like "What do I want to be?" A middle-aged or spiritually mature man ought to ask himself, "What am I doing?," just as Vernell began asking himself as he worked hard but seemed to make little progress. And men during the third and fourth quarters should consider "What have I done?" and adjust accordingly. I'll be the first to tell you that none of this reflection is easy; however, the answers you obtain and the results will be worth it.

As Vernell dealt with his struggles, it hadn't dawned on him that Mark had been admiring his commitment, diligence, and loyalty. Mark worked at a university. He had a job opening. And though it paid less that Vernell had been making as a cook, he suggested that Vernell consider the opportunity. Though it would require a pay cut and a long commute, Vernell and his wife agreed to make some adjustments, giving him the opportunity to dash through the door.

"Working for Mark gave us more time to talk," he says of his experience. "It also gave me time to think about what I wanted for my life. I was beginning to see a little blue between the clouds and was working at becoming a better version of myself."

As you take stock of where you are and where you're headed, eliminating distractions will help you keep your life simple. You will need to prune and weed out the aspects of yourself and your life that don't reflect who you've become or fit with where you are going. This should include the parts of yourself you outgrow as you get clearer about your own path and less interested in chasing other people's dreams for you or conforming to societal norms. Expect this pruning and weeding process to require you to sacrifice some of who you were and what you have in order to get to your next level. Some things we have to sacrifice can disrupt our lives and unsettle us: leisure time, comfort, familiarity, material possessions, relationships, and so on. Letting familiar people, places, and things go isn't always easy; it can even be painful.

In the midst of life's chaord, it's important to lean into your faith that something greater than yourself is going on at a higher level. Because the more you commit to following your destiny, the more you will find yourself set at odds with the world. And a person's faith typically corresponds to the person he used to be, not who he is required to be today. Few of us have already developed the faith we'll need for our next level of life. No wonder change and growth tend to frighten so many of us.

Developing and practicing faith helps us walk through the door and into our next season of life. But increasing our faith is a lot like lifting weights: Every man is strong enough to lift the amount of weight he's already been pushing. But if he wants to get stronger, he has to add more plates, heavier plates, or increase his reps. To get to your next level, don't just talk about it, *be* about it, too. Go to the gym of spiritual, mental, physical, and emotional development. Get on the machine, do the work, endure the discomfort, grow stronger, and gradually increase the weight. You have already mastered earlier levels so push yourself even higher.

In the process of enduring discomfort, you will become an increasingly more integrated human being. The word "integrated" comes from the Latin root *integer*, which means "whole." In math, an integer is a whole number. For example, one, two, eleven, twenty-four, and thirty-seven are whole numbers. An integrated man is a whole man. He doesn't feel like he's missing anything. No one but God completes him. As he deepens his understanding of his Power, Place, Purpose, and Parameters, he gains a better sense of who he is as well as who he is not. He knows the game he is playing and excels upon that field. He does not wander thoughtlessly into adjacent lanes—or start playing a different sport altogether. As he gets clear, life begins to flow to him.

To help pay the bills while he worked for Mark, Vernell continued his side jobs, including personal training. As he interacted with his clients, he discovered that several needed help eating healthier. He started out by creating meal plans for them, but when he discovered that they didn't have time to cook, he transformed his culinary skills into a personal chef service. In other words, as he asked the 5P questions and built a strong brotherhood around himself, Vernell's seeming chaos began to fall into order.

Righteous warriors can thrive even as seasons change, life gets uncertain, storms unfold, and they make mistakes. They know that the fastest, strongest, or nicest guy doesn't win every fight. But they know that they will persevere until the end.

Spring Forward

Sometimes men experience challenges because a season is over and it's time to move on, as Vernell did.

A man cannot bear fruit in the same way forever. Just as in nature, sometimes a fruitful thing grows as much as it can in that way. To become more fruitful, it has to be pruned or replanted or fertilized so it can grow in a new way. The pruning and replanting may be uncomfortable in that moment, but over the long term the plant thrives.

When I talk to men about what they need to cut back or let go of, they rarely need to engage in a battle between good and bad, darkness and light. There is no impropriety, outrage, or scandal. Most times they need to make a couple of meaningful sacrifices that would allow them to move from being good to being great. Some may need to let go of materialism; for others it's bad habits, unsupportive people, unforgiveness, whining, foolishness, pride, partying, or not studying. They often need to find a new set of friends and build relationships with people who can accompany them into their new season. It's also not unusual that they need to stop wasting money and set financial goals. Cutting back on junk food, eating more healthfully, and exercising often show up on their list. So does getting online or back into the classroom to retool for their new future.

The definition of what's holding them back, or what's baggage or a distraction, differs from person to person. Some of us frustrate our progress because we haul people or stuff from an old season into the new time in our lives. Suddenly, the same folks or things that used to be okay begin to get in the way. Other times, we slow ourselves down by not dealing with important issues. As a result, our unaddressed stuff comes up repeatedly, until we deal with it. But don't be afraid to say good-bye to the previous season. Your destiny is in the next place. As you attempt to go up a level, you will experience periods of challenge. You should expect to go through seasons that may consist of a series of trials and tests. Don't get discouraged. Trials and tests merely measure your ability and provide an opportunity to demonstrate what you've learned. It's very similar to when my girls were in Kumon, an after-school academic program designed to strengthen children's math skills. Their teacher knew they were ready to advance when they passed a test with a score of 100.

Similarly, when you are wrapping up one season and about to graduate to the next level, expect to experience some difficulty in the form of a trial or test. Just think of it as being a lot like when you play a video game; right when you get close to the door to the next level, you face a burst of opposition. In fact, you know you're close to the door when the opposition becomes particularly fierce and takes every weapon and skill you have. If you've mastered those skills, you win the battle and get to progress. If not, you have to go back and try again—but this time armed with more knowledge. The same thing happens in life, so don't take it personally. This, too, is part of life's chaord.

Not only do tests signal good things—that you're nearing the door or walking through it—they also prepare and strengthen you for the challenges you'll face at the next level. Trials are for your good even though they may not feel good. If you don't pass the first time, just have another go at it. How do you know if your experiencing a test? One way is if, after being exposed to new information, you are presented with an opportunity to solve a related problem in new ways. For example, I have been having conversations about race relations within American churches comprised primarily of Black people for a couple of decades. I'm fairly practiced at it. Recently, I've been working on an international level, which has given me the opportunity to talk about race with Black people from other parts of the world and to learn about their challenges. Both of these experiences call me to learn new information and test my ability to speak about the Black experience in America and the experience of Black people within a global context.

Another way to know if you're experiencing a test is if you're having the same experience repeatedly. Yogi Berra once referred to it as having déjà vu all over again. Do you keep having the same kind of boss over and over again? Or have the same problems with your second (or third) wife that you had with your first wife? Or run into the same situations, only the people have different names? If so, there is something you're being called to learn in order to progress. It's time to dig in, learn the lessons, and apply them. Once you pass the test you'll be able to move forward.

The Calm Within the Storm

At some point in a man's life he should expect to experience at least one season of troubles and storms, where life becomes overwhelming and things feel out of control.

During their pregnancy, Leroy's wife Felicia's water broke at only twenty weeks.

"We rushed her to the hospital, and they put her in bed and on monitors and were trying to get to at least twenty-five weeks," he says. "This was back in the day before hospitals were family friendly. They kept telling me, 'Sir, you can't stay. Visiting hours are at a certain time.'"

"I'm not leaving my wife," Leroy would argue.

"Well, you're kind of in the way."

So Leroy went to an REI sports store and bought a sleeping bag and a mat. He asked the hospital staff to raise her bed up, then he lay out his sleeping bag and mat under her bed.

"I'll be here," he told them, "but I'm out of the way."

He slept under Felicia's hospital bed for two weeks, leaving periodically to care for their then-two-year-old, who was staying with his mother-in-law.

"We knew our baby would be a girl, so we decided we'd name her Faith," he says.

But one day the doctor came in and told them they had an awful decision to make.

"He said, 'At this point in the pregnancy, we're not seeing what we want to see.' We had to make a decision: It was either my wife or the baby. And for a split second in that moment, the thought passed through my mind that this was God responding to my prayers by saying, 'Okay, you really wanna have a deeper relationship with me? This is what it looks like. Trust me.' "

This is when all the difficult work Leroy had been doing to be a better husband, father, and man really showed up.

Leroy says, " 'You decide,' Felicia told me. I was like, 'Really, Felicia?!' Because I believe in the saying 'happy wife, happy life.' Like ninety-six percent of what we do is because Felicia says so. I really don't even care; I ain't that deep. I'm like, 'Whatever you want, babe.' So everything else she gets to decide, but the heavy, crazy deep stuff now is on me. On top of that, she's a professional woman; giving me the authority to make that decision flies in the face of women's lib. I didn't really understand until that moment that she literally trusted me with her life.

"All I know is that in that moment, I wanted to go to church," Leroy says. "As soon as I arrived, I got a message that the hospital had called—this was in the day before cell phones. In those twenty-five minutes, Felicia had delivered. My daughter was alive but her lungs were not fully developed, they told me. I rushed back to the hospital, but by the time I got there it was over. Faith . . . I missed it. But they cleaned her up and we held her and started to grieve. Even for the short hour she was with us, Faith changed my life."

Though difficult, storms play an important role in a man's existence. Some storms roll in to redirect you onto a different path. I experienced this when my brother died. His death pushed me away from my nonsense during college and caused me to accept my calling into ministry. Other storms teach you what you're made of.

As Felicia and Leroy experienced, some storms take place publicly, providing a teachable moment for others. From the hospital staff, who were moved by Leroy's devotion and commitment to his wife and unborn child, to many members of our church, lots of people knew that Felicia and Leroy were pregnant. As people learned about their great loss, their grieving took place semi-publicly and provided a tremendous model of love, courage, commitment, and dignity.

Still other storms can tear up a man's entire life. These tend to occur when we've repeatedly ignored the warning signs that we need to change our ways because we've gotten involved in something immoral, or illegal, or that we never should have engaged in in the first place. A man will survive a destructive storm like this, but he won't be unscathed. The storm will tear up things he didn't need and blow them away, leaving him only with what he needs for the next season. He will have to rebuild.

But while it might appear that life's storms create problems, storms are actually resolutions. In meteorology, rainstorms, snowstorms, and even hurricanes resolve unsettled atmospheric conditions. Similarly, life's storms tend to resolve instability and imbalances in the various aspects of our life. So, though the storm may bring a fusillade of hail and wind, the storm itself is not the problem. The problem is the atmosphere that precipitated the storm. Though burdensome, the storm actually arrives with the answer. After the billows blow through, the sky is blue and the air is clear.

When you have organized your life around spiritual principles, you can ride out any storm. Not only that, the storm itself can actually help you move forward. Because life is not merely about what happens to you, it's also about where what happens to you takes you. Though a storm may seem destructive while you're in it, once it's over you may discover that you're better off. Sometimes getting fired, or losing the love of your life, or surviving a heart attack pushes you into a vital next phase of development that you'd perhaps been resisting. While it's happening, it feels like the worst thing in the world, but if it hadn't happened you wouldn't have had a new chance at life. In the end storms are a lot like eating your vegetables. Though they may not feel good, spiritually they are good for you.

"Even as painful as that moment was, I said to God, 'I get it; I'm all in,'" says Leroy. "That was the point when I stepped fully into my calling." Today Leroy leads our church ministry for people who have lost a child.

He is also a chaplain at a children's hospital working with families who have experienced stillbirth, lost their children to sudden infant death syndrome, and have experienced other tragedies.

What in the Devil?

Every person has his or her own way of understanding positive and negative energy. The way that I understand the world, it has a God, devil, angels, demons. These words and ideas may or may not be your language. Many people think in terms of concepts like karma, which is rooted in Buddhism and Hinduism but is often used in a more mainstream context to refer to the dynamic of cause and effect, or what Christians often refer to as "sowing and reaping." Other people focus more upon negative energy. No matter what you call it, the concept is universal. But while Satan, bad karma, or negativity can have the power to distract a man, they do not have the ability to destroy him. What they can do, however, is cause him to destroy himself.

Whereas a test or a trial merely measures your ability, temptation entices your brokenness. Many men see evidence of the devil in that. Temptation occurs when you have a preexisting inclination inside of you that matches up with a force in the world. In other words, you can only be tempted if a little bit of the thing that tempts you already exists inside of you. If you don't possess the thing, it cannot tempt you. That's why nonsmokers don't understand the smoker's struggle. Or why one person can enjoy a glass of merlot while if another partakes he will go on a bender. Yet the fact that you feel tempted doesn't reflect a deficiency on your part or mean you have sinned; don't feel guilty about it or beat yourself up. Sin only occurs if you give in to the temptation. Remember, sin merely means that you're missing the mark in terms of God's will for you. So an appropriate response includes making the kind of adjustments that will move you back on target.

If you are ever feeling tempted about something, know that that thing is not a part of your spiritual path. God will test you; God doesn't tempt. God would never put a bottle of liquor in front of me. When that happens, from a spiritual perspective it's the devil trying to pull me back into active addiction. If you fail a trial or test, the consequence you experience is that you don't go to the next level. If you fail a temptation, it will cost you something. Depending upon the temptation, it may ruin your life. But succumbing to temptation isn't always scandalous. It's not unusual for a man to feel tempted as he's going through a transition. People are often tempted by food, cigarettes, and what we sometimes refer to as bad habits just as they're trying to quit. Indeed, one of the most common urges that any human being feels is the lure to return to what is comfortable. That can be enticing though not necessarily dishonorable. Also, if you've ever been inclined to deal with the "devil you know"—staying in a job you've outgrown rather than relocating for a new opportunity—you've experienced this. Indeed, many of us would rather return to a known hell than into the promise of an unknown tomorrow, no matter how bright. This can be especially true when we're feeling afraid.

Scandalous or not, temptation knocks many men off their assignment. Even if you wrestle with temptation, as I do, be encouraged. The devil cannot make any man do anything. What he can do, however, is make doing the thing that's got a hold on you seem like a good idea. One way I suggest you protect yourself from temptation is not to keep secrets. Mental health professionals often say that we're only as sick as our secrets. I strongly believe that. In other words, whether we understand it or not, the unconfessed stuff of our lives runs the show. Rather than talking about things, many of us keep them to ourselves. They often play out in unproductive habits and passive-aggressive behaviors. That's why it's important to talk about the things that are on your mind, especially those things that trouble you. When I am wrestling with my addiction, I have learned that it's far better to talk about my struggle that it is to keep it a secret. When I name it, it no longer controls my brain space and begins to go away. That's why so many spiritual and religious traditions teach that confession is good for the soul.

So when you feel tempted, talking to your romantic partner, a trusted friend, a counselor, or spiritual adviser can help break the spell the temptation has over you. That said, you have to be careful about a person's ability to handle who you are to them in their life. While people think of me as being a very transparent person—and I am—because I'm their pastor there are some things I should not say to my church. It's just not right to dump on people who may not be able to handle your less attractive parts. When some people are about to die, they dump all sorts of secrets on their loved ones. That's not honorable because they won't have the opportunity to discuss the new information with a dead person.

It's not unusual, right before you have a great experience, to undergo what is known as a spiritual, or demonic, attack at your point of vulnerability. Some men have an experience known as spiritual warfare. This is when Satan will try to fool you into thinking the person or situation you are in conflict with is your enemy. In reality it's not about the person or situation you see, it is about something in the invisible, spirit, or supernatural realm. Ultimately, spiritual warfare's a head game to see if you'll lose faith if you take enough shots to your righteousness, similar to how a fighter will drop his arms when he's tired. In this example, losing his faith sets the man up to get knocked out.

Dig Deep

During times when you're experiencing difficulty—trials, temptations, or attacks—it's important to dig deeper into your spirituality. The challenge becomes how not to succumb to it. The righteous man must engage in battle.

Times of challenge can be a great time to deepen your prayer life so that it feeds you and becomes a source of your sustenance, or develop one if you don't already have one. I recommend that you start praying when times are good, so that your prayers will have power when times get tough. Prayer will also help to give you peace, even during the storm. In fact, one way to determine whether or not you are making the right decision in a circumstance is by whether the decision gives you peace. You can experience joy in the midst of great difficulty as well. Indeed, joy comes from doing what's right even in the worst circumstances. Over the long run, righteousness and Truth will prevail. As Rev. Dr. Martin Luther King Jr. said: "The arc of the moral universe is long and it bends toward justice."

Far too many people mistake the difficulties they face in the aftermath of their poor decisions as the devil or God's judgment or punishment of them. Not everything that happens is as result of either the devil's or God's wrath. Whether positive or otherwise, our behavior has repercussions. So we are much more likely to be reaping the natural consequences of our own choices. Sometimes we make things hard on ourselves.

Though you may struggle or experience hard times or become demoralized, the consequences of your mistakes or bad choices will not destroy you. Indeed, while Satan, bad karma, or negativity have the power to distract a man, they do not have the ability to destroy him. What they can do is cause him to destroy himself. The hard times that follow the bad choices we make are more like a warning shot signaling that we have strayed off our path. There is a higher purpose for your life, but pursuing it requires your spiritual obedience. As long as you line up with it, nature and life's circumstances will align to support you. But when you sin, or stray from that path, you will leak joy, power, and peace. In fact, don't be surprised if you experience a lot of drama. These are merely by-products of being off the mark; they are not God punishing us. If you continue to wander off your path, the spiritual warning shots are likely to escalate. To protect you God may even shut down that aspect of your life. You can always tell when

God has shut a thing down. No matter what you do to make it work, the door is slammed shut; nothing will budge.

As Leroy experienced, sometimes life gets so hard that all you can do is hang on. During these times use your history as both a source of your help and your hope. When this happens, I encourage you to look back over your life and reflect on other situations where you barely scraped by. You thought you weren't going to make it back then, but you did. As uncomfortable as your current position is, you've made it here. A popular passage of scripture, Psalm 23, says that though you may pass through the valley of the shadow of death, God is not only with you, God will also prepare a table for you in the presence of your enemies. That means you can be surrounded by antagonists and adversaries yet grow and develop in the midst of them if you stay in the fight.

It may not be easy and it may not be comfortable, but even in the thick of life's battle, you can feel tremendous satisfaction in the fact that you haven't folded.

Be a Family Man

Understand that you must fight both to have a family and to keep your family. This is an uphill battle, but you have the tools to turn the fight.

HE WAS BIGGER and stronger than I was and that's how I knew I could take him. You know those really strong dudes who breathe protein powder, live in the gym, and like to show off their pecs? Well, he was that guy. And truth be told, he was a lot stronger than I was. He was also way better than me; there was just no comparison. Yet I was confident I'd be able to hold my own, if only for a short while. Long enough to earn his respect, but not so long that I'd make a fool out of myself.

We were at Greg Jackson's Martial Arts & Fitness Academy in Albuquerque, New Mexico. Greg Jackson is the foremost MMA trainer in the world. Jon Bones Jones and Holly Holm are among the fighters in his camp. We'd come to learn more about MMA fighting. For the past several years, I'd been the assistant wrestling coach at our church's neighborhood high school. Back when I graduated, a wrestler's only option was to go to the Olympics or the Pan-Am Games, but when these guys graduated some of them wanted to try their hand at becoming professional MMA fighters. For a strong wrestler, that had become a legitimate path. But the way the wrestling world is set up in Philly, the only place they could train was on the opposite side of town. Since Enon is "unapologetically youth oriented" and already offers Naphtali and CKM to our members, we realized that by getting trained and buying a few mats, we could easily create an avenue to help young men in our area pursue it.

So now here I was on the practice mat with a professionally trained MMA fighter leaning into me. I knew what I was up against, but I sensed that I'd be able to pull off a Mongolian attack, a tactic where you tempt the other fighter into a trap. You've witnessed the Mongolian attack in the movies. It's when you see Mongolian warriors on horses galloping away from their enemy. Because the horses are galloping, it appears that the fighters are running away. But what the enemy can't see because of the distance is that the warriors are facing backwards on their horses—they are turned toward their pursuers. At some point they slow their horses down, intentionally allowing their enemy to gain ground on them. Then when their pursuer draws within range, they pull out their bows and start shooting arrows. Their attacker and his horse gallop right into the arrows. Needless to say, they're done!

So as the big guy leaned into me, I pushed into him, knowing that he'd want to throw his weight around and would push me back. Then I pushed a little harder, aware that would make him want to show me how strong he was. Little did he know that, in wrestling, I am known for my throws. I enjoy executing throws and can do them from many angles. I figured that by pushing him I would lure him in, then I would do an over/under hook and throw him. So he leaned in one too many times, and I threw him. *Boom!* The big guy landed on the mat.

Of course, he was a professional and I am not, so eventually he got the best of me. But I held my own and had earned respect in a battle with a guy who was significantly larger than me.

In martial arts you need techniques to help you fight against opponents who are larger and stronger than you. That mind-set and skill set apply in our society and culture, which tend to be at odds with and even fighting against healthy and enduring relationships, marriages, children, and families. You need to prepare yourself to engage in a dogfight.

Get Ready to Rumble

If you want to experience love that lasts and a family that endures, you're going to have to pull out your boxing gloves. Throughout society, meaningful romantic relationships, marriages, and families are all under attack. It's still possible to have a fulfilling love life and a happy family, but you will have to take up arms. To win, a righteous warrior must be faithful.

Consider some of the forces many of us are up against. Those of us trying to find a meaningful love relationship are forced to deal with the fact that our culture socializes men and women to evaluate and swipe past each other based solely upon whether a person looks "hot or not"—as though a human being is an object rather than the heart of humanity. In the workplace, many of us, especially young adults and men of color, struggle to earn a living wage. Long and irregular work shifts undermine our ability to connect with our loved ones and raise our children. These days technology and entertainment are so enticing that we often focus more on our screens than the loved ones watching alongside us. Brands sexualize transactions that aren't inherently sexual—think putting on deodorant, shaving, and styling your hair—distracting us from what's really important, such as our character. Some members of the media dispense false information, perpetuate stereotypes, and even incite people with similar interests to resent each other and compete when they would be better off cooperating. All of these forces push against us—and more.

If that weren't enough, our culture also pits people against each other during difficulties and breakdowns in their relationships, marriages, and families. Throughout our society and in many extended families, support systems to help people through life's inevitable challenges have broken down. So it's no wonder more than forty percent of first marriages end in divorce (the rates are significantly higher for second and third marriages). And while some marriages may need to end, we also now have a situation where a large percentage of our population is dealing with the unintended consequences of broken families. Across generations, many people deal with feelings of emotional abandonment, struggle to heal from heartache so they can form new relationships, feel heartsick, deal with trust that has been destroyed, have drained bank accounts, live in families with impossibly complex structures, carry heavy financial burdens, and deal with unprecedented rates of loneliness. People survive all of these types of situations, of course. And the truth of the matter is, some folks find tremendous meaning in their difficult circumstances and go on to thrive precisely because of them. But far too many of us get knocked off our path and lose precious time, money, and love as we regroup. Lots of people become permanently scarred and unable to recover. Though we live within our society, I believe we need to gallop away from these belief systems.

Fortunately, society's approach to building relationships and family is not a man's only option. Living by righteous principles separates you from everyday mind-sets that lead to unwanted outcomes. They also arm you with weapons to experience love and family in a healthy way.

Are You a Male or a Man?

One of the areas where you will have to fight is to develop yourself as a righteous man. Your ability to carry this intention through will be key to finding fulfilling love and building a healthy family, whether your own biological family or a family of people whom you love and who love you that you create by choice.

People use the terms "man" and "male" as though they're interchangeable; actually, they're not. All that it takes to be a male are XY chromosomes and the resulting male sex and reproductive organs. However, everyone who is a male isn't necessarily a man. From a legal standpoint, there's an age component to manhood. In many states adulthood (and therefore manhood) is defined as either eighteen or twenty-one, depending on whether you're trying to vote, join the military, purchase alcohol, own a gun, or do something else. But while the fact that you can buy a brew or a gun may make you a man in the legal sense, neither the ability to cast a ballot, drink, or carry a weapon—mean that you are a righteous man.

A righteous man also accepts the social responsibility to be connected to other human beings. Here's what I mean: Manhood plays out within a web of relationships. You are somebody's son, someone else's brother, another person's father, uncle, cousin, classmate, student, coworker, employee, community member, and so on—all at the same time. Righteous manhood acknowledges the fact that you are both a part of this matrix and have responsibilities within, and because of, it. In an ideal situation, you are accountable to and support your parents, your siblings, your children, your classmates or coworkers, and so on—and they are also accountable to and support you. Of course, a sizable percentage of families deviate from this ideal, even in families where all of the members appear to be in place, including my own family of origin.

As I press this idea a little further, I'd like you to consider the possibility that these people might be part of the extended family of humanity, in which you could grow and share and express yourself. Together, all these people can help you be a whole human being. And if I take this idea a couple of steps further than that, I want you to chew on the idea that a righteous man should actually think of himself as a Family Man. Now, traditionally the phrase "family man" means that you have a wife and children, which is why I'm capitalizing it; I'm not talking about that. And I admit that it's a difficult concept to convey in a world where many men refer to marriage as a "sentence" or would rather just live together. I get it that lots of young men are struggling to get the foothold that would allow them to support themselves and a family. Still others don't want to get "tied down" with either a woman or children. However, when I use the phrase Family Man, my definition extends beyond its traditional use. When I talk about being a Family Man, I mean that you not only understand that you are a part of a complex nexus of humanity, but that you actively seek opportunities to participate in and contribute to humankind, whether or not you are married or have children. Why do I suggest this approach? Ultimately, adopting this posture makes you stronger internally. In addition to that, it strengthens your family. Finally, it also builds up your ability to influence others and creates contexts for you to share your gifts with the world. Each of these things represents a win for you. No matter the circumstances you were born into—and whether you have a traditional or even healthy family construct or not—they can help you build a life where you will thrive.

Now, I'll be honest: As is the case with other righteous warrior attributes, identifying as a Family Man runs counter to the messages purveyed by popular culture. Among other things, our society encourages us to define our self-interest in the smallest terms possible. It teaches me that I should "get mine" and "take care of my own" and you should "cover your ass" and "look out for yours." Allow me to draw your attention to a couple of examples circulating around society right now. If you are White, you may receive the message that you should fear me as a Black man—or Latino, or Muslim, or immigrant—and that we are taking something that is rightfully yours. If you are a man who is a member of one of these marginalized groups, you may receive the message that White people won't give you a chance.

I have to admit that I've been very saddened to learn how many people believe their way of life is being endangered by those whom they (rightly or wrongly) believe are different from or even a threat to them. On the one hand, I get it. Because there are ways in which I believe that Christianity is under attack. However, a man need not view people of other backgrounds as a threat to himself. I work with people of all different faiths. As a Christian, how do I reconcile that? Because I don't need to agree with all of their religious beliefs. I recognize good men doing good work, and I honor that. I'd like you to consider that when a man embraces the Code of the Righteous Warrior, his Power does not depend upon the absence or presence of any other man (or woman). No other person can occupy or take from him his unique Place in God's ecosystem or deprive him of his Purpose. As long as he lives within his Parameters, no one can occupy his Eden but him. If you feel you are being threatened by others, I invite you to keep doing this work so that you can unlock your own unique masculine potential and see that no other man or group of men (or women) can stand in your way.

Sadly, too many guys move through life with these types of mind-sets, not understanding that their own narrow outlook is what traps them in a world too small to accommodate their spirit. Not only do such beliefs limit a man's ability to access his destiny, but good men who deserve great relationships miss out on the chance to learn from and feel connected with others who may appear to be different on the surface, but with whom they likely share much in common on the inside. This disconnectedness, not other men, is what limits their ability to feel fully satisfied with their lives. While it's easy to blame others, the choice is really our own. Worse, these limiting belief systems weigh down entire communities, pinning so many men against life's wrestling mat that they think that's just "the way it is" and don't even know they're complicit in their own entrapment. But when you sidestep these types of mind-sets, you discover that they often fall under their own weight, leaving you feeling lighter and freer to follow your spiritual path.

Furthermore, men who are loners or have a loose sense of connected-ness tend not to experience the depth of life's riches to the degree that guys who are more tightly connected do. This makes it more difficult to access the path to their destiny. Furthermore, it's not unusual for guys who carry this mind-set to find themselves in trouble of one sort or another—whether "swimming with the sharks" at the top of the business world leaves them feeling lonely and isolated, or they miss out on their chances to get to know their children or other relations because they're overworked or have a complex family situation, or because their imma-ture and selfish decisions land them in legal hot water, as Rich experi-enced early in life.

Beyond the Lone Ranger

The path to becoming a Family Man isn't a simple or linear process. In-deed, many of us need a nudge, whether from God or from our loved ones. Ellyn and I got married after my second year attending Southern Baptist Theological Seminary in Louisville, Kentucky. During the week I went to school; on Sundays I was the minister of music, playing the organ for $50 a week at Canaan Missionary Baptist Church. Even after I graduated, I spent far too many afternoons hanging with my buddies, drinking Jack Daniel's, eating Papa John's Pizza, and somehow expecting that work would find me. (Louisville is home to many distilleries; back then, alcohol flowed on campus.) In the meantime, Ellyn was teaching; I was on her insurance. One day she looked at me and said, "I am getting up every day and teach-ing these children. I know you have a master's degree, but you are going somewhere today, too, aren't you?" In other words: You will not be laying around here and hanging out with your friends. "The Ryan's Steakhouse up the street is hiring," she added.

At that point in my life, I clearly understood my responsibility as a son, brother, teammate, and friend. But the time had come to deepen my identity as husband and walk into my soon-to-be identities of father, minister, community leader, and (twenty years later) global citizen. So I dragged myself over to Ryan's, filled out an application, and was hired to wash dishes, bus tables, and work the French fries. Truth be told I thought the work was beneath my master's degree; sometimes doing things required me to engage in a mental and spiritual fight. Fortunately, my father had already taught me that working hard was part of manhood. Though this wasn't the work I aspired to, I started feeling the pressure of becoming a provider. So I became serious about my fries and took pride in my work.

That phase of life really challenged my understanding of manhood. My check from Ryan's was $150 a week, plus the $50 I earned at church. Ellyn's was $650 every two weeks—in other words, she made almost twice as much as I did. And because my beliefs about manhood that I had yet to outgrow encumbered me, on some days I engaged in a lot of mental gymnastics just to be able to look her in the eyes. I'd tell myself, "I'm on fries now but I'm soon gonna be . . ." a music minister, a pastor, leading a church, fill in the blank. I was doing a lot of psychological wrangling. My development occurred unevenly, but I was growing. I was beginning to understand myself as a Family Man in the traditional sense of the term, which was the only definition I had. This is where my thoughts about the righteous use of the phrase—the one that I capitalize—began to develop.

A righteous warrior embraces each of his manly identities—from son, to husband, to father, to community member, to coworker—as well as the responsibilities and opportunities that come with each role. Along the way, he learns how integral he is not just to his nuclear family, which is tremendously important, but also to his neighbors, classmates, school, coworkers, workplace, town or city, country, and ultimately the family of man. He is able to experience the richness of this life whether or not he has or wants to have children. Building a robust life in each of these roles will allow you to leapfrog over the uptick in loneliness and alienation that has become so common among men that it is now an epidemic. When you adopt the identity of a Family Man you can break the chains of separation that may hold you apart from family, friends, a spiritual community, and a purposeful life.

Vernell experienced several decades where he felt a pervasive sense of aloneness.

"Even though my grandfather and uncles were in my life, not having a father meant that I didn't have a man who was there just for me," he recalls of the years after his dad died, which happened when he was three. "I was also an only child. For a long time, I sought after a father figure, and I always wanted friends. Naively, I was one hundred percent of a friend to people who were fifty percent friends to me. Some of them took advantage of me."

For several years during his teens, Vernell also felt that he had been deserted by his closest uncle, who became a minister and embraced his entire community, with the unintended result that Vernell felt cast aside. "Then he ended up dying as we were working it out during my adulthood," he says. "I felt like he abandoned me, every friend I have seems to leave, every time I try to make friends someone takes advantage of me, and so forth. It caused me at different times not to trust. I started thinking, 'I'm a loner, I'm gonna be a loner. I don't have no new friends; I don't have no old friends; I just don't like people.'"

Vernell's experience is common to many men and causes lots of guys to buy into what I call the Shaft, Marlboro Man, Jimmy Dean, Luke Cage, Lone Ranger mind-set.

"On the outside, you never would've known that I was struggling," he says. "But deep inside, because I didn't have relationships with other guys, I saw them and I wanted them."

Even if a man's family upbringing wasn't ideal from his perspective—if he was raised by someone other than his parents, or was orphaned, adopted, placed in foster care, if his upbringing was inadequate or his family members passed away—he does not have to live disconnected from other human beings. God is inherently social so God wants us to enjoy relationships with friends, family members, and mankind. Innate within him, every man is born with the ability to connect with others and build relationships. Like a puny muscle a guy works on at the gym, his social muscle may need to be strengthened (or even repaired and restored), but it does exist and it's naturally in him.

The Circle of Life

We men gain our power in concentric circles. By that I mean our power ideally begins in our family of origin and radiates outward from there into the world.

In other words, we learn about relationships from our formative experiences, especially the behaviors and themes we learn within our family and that, if not contested and reconciled, play out in our relationships for much of the rest of our lives. What we learn from our parents we practice first with our siblings, cousins, and extended family. We then carry those learnings outward from our home to our spiritual family and school. Eventually, we bring those beliefs to our community, the places we work, and the wider world. In that sense our nuclear and extended families are places of training and preparation. They provide a practice ground that can either help or hinder our life, depending upon our experiences. This is one of the reasons why a man's relationship with his father is so important. Ideally, your relationship with your dad teaches you how to relate to older men; your interactions with your mom trains you to interact with older women; your relationship with your sister shows you how to relate to female peers in a platonic, nonsexual way; and your bond with your brother prepares you to get along well with other guys.

Under the best of conditions, love begins at home. And because love is the world's most powerful force, your power in life emanates outward from the love you've experienced or created in the everyday interactions within your family and inner circle. A man who has good relationships with his mother and father is situated for his influence to extend into the world. He's also well positioned to attract a Partner who honors, supports, and believes in him. However, not every man knows his mother and father. And even among those of us who do, not every man's childhood home life was perfect. A man's relational brokenness often plays itself out in the challenges he experiences in his relationships. So, for instance, a man who finds himself repeatedly experiencing run-ins with male authority figures—whether his teacher, his boss, or even the law—might want to go back and examine his relationship with his dad rather than continuing to tell himself that every boss he has is bad. He may or may not be able to fix things with his father, but he still needs to reconcile the fact that the root cause exists within himself and it is he who must be healed. He needs to ask God to bring some older men alongside him who will help him work that out.

Because Vernell's dad died when he was three, he hardly had the opportunity to know him. He reached a point in his spiritual and emotional development where he made the decision to challenge the belief he'd unknowingly internalized—that men would abandon him—and took the chance to build relationships with the men in our band of brothers. Even though I come from what is a wonderful family, the truth of the matter is my father essentially had three different families. He had Alfred and Alexander with his first wife, who passed away. He remarried and had my sister, Wendy, who is seven years older than me, but he and Wendy's mom divorced. Then he married my mom and I was born. Not surprisingly, all three of my siblings have a different experience of our father than I do. When my brothers were growing up, my dad was a young, struggling, but promising preacher who had once been a good athlete and was young enough to want to play with them. Wendy experienced my dad as an absentee father who divorced her mom, married a much younger woman, and moved to a different state. I didn't meet Wendy until I was ten, when she came to live with us for a couple of years. If I'm honest, back then I resented her. By the time I came along, my father was a famous civil rights leader, a leading pastor, a hero, and a resourceful man. So while I got the best football, the best bat, and the best glove because he could afford them, he was also older, didn't have much time, and didn't feel like getting out and tossing a ball with me. In fact, I can't recall ever playing catch with my dad. I threw my brand-new Spalding football with my brother Alfred, who had gotten lots of Dad's time but had never gotten a new football.

Furthermore, even guys who get along great with their folks are taught by society and perhaps even their dads to idolize the Lone Ranger. No matter their redeeming qualities, ultimately the disconnection leaves them feeling lonely and misunderstood. Every year as Mother's and Father's Day roll around, I have conversations with a lot of guys who struggle to celebrate one or both parents. Because of a number of situations that may have taken place during their childhood, they are left to wrestle with loneliness, heartbreak, disappointment, anger, and resentment as adults. Unresolved anger or heartbreak trips them up as they attempt to achieve their destiny. Beyond that, you can't be both a good Partner and a hurt or angry man. To thrive you must engage the very necessary journey of forgiving your parents and healing, as Vernell ultimately did. We will talk more about that in Principle 8.

Finding Your Partner

Identifying as a Family Man as you develop your Power, Place, Purpose, and Parameters prepares you to discover your permanent Partner.

A man becomes a complete human being once these foundational pieces are in place. With these principles as his base, he can operate as an independent entity within the social fabric of humanity. He can obtain full value *from* society as he also brings his full value *to* it. So as you become increasingly clear about the first four Ps and the complementary concepts of Identity and Industry, you will notice that you begin to attract the type of woman who could potentially become your Partner. In other words, the type of woman with whom you will share Intimacy.* If you fol-

---

*I don't mean to offend my friends in the LGBTQ community as I speak about a man's Partner; however, I am speaking from the context that I know: heterosexual relationships. These foundational principles could be very useful to people with other identities; however, I just don't know that experience.

low this process, you will meet your ideal Partner along your spiritual path. In fact, you will likely stumble across her as you carry out your assignment. Said another way, you won't need to go on Match or Tindr or to the bar to find her.

"Les and I are both educators. We worked at the same job," says Jerome of the woman who is now his wife. "I was in a relationship with someone else and so was she, but after a few months of knowing her, I fell in love, and I told her. Fortunately, she was in love with me as well. We got married just a few months after that even though we'd known each other for less than a year. At this point, we've been together for more than thirty years."

Before you profess your love to your coworker today, it's important to note that times have changed. Dating on the job is more of a risky proposition now than it was back then. If you do date someone at work, I encourage you to approach dating with Integrity.

But it's essential to get clear about your Power, Place, Purpose, Parameters, Identity, and Industry first, because a man must figure these things out for himself. A woman cannot give them to him. In other words, if you need someone to tell you who you are and push you to have a spiritual life or attend religious services—if you need a woman to try to give you your Power—eventually the pressure of that will weigh the relationship down. (By the same measure, a woman who doesn't have a spiritual life—and who can't be alone with herself for long enough to figure that out for herself—isn't ready to be with you.) And no matter how kind or beautiful or generous she is, if you need a woman to tell you about your Place and Purpose, the day will come when you resent her. Nor can your Partner give you your Parameters. No well-developed guy needs someone to tell him what he can and cannot do, where he can and cannot go, who he can and cannot be around. Indeed, if you already set your own Parameters, anyone who attempts to do it for you will leave you feeling emasculated. And, let's be honest, if you can't set Parameters for yourself, you can't be trusted in a serious relationship anyhow. In my experience, when a man needs a woman to tell him these things, the relationship is doomed. It is extremely difficult to build an enduring Partnership when either party believes that another person "completes" them, as Renée Zellweger's character told Tom Cruise's in *Jerry McGuire*. For a marriage to go the distance, the partners must be "complete" before they tie the knot. A marriage consisting of a "half" person who connects with another "half" person is unlikely to endure. But when one whole person marries another whole person, that relationship stands a good chance of making it to the finish line.

So let's deepen our conversation about love and family by digging into the concept of Intimacy put forth by Professor Schreck, my former Palmer Theological Seminary teacher. In our inquiry into Intimacy we must ask which voices in our life we value most. Ask yourself: Who do you want to have in your corner? Who will you allow to have your ear? It's important to consider things like: Who really loves you? Whose ideas tend to be the most meaningful? Which relationships do you want to nurture? Who encourages and sees a positive future for you? Who needs your permission to tell you the truth no matter how much it hurts? Whose words need to go in one ear and out the other or bounce off you so they don't bring you down? The answers to these questions will help you identify the people to develop close relationships with—the people who will form your inner circle.

For some of us, loved ones will be our biggest cheerleaders. But we can't assume that the people we are closest to will necessarily understand our dreams much less encourage us. Some loved ones will cheer us from start to finish, but others may struggle to envision us in our dream life or worry about how our change will affect them. Our goals may even scare some people who are close to us. We may experience loved ones who discourage us. So don't just stop with your family. Indeed, a person outside of your inner circle—a mentor at work, your high school accounting teacher, or one of your basketball buddies—may understand your vision better than anyone else and encourage you to go for it.

Not long after he met the fellas, Jerry began applying the administrative strengths he'd developed in the military to our band of brothers' dreams.

"One of the guys in the crew might come up with an idea, and I'd think, 'If he brought it up, it must be something he would like to do,'" Jerry says. "Right away, I'd go on a kind of a fact-finding mission to research whether I could put it together."

A Love Supreme

Being able to distinguish between and deploy the various types of love will help you experience the love you deserve and fulfill your identity as a Family Man. We live in a society that sexualizes razor blades. The entire society is affected by the eroticization of everything: In short, sex sells. The ability to see this marketing tactic helps you not get swept up into it and frees you to seek and receive meaningful love. There are four types of love I believe you need to understand the difference between. I write about them using their Greek root.

Storge love. When you're taking your grandmother to her doctor's appointment, consoling your son after he scraped his knee, or helping your nephew move into his college dorm, you're expressing *storge*, the deep and abiding connection that exists between family members. This includes parents and children, sisters and brothers, and extended relations including the people you call "auntie" or "uncle" even though they're not blood relatives. Most people first experience *storge* love when they are children, then you express this love to your own children when you become an adult.

"From the time he was eight years old until he was in his twenties, my son and I used to wrestle," says Jerry. "It was important to me that he knew he was loved; this was a love wrestle. Sometimes he'd bump up against me or I'd bump up against him and it would just start. I would grab him and pin him down. He'd say, 'Okay, Dad, that's enough,' but I'd say, 'Tell me you love me' or 'Give me a kiss!' He'd say, 'I'm not kissing you!' We could have a house full of people on Thanksgiving yet be in the middle of the kitchen floor. I always wanted him to be able to say, 'I used to do this with my dad.' This was how we connected."

"My grandfather was stern and I have that stern demeanor. My wife isn't as stern, so sometimes they look at me as if I'm the Grinch Who Stole Christmas," says Vernell, who approaches parenting somewhat differently from Jerry. "I'm always on the same page providing consistency. I'm the father that doesn't allow his sons to get away with things, who makes sure they clean up their room, who makes sure they say their prayers at night, who makes sure that when they get up in the morning they do specific things. I believe that if you train them the way you were trained, then those values will seep into the next generation. If you lag, then it becomes harder."

Phileo love. Though both men and women are social beings, most of our relationships should not be romantic. Every man needs nonphysical, nonsexual, friendly relationships with women—relationships that express *phileo* love. In other words, we need to develop the skills to love women platonically. Men's friendships with women are very important. In fact, most men are not missing mates in their lives, they are missing relationships with people who feel like sisters and brothers. *Phileo* love transcends sexual attraction so that people can talk, share, learn about each other, be honest, and discover what the other thinks. When you participate in a *phileo* relationship, you love and honor a woman's insides.

Eros love. Anytime you fall in love with a woman's appearance, you're experiencing *eros* love. Popular culture pushes *eros* on us—in hair gel, in razor blades, in deodorant, in toothpaste. You name it and marketers will make it sexually alluring. And while there's nothing wrong with physical attraction, a man needs strong Parameters to rein *eros* in. Especially when you're searching for long-lasting love, it's important to distinguish between women who are attractive but distractions and the one woman who is your destiny. *Phileo* love keeps *eros* from flaming out. Our society lies about romantic love, including conveying the myth that our Partner is the only friend we will need ever. As a result, many men and women abandon all other relationships for the sake of one woman or man. Then, because they no longer have platonic friends, they look to one person for everything. Before long, they discover that one person is just not enough, which tends to lead to anger if they gave up all their other relationships. *Phileo* love is also important within *eros* because no matter how beautiful a woman's outsides are, a lot can happen between now and the time she's eighty years old—from childbirth, to accidents, to wrinkles, to diseases. When you marry a woman, you love her insides no matter what happens to her external appearance; ideally, she loves your insides, too. Even if you're not married but are raising children together, *phileo* love will help to hold your family together.

Agape love. The universal form of love, you express *agape* when you care for the family of people who are not related to you. You love people of all races, religions, colors, nationalities, sexual orientations, and so on because they are human beings. When you practice *agape* during the dating process, you treat each other respectfully no matter what happens. Even if you decide that they are not right for you—or vice versa—you part peacefully and courteously.

How can knowing this help you find a romantic partner? I'm glad you asked! Popular culture teaches us to progress straight from our family's *storge* love to love relationships centered in *eros*. However, following this path makes it more difficulty to cultivate long-lasting results, so you'll have to push back against that also. This is where your Family Man identity can be very helpful. I want to suggest that in an ideal situation a righteous warrior travels the path to marriage differently from the journey expected within popular culture. After experiencing the *storge* love of his family during childhood, he next expresses *agape* love toward women, loving and appreciating their humanity. After that he moves to *phileo*, by developing a friendship. Most of his relationships with women will stop here. In this paradigm, the righteous warrior arrives at *eros* last. As he has children and a family of his own, he cycles back around to *storge* again. Following this process runs counter to popular culture, but it allows him to develop a relationship that will withstand life's challenges. I believe this sequence is important because not every relationship with a woman is meant to be romantic. Most should stop at *agape*; some should progress on to *phileo*; ideally, one will end in marriage. When you follow this progression, you avoid unnecessary wear and tear, disappointment, betrayal, and loss upon your spirit, especially in the romantic department—not to mention getting ghosted or trashed on social media, or dealing with cut clothes, thrown plates, keyed cars, or slashed tires. This slower approach protects your spirit and keeps you from losing trust in women and becoming bitter and jaded. Even if your dating relationship or marriage breaks up, you respect and love each other enough that no one cuts up the other's clothes or flattens their tires.

Like Jerome, Leroy, too, met his wife at work.

"We started working at a new job on the same day," he says. "She says that I was wearing a too-small suit and carried a briefcase with nothing in it—she was so unimpressed with me! I tried to give her my Mack Daddy vibe, but she wouldn't give me the time of day. 'I don't date on the job,' she told me. Thirty years, two college-age daughters, and Faith later, there has never been a day that we've not worked together."

Thinking of yourself as a Family Man positions you to have a marriage that lasts. Back in our grandparents' day, it wasn't unusual to encounter couples who had been married for forty, fifty, or sixty years; today that is extremely rare. Though people often joke about marriage being a sentence, there is a lot to be said for the man who wins the fight to preserve his marriage and keep his family intact. Though we love and embrace every blended family, there's something noble about maintaining a marriage for forty years. It is important that we honor the man who has been victorious in the marriage fight.

Fellas who do fight through the challenging phases of marriage gain incredible power. Indeed, something powerful occurs in the inner life of a man who goes places—mentally, emotionally, and spiritually—he promised he'd never go and forgives things he vowed he'd never forgive, and who wants to leave from time to time but chooses to stay with just one partner. In time he reaches the other side with that partner, their marriage intact, and can see that it was all worth it. His life may not be perfect, and it certainly wasn't easy, but it is full and rich. He can sit back and enjoy his children and grandchildren—the fruit of standing in the face of difficulty and loving his wife through all of it. This accomplishment requires tremendous commitment and strength. It also creates strong and powerful children. Indeed, keeping your marriage and family together for long enough to enjoy your grandchildren as one intact family is a righteous man's greatest accomplishment.

But a lot of people are on a relationship clock. They want to get married by a certain date and feel like they're getting old if they haven't found their Partner by their internal deadline. As a result, lots of guys rush things, cut corners or lower their standards. This often leads to one sort of mess or the other. Resist those societal expectations. Take your time and let the right woman come to you. Having said that, the old folks used to say that there's someone for everybody. I think that they were being overly optimistic: Every pot doesn't have a lid and every man doesn't have to get married. Married or not, you will be far better off by following the spiritual path that's for you.

Separate and Equal

Not that marriage was ever easy, but many men are finding that they are facing challenges as they attempt to build an enduring marriage with to-day's woman.

To help him succeed in that most important relationship, I believe that a righteous warrior should approach his marriage from an egalitarian, complementarian framework. When I use the word "egalitarian," I mean that he understands that men and women are equal in value. "Complementarian" means they are different in their roles. In other words, a man who follows this framework believes that men and women are equally important; however, they are not the same and the parts they play within a family should differ. In a marriage, they should harmonize with and enhance each other.

Now, let me start by explaining that historically Christianity has been taught from a Eurocentric, masculine, hegemonic perspective. In other words, White men have almost always been in charge and they have often used their power to dominate others—whether in their household or in the Church's involvement around the world. Indeed, many men have been taught that they should be the head of their household and that being the head involves requiring their wife and children to subordinate themselves to him. Indeed, lots of guys are taught that they should be "king of the castle" and many women are told that they should do whatever a man says. I strongly disagree with this approach. In fact, I believe that this doctrine of family leadership, called headship, is a very abused topic in conservative Christian circles. It causes families to get built in ways that hurt both the family as a whole as well as its individual members. I, too, am conservative and I believe in the headship language. But I take a far different approach than the Eurocentric model that we so often hear about.

In many conservative Christian circles, women are told to submit to men and men are told that they are the boss. One way that *Merriam-Webster's Dictionary* defines the word "submit" is "to yield to governance or authority." Seen in that light, almost everyone practices submission and we do so in a number of contexts. For instance, we submit when we follow the laws of our society; we submit to the rules at school and at work; we submit when we obey the rules of the road, and so forth. In other words, though we don't use the word in conversation very often, submission is neither limited to wives and husbands nor is it a bad word. Indeed, there are ways in which our obedience provides the kind of framework or structure that allows humanity to experience great freedom.

Submission is also a Christian spiritual principle often tied to a conversation about men's family leadership. The New Testament, where the language about men's headship is found, was originally written in Greek. In the Greek language back then there were two words for "head." One, *arche,* carried the connotation of being "over" someone or something; the second, *kaphale,* meant "source," "point," or "out front." The conservative Christian teachings about a man heading his household are taught from an *arche* perspective. They suggest that a man lords over his wife and children and has the right to tell them what to do. From this perspective he is the nucleus of the family and everything and everyone revolves around him. However, *arche* wasn't the word used in the original Greek texts; that word was *kaphale.* A man demonstrating *kaphale* headship leads his family in a manner similar to how the head goose leads a flock or a cyclist leads a bike race: by positioning himself out front and working harder in order to cut through life's headwinds to make the experience easier for others. The *kaphale* leader serves as a source of spiritual vitality, strength, security, and provision; however, he is not fundamentally more important than any other member of his household, nor does he lord his power or strength over them. The Bible calls Christians to submit to each other's gifts, not each other's gender. Ultimately, everyone is also required to submit themselves to God.

So whether they're merely unaware of this Truth or enjoy the advantage that the doctrine gives them, a large number of conservative Christian ministers and leaders, most of whom are men, teach women to subordinate themselves to their husbands. In fact, the church teaching that women should be submissive to men is so widespread that many people believe that it is Christian theology. It is not. Furthermore, some ministers teach not only that wives should subordinate themselves to their husbands, but that all women should subordinate themselves to all men. Interestingly, that's not in the Bible, either. Some preachers even go so far as to assert that women shouldn't do certain work—preach, serve in the military, be president, and so on. None of this can be found in Scriptures. In that respect, it is neither true nor True. Instead, these assertions reflect the spiritual principle of headship presented inside the framework of the Eurocentric beliefs that men should dominate and reign supreme over others. This is not righteous manhood.

The Truth of the matter is that a woman is capable of being president; she is capable of being a preacher; she is capable of being an astronaut—she can be anything she wants. No hierarchy exists between a man and a woman. We are different, but each gender possesses something the other needs. Beyond having different body parts and chromosomes, each gender brings something unique, important, and complementary to the table. Both men and women have gifts and talents, skills and abilities.

A righteous husband and father fights to create a context in which everyone in the home can express their gifts and where all of those gifts work together for good. He understands that individual gifting drives the principle of headship. As a result, he practices situational authority around individual gifts and everyone in the household subordinates themselves to whoever has the strongest gifts in a particular area. So rather than oppressing his wife and children, a righteous husband behaves more like a benevolent manager. By that I mean that he takes care of his loved ones, but doesn't require them to submit to him. It implies "living with," rather than "living over" others or subjugating them. It requires rejecting the traditional mind-set that says "I am the boss," and instead embracing the identity that "I am the manager of our household." When you do this, you create an atmosphere that others can thrive in. Leroy did this as he prayed to be a better husband and father. The outcome was that at her most vulnerable moment, Felicia trusted him with her life.

My wife, Ellyn, is one of the most intelligent human beings I know. She is smarter than I am. Period. Though I am a man, I am not Ellyn's boss. Together we made the decision that we would be a pastoral family who would go wherever the church sends us. So I am responsible for the welfare of my family and Ellyn submits to my leadership on the major decision of where our family goes. Biblically, we believe that on judgment day, God will hold me accountable for the condition of our family. That said, Ellyn is a financial genius. I submit to her in terms of financial planning, budgeting, and spending. Everything I earn I turn over to her. Then, because I am a good negotiator, I broker all of our major purchases (cars and houses) and handle contracts. So as a husband who strives for righteousness, I practice teamwork with Ellyn. Anything else in our relationship would constitute abuse.

What has this looked like as a practical matter? Though we both had high aspirations, in the beginning of our marriage Ellyn and I agreed to push me forward educationally and professionally before we pushed her. For several years, when our daughters were little, she put her professional goals on hold and raised them full-time. We struggled financially as I gained my foothold in the ministry, but in short order Ellyn returned to work and we were fine. After Ellyn resumed teaching, I had the more flexible schedule, so I dropped off and picked up my daughters from school. There were times when this felt uncomfortable for me. Number one, people would often comment about me babysitting when I'd drop them off and pick them up, but it's not babysitting when you are the dad. I took my little girls to school because being a righteous partner to Ellyn and father to our girls required it. And it was my responsibility to create a context in which all of us could excel.

When the girls grew a little older, Ellyn returned to school to pursue her doctorate. It was my responsibility to facilitate that, especially because early in our lives and during our children's teen years, Ellyn spent much of her time following me around. Now Ellyn has earned her Ed.D. In fact, when someone calls for Dr. Waller, they are often talking about her, not me. She receives a lot of invitations to speak about ending human trafficking and I often follow her. I am very proud of her and the work she does around the world, even though it has taken an adjustment on my part. I'd be less than honest if I didn't admit there is a part of me that struggles with my traditional masculine socialization and still feels that, as the man, I should be the primary provider. Yet the bigger part of me knows that I am accountable for supporting her dreams as enthusiastically as she has supported mine.

A rule of thumb I practice as a benevolent manager in my household (and beyond) is that if I'm getting what I want more than eighty percent of the time, I am probably oppressing somebody else. So I've learned to be "water" and to live with a number of things that make me uncomfortable so that other people can thrive. As a righteous man, your job is to create a context in which your family can flourish. You are very responsible for your children's upbringing and your romantic partner's well-being. One way or another, life will hold you accountable for how well you manage your household as well as whether you oppress your loved ones or any other human being.

Indeed, to thrive in today's society, every human being must learn both to lead and to be led by members of the opposite sex. As a practical matter, conservative Christian or not, most men cannot afford to define headship in the old-fashioned hegemonic way. For most of us the era when men go to work and women stay home forever is over. That way of life no longer reflects the economic reality that most families will sink if all the adults are not earning every penny they can.

So if you were raised to believe that your wife shouldn't work, it's time to let yourself off the hook. A righteous man positions himself out in front of his family—physically, mentally, emotionally, and spiritually. He does this not to make them lesser than him, but to lead, protect, and create opportunities for the people who live in his home. Honor, rather than dominate, your family members as you guide them. In the meantime, celebrate the fact that you've married a queen who is strong and able to provide for her household. This is what makes you a Family Man.

PRINCIPLE 8

Play Hurt

Come to terms with your weaknesses and imperfections, work on them, live in the tension of their existence, and stay engaged in the fight even when you're hurt—it's possible to live your best life both with and because of your shortcomings, heartbreaks, and pain.

I LAY ON the floor curled up in a ball. My eyes were blindfolded. My hands were tied together. I couldn't protect myself. My imagination was just going crazy. I was scared—I had no idea what was going to happen to me. Every time I heard a sound I flinched.

I had advanced through the levels of CKM one by one. At each level, I'd learned a number of new techniques and had had to fight a little longer and against more opponents. I'd started out with four-minute fights against three guys. To pass the Level 7 test, I'd have to fight three guys for a total of fifteen minutes. I hadn't necessarily learned any additional techniques. I mean, we'd learned how to disarm a person carrying a rifle, but that's kind of impractical. A guy with a rifle is probably not going to get close to you like someone who's carrying a handgun might. The likelihood I'd have to wrestle a shotgun from someone seemed pretty slim to none. Then again, church shootings . . .

So here I was on the floor with my eyes closed and hands tied, waiting for my beating. More important than that, I'd have to do it hurt. Before the battle goes down, three other fighters ceremonially beat you with half-inch-thick wooden rods, clobbering you on your shins, legs, back, and chest. Your body feels like it's on fire. After they beat you for one minute, the fight begins. In essence, the test is asking the questions: Can you control yourself when someone is hurting you? And can you fight—and can you implement all the defensive techniques you've learned—when you're hurt?

I knew that I needed to pass this test the first time; I wasn't going to put myself through it twice. Not only did I want to reach the next level without having to undergo this beating again, I also understood it as a metaphor. At fifty, I knew that I was living with wounds. Things may look good from the outside looking in, but from the inside looking out I know that I am scarred. My ability to pass the test while beat up and hurt had a lot of symbolic meaning. So I lay on the floor, not knowing when each blow would come. Instinctively, I found myself flinching to protect myself every time I heard (or thought I heard) a sound. I knew the beating was coming, I just didn't know when. Amidst that uncertainty, I laid there flinching over and over. For no reason. Then they started beating the mess out of me.

The first couple of licks hurt really bad. The blows hurt and my flesh stung so much that I wanted to cry. Of course, there's no crying in Krav Maga. After a few hits, I realized, "Okay, I'm getting hit and I can survive this"—and I just took it. As suddenly as they had started, the hits ended. But were they really done or were they just going to start again? When my opponents told me to stand up, I still wasn't certain. I only knew I was sore and my body bruised. When they removed my blindfold, I looked at my skin, covered with cuts, red marks, and welts. Now it was fight time.

For the next four minutes I gave everything I had against three guys who were lighting into my red-hot skin. Then we took a one-minute break, during which we did some calisthenics. Then we fought for four more minutes and did calisthenics for another minute. Then we repeated the routine one more time. Somehow I made it through this process. Once we finished, I rose, bruised and battered, to fight again, just as every man must do in his life.

Making YAC

A righteous warrior keeps moving forward even when he's wounded.

Whether his wife tells him she's leaving and taking the kids, the pipes burst while he and his family are away on vacation, or a tornado levels his neighborhood, as he deals with life on life's terms, some situations will overwhelm him. A warrior accepts that he lives in a chaordic world. He also acknowledges that he is a human being who has personal weaknesses, a man who will occasionally use poor judgment and every now and then make a major mistake. In other words, he comes to grips with all that's wrong with him, but continues to move forward in the tension of that. He refuses to join the ranks of the guys who have thrown in the towel or bailed on the people who love and rely on them. Nor does he run away from life's challenges by hiding behind *SportsCenter*, Fox News, Netflix, *Grand Theft Auto*, the NBA playoffs, or the World Cup.

When we exercise the warrior mind-set even when we're hurt, we are acknowledging that every guy who has achieved any level of excellence has suffered defeats, humiliations, rewrites, and do-overs. In fact, the very successful men whom we admire on the field and screen have been told no over and over. They have cried and bled and risked ruin and gotten up again—that's just the stuff of life. Nobody who has done anything worthwhile has skated through without hard times. Even the most righteous man plays at least part of life wounded. But don't take my word for it, you give me the name of a champion and I'll show you a man who has given his all while he hurt. In Game 5 of the 1997 NBA Finals, Michael Jordan dropped thirty-eight points on the Utah Jazz while he was so sick with the flu that he was staggering up the court. Curt Schilling pitched in the 2004 World Series shortly after surgeons had reattached one of his ankle tendons to the bone—he even had blood on his sock. Tiger Woods won the U.S. Open with a torn ACL. And Nate Robinson dropped forty-two on the Boston Celtics right after throwing up on the sidelines.

Because here's the thing: There are 16 games in a football season, 82 games in basketball, and 173 between opening game and Game 7 of the World Series. Everyone's hurt and banged up when the end of the season rolls around. Yet they have fought to make it to the playoffs and have been dreaming about and sacrificing toward it since childhood. At the height of their career, their record and reputation are on the line. The time has come for them to perform at their best. In other words, come playoff time, every athlete is facing the most difficult competition when their body is the most banged up it has been all season. Nevertheless, it's show time and everyone has to perform. Superstars know how to play when they're hurt—and we admire, are inspired by, and even worship them because of it.

Former football coach John Madden once commented about the legendary Emmitt Smith. Over the course of his career as a running back, Smith ran for ninety-five yards or more an incredible twelve times—and I don't mean ninety-five-yard games, I mean ninety-five-plus-yard runs! But those long dashes down the field, as impressive as they are, aren't what made Smith so celebrated. What made Emmitt Smith so powerful was that he could take a hit and keep powering forward. The first hit never brought Emmitt Smith down. His celebrity came from his ability to make yards after contact, or YAC, as Madden called it. Of course, any player can score a touchdown if nobody hits him. But that's not how the game of football is played. As long as a player possesses the ball, guys will come after him and try to tackle him. He's going to take some hits. The question becomes whether he keeps going.

The same question applies to you and me. When we're down, when we're disappointed, when we're depressed, when we're heartbroken, what do we need to do to make YAC? Because not only does the ability to make YAC make a running back great, it's also what transforms an ordinary guy into a warrior who can fight through the battle at the door to the next world and access the subsequent season of his destiny. Let's be honest, there are times in life when you don't have it together—you don't have the emotional strength to continue, or your health has failed you, or you're bewildered about why something has happened, or you can't see where life is taking you.

In CKM, at the upper level, in addition to undergoing ceremonial beatings, the training also involves the instructor picking an appendage that you can't use. Your right leg may be "injured" or your left arm "broken," yet you have to fight your way through it. You still have to pass this "pressure test." Simulating conditions when you're hurt causes you to draw on undeveloped aspects of yourself. If you can't use your left arm because it's tied down, you're forced to focus on what you can use. In the process you discover new things about yourself. From a martial-arts standpoint, this is one of the ways that you prepare to fight hurt. A righteous warrior is resilient.

Your Crop, Your Cross, or a Coup?

From a spiritual standpoint, every man is a combination of the Divine and the dirt. God created him and God lives within him, but he exists within the "dirt" of the physical world. That's where the challenges come in. All of us grapple with some combination of the external pressures we feel from the world—whether school, work, finances, partners, children, or other sources—and our own internal brokenness. Again, when I use the term "brokenness," I am referring both to the serious traumas and tragedies you've been through as well as the garden-variety heartbreaks, hurts, and disappointments of life. I also believe that each of us is innately born weak in certain areas—whether we are quick to anger, are disposed toward addiction, or have a propensity for prostate problems. Internal and external pressures such as these play out as our life's dramas. But not all turmoil is the same. A man's crises tend to come from three places: his crop, his cross, or a coup.

Your Crop

A man's crop consists of the seeds he has planted that eventually ripen into his harvest. A righteous man usually reaps positive things: a loving family, good friends, a supportive community, and so on. But he may also sow some things he didn't intend to, doesn't want, or may have thought he wanted at the time but now he sees all the consequence. Harvest time eventually rolls around and he must deal with unwanted repercussions. This happened to Rich, whose criminal behavior fueled by addiction got him locked up for thirteen years. It also happened to Jerome as he repeatedly made decisions over the years not to take care of himself.

"I used to be able to eat a whole cheesesteak," he says about reaching three hundred pounds and developing high blood sugar. "I loved my Tastykakes. I used to love fried chicken, especially fried breasts and wings. I used to love McDonald's French fries. That's basically what got me in trouble." Eventually he decided to have weight-loss surgery. "I knew that this was gonna be my last-ditch effort to get it together."

There may also be situations where enough time has passed —it could be months, years, or even decades—that we forget the role we've played in the situation by the time harvest season rolls around.

Of course, every mistake you make won't take you out. Most things eventually work out one way or another. God will forgive you when you feel remorseful and try to make amends after planting a bad seed. That said, your crop may still grow in ways you will have to contend with; what goes around eventually does come back around. Indeed, most of us are complicit in at least some of our struggles. I include myself.

I have always enjoyed the peaceful way alcohol made me feel, though for much of my adult life, I've had a love-hate relationship with it. Because I am a minister, for a while I wrestled with the theology of drinking and studied the Bible to figure out whether it was a sin. But even though I reached the conclusion that, theologically, drinking is okay, I would hide the fact that I drank. The story I told myself was that I wanted to be discreet, and though there was nothing wrong with enjoying a glass of wine with dinner, everyone didn't necessarily feel that way, so I probably shouldn't have any at a church banquet where my members would be watching—that's how I explained it.

Indeed, over the years there have been times when I was okay with having a drink and phases when I didn't drink at all. There were also times when I would drink too much. From time to time, I would experience warning signs that I'd gone overboard, but I didn't pay enough attention. What I didn't know back then was that because I have a gene that predisposes me to alcoholism, I shouldn't have any alcohol at all.

Then there was a period of time after we'd built our new church when I was burned out and should have taken some time off; however, I was afraid of what might happen if I wasn't there. My profile in the city had risen significantly. In addition to the added responsibility of our church mortgage, I experienced a lot of envy and criticism. I found this difficult to take because part of what comes with my addictive personality is a desire to be liked. I didn't know how to handle all the pressure. I would allow myself to drink from time to time, telling myself the lie that I could manage it.

Then a celebrity mentor who had been helping me navigate life as a newly well-known person suddenly passed away. The tsunami of emotions I'd failed to process when my dad and brother had died overtook me. Shortly thereafter, a young man I'd been mentoring and viewed as a son became deathly ill. I started drinking and it got out of control. I was in my spiritual mentor's church when I completely succumbed, and I am ashamed to confess that I went totally off the rails. I consumed three gallons of vodka over the course of a week. Worse, I was so drunk that I thought I could still preach a revival. The situation was very ugly. Indeed, I am lucky to have survived. To this day I am very ashamed and will have to live with the consequences of my behavior—and there have been some tough ones that I will have to live with forever. Fortunately, God knew where to let me fall; my friends were there for me. Ellyn came to get me and I went straight from the church to the Betty Ford clinic. There, I detoxed and began to engage in the deep work that recovery requires.

The young man whom I'd been mentoring died shortly after I returned home. I preached at his funeral and we buried him. Then I went off the rails again. Eventually, I got it together. It took me a while to submit to the Alcoholics Anonymous (AA) process. I had become well known enough in Philadelphia that I was afraid of who might see me if I went to an AA meeting. If the word got out, what would everyone say? Would people abandon my family and me? Would they think that as a minister I was a fraud? Would anyone even want to come to my church? I felt the pressure of all the people depending upon me. Eventually I realized that I could be much more effective for myself, for my family, and everyone else if I surrendered that fear to God. Working my program has helped me develop the discipline and commitment to live life differently. The bottom line is, AA works if you work it. Ultimately God is the healer, but he invites you to partner in your healing.

Your Cross

Just as carrying the cross to Calvary was part of Jesus Christ's assignment, every righteous man has some sort of burden to bear. Though the root of this concept exists in Christianity, this idea is common across spiritual traditions. So when I talk about a man's "cross," I mean the problems that come with the territory while you are alive. Even when we are pursuing our destiny, getting there isn't always smooth sailing. As a man carries his cross, he will go through some dark places that will teach him lessons and develop skills that the good life and sunshine don't foster.

"Devon was twenty-three years old, a rising college senior and studying criminal justice. His goal was to be in the Secret Service. He had even completed a few internships with the DEA; they were waiting on him to graduate. He wanted to be that guy in a black suit, black sunglasses," Jerry recalls. "But at one a.m. on Saturday, August 21, 2015, the doorbell rang and the dog barked. 'Our door?' I remember asking myself before getting out of bed and going downstairs. When I opened the door, two police officers I knew stood in front of me. I knew what they were there to tell me; I fell to the floor. I had never ever dreamed in ten zillion years that that was going to be who stood on the other side of that door.

"You see, back when I was a first sergeant in the Army, I had been the casualty officer in the dress uniform who knocked on the door at six a.m. waking parents up and greeting them with the sad news, 'On behalf of the president, we sorrowfully are here to inform you about the loss of your son or daughter.' I had done it in 2005 when the Pennsylvania National Guard of Philadelphia lost eight soldiers in one firefight in Iraq. It had been one of my duties. Now somehow the tables had turned.

"My wife came to the top of the stairs. She, too, saw the police officers. She screamed, 'Not Devon!' then collapsed."

I was in Florida when Jerry called to tell me that Devon had lost control of his car and lost his life. Needless to say, I dropped everything and flew home. By the time I got there, my wife, Ellyn, Leroy, Rich, Vernell, and other members of our church family were already there to help comfort them.

"Devon was my only biological child," Jerry explains. "It was like taking a rib out."

But as devastating as their experiences are, it may shock you that Jerry and Leroy are not the only guys in our group who have experienced shattering loss and have had to learn to play hurt.

"In 2007, I had joined the church and was turning my life around. My daughter had just had a baby. I had just gotten my son a job and into the union at nineteen, and everything was working out," Rich says. "One day, we all were just in the living room talking. I looked at my son, who was sitting on the steps and said, 'Son, I want you to come to church.' He said that he would, but when I looked back at him again, he looked a little funny. I said, 'Son, how you feeling?' He said, 'Dad, I got a little headache.'

" 'Well go on upstairs and handle it,' I said, thinking he'd run to the medicine cabinet and grab an aspirin. But then he looked at me and he looked at his mother, and he slid down the steps and that's where he died. Later we discovered that he had arrhythmia; unfortunately, nobody had known about it."

Making Rich's grief worse, some of the people he used to hang out with told him that this was his payback.

"I couldn't get that out of my head—that this had happened because of something I'd done," says Rich. "I kept asking God if it was true, because I was new to religion. I'd just joined the church and gotten baptized, but now my son's dead."

Our band of brothers supported Rich through his heartbreak.

In addition to the fact that many people encounter unexpected tragedy, you should also expect to experience difficulty as you follow your destiny because following a spiritual path will invariably set you at odds with the consumerism common to our society. No matter how your life's journey goes down, if you go where you are supposed to go and do what you are supposed to do, you will experience divine support—often right when you reach the limitation of your abilities. Keep your eyes peeled for assistance both from heavenly emissaries and other human beings.

"On the day of the funeral, I shied away from everybody. I didn't want to hear that tomorrow's a better day, joy comes in the morning—none of that," Rich says. "I was up in my room with the TV on. Before I knew it, I had stuck my hand in my drawer and put my nine-millimeter in my mouth with the safety off, gun cocked.

"I was about to pull the trigger, when I heard a faint voice saying, 'Daddy, Daddy.' It was my daughter.

" 'What do you want?' "

" 'It's the telephone.' "

"'Who is it?'"

"'It's Reverend Murphy.'"

"I put the gun down beside me. This was the same man who'd taken a special interest in me back when I was still drinking and when I was finishing my introductory classes at church. Now he was calling to check on me and tell me he would be preaching my son's funeral.

"'I love you. You called just in time,' I said. "Almost ten years would pass before I told him that his call had saved my life."

Rich's help showed up right on time. If you are struggling, but your help hasn't yet shown up, there's more that you are capable of doing by yourself. You can make YAC on your own.

There is a very well known biblical passage of scripture, Psalm 23, that talks about dealing with tremendous difficulty. It uses the language, walking "through the valley of the shadow of death"; however, the Hebrew root word that is typically translated as "death" actually means "darkness." You are likely to suffer, but the word "shadow" in that context is very important. I am only five feet eight but at four in the afternoon, my shadow is bigger than me. If you could see only my shadow coming, it might scare you. But my shadow isn't really me, it's merely what happens when the sun is behind me.

Though your heart may be breaking or your head spinning, during tough times it's important to understand that some of the stuff you're experiencing looks really big right now; however, from a different perspective—whether when you calm down and don't feel so afraid, or with the benefit of time, from a higher or just from a different perspective—the challenge isn't as big as you think. Spiritually, you and God are a majority in any situation you face, so dig into your faith and demonstrate discipline around it. In many religious traditions, as in Christianity, there's a lot of wisdom or scripture that advises "fear not," or "be courageous," or "be of good cheer." Even the greatest difficulty cannot destroy you spiritually unless you allow it to.

"Everything in my life is about a mission," Jerry says. "I knew that someone had to step up to handle the family business. There was a mission to be accomplished. This mission was to take care of Devon at all costs. There was so much stuff that had to be done—from finances, to car insurances, to attorneys, to Sallie Mae, to stuff I'd cosigned for him. I knew that all that stuff had to get accomplished. I knew it had to be done. You hear the old cliché 'life goes on,' and that's true. Handling everything well administratively to close out his life, this was one of my ways of honoring Devon."

So fight through, learn what the situation has come to teach you, and stay humble. You will emerge more powerful than when you began.

A Coup

Sometimes a man encounters a coup, when people he knows and trusts let him down, leave him, or perhaps even turn on him. Many men will encounter enemies or even "haters" along their way. Opposition is just part of life. It is an affirmation of who you are—and may even propel you forward along the path to your destiny.

But do you remember the sports posters you had in your bedroom when you were a child? Whether you had Jim Thorpe, Muhammad Ali, Michael Jordan, Jeremy Lin, Alex Rodriguez, Cal Ripkin Jr., or Pat Tillman on your wall, these posters tended to depict that superstar overpowering some unlucky defender who will forever be "posterized," a slang term that describes the poor guy who will always be remembered for getting burned. Now, we remember that star for his amazing play, but we may not realize that we wouldn't have been wowed if he hadn't had an opponent. Having opposition is necessary because it forces us to strengthen ourselves and become better. Similar to what happens near the door to the next level of a video game, resistance also affirms both that you're nearing something valuable and that what you have to offer is of value as well.

Whether your crop, your cross, or a coup is causing your struggles, just as a hit didn't take down Emmitt Smith, your struggles, stumbles, or tragedies don't have to stop you. No matter where your drama comes from—whether you caused it, it comes with the territory, or you're being betrayed—as grueling as the process may be, you can persevere and push through. You must do this not only because you depend upon yourself, but also because your family, team members at work, and your community depend on you, too. So while you may not suit up and step onto a professional football field, you must earn YAC in your own field of play.

Off the Mark

Whether our family of origin's story or our partner's psychological projections, it's also not uncommon for men to star in dramas that were written for them by somebody else. For instance, your parents or wife may tell you that you should keep your job for security even though your heart has been telling you to start your own business. This often sets up a situation where we meet other people's needs but fall short of our own possibilities and destiny.

"When I was in my twenties, I wanted to be a police officer," Vernell recalls. "But my mother and then-girlfriend were very instrumental in my thought process. They were real big on, 'No. Don't become a cop, you're gonna die! My child, oh my god, my child!'"

Other times we get in trouble because we've developed bad habits and can't break them. Whether smoking, watching Netflix when we should be working out, or eating too much fried food and not enough veggies, I see this a lot where it comes to men's health. Sometimes habits get passed down through the family. Just as green eyes can be inherited, so, too, can temperaments, behavioral patterns, predispositions, and even unhealthy recipes. Brokenness can be learned, inherited, or genetically transmitted, as well. Personally, I know what it means to have been born with a gene that leans you in the direction of alcoholism or chemical abuse.

Get Back on Target

A righteous man doesn't beat himself up when he falls short of any target. Remember, your goal is not to live in sinless perfection but to be the best human being that you can be. When I use the word "sin," I am not saying you're going to hell. I merely mean that you are "off the mark" or have strayed off the path to your destiny. The proper response to sin is just to get back on the path.

"Now my focus is different; I'm thinking about a career, not just a job," Vernell says. "I'm forty-five and my credit is in a wonderful place. I'm applying to be a police officer!"

One really important thing to understand is that sin is subjective. So something that is a sin to you may not be a sin to me. What tugs you may not pull on me. It may not bother you to have a glass of wine with your dinner. I, on the other hand, could have that exact same glass, but it would trigger a "life or death" struggle with my addiction. Sometimes we have an internal battle going on. The voice that's going to win will be the one that we feed. So, in order to be victorious, you have to get at the root cause of every battle you encounter. That means you also have to figure out what triggers you to be less than your best. In other words, your ability to earn YAC depends on how well you understand your triggers. Understanding what sets you off will help you get clear about some of the things that you need to let go of.

Though a righteous man is not sinless, he should still strive to sin less. When we fall short—and we will—we should take the necessary steps to get up. All of us fall short of everything that's possible for us. Depending upon what we've done, our crop could cause us to lose yardage and have to start from our backfield, the "red zone" or even up against our own goal line of our life. The outcome for you really hinges upon the degree to which you're trying to get back on track to your Purpose. There is a difference between weakness and wickedness. Men who are weak eventually get another chance. But if you keep sinning, that will become normal for you. Because each time you engage in sin it makes it easier to do it the next time. The more you do a wrong thing, the less it bothers you. This can lead to a point where sinning no longer bothers you. Indeed, sin is different from inequity, which means you're not even trying at all. Confession helps reset your sensitivity so that you will feel bothered when you sin again. Some sins take you further than you planned to go and cost more than you planned to pay. A lot of dudes are just in plain old D.E.N.I.A.L. They've been out there for so long, they *Don't Even kNow I Am Lying*.

Only the Lonely

Whether as a result of the crop he planted, the cross he has to bear, or his coup, after a man takes a hit, the amount of YAC he earns depends upon how he recovers from it.

"It helped me knowing that the fellas were there without me asking," Jerry recalls. "I didn't have to say, 'I'm not feeling well today, will you come sit with me?' I didn't have to do that. There were some Saturdays when I'd get up and Leroy would be knocking on the door saying, 'I felt like you needed some air, let's go for a ride.' Leroy lives over an hour away. He didn't call me Friday night; something told him he needed to get to me. The same with Alyn and Ellyn. Ellyn almost moved in with us. She was there every day in the week leading up to the service. She was with my wife and girls, on her hands and knees, wiping down toilets, cleaning bathrooms and kitchens."

A righteous man who has taken a hit or a guy who's on the rebound from his sins should not be surprised if he experiences a season where he finds himself walking alone. This may also happen when he's being spiritually prepared for a role or a season that he and the people around him may not yet understand. During this transition period, he may doubt himself and others may challenge or even attack him.

All human beings move back and forth across a continuum between aloneness and group activity. But being alone is not the same as being lonely. Being alone merely means that no one is around you. It can restore you and be quite clarifying. Times of aloneness and solitude can even be a source of great Power.

"I'm more of a prayer, a silent prayer; I can contain it," says Jerry. "I can go there all by myself. I don't need anybody; I don't need to be in church. That's why I had a bench installed by Dev's stone. It's eight miles from my house, so I ride down there all the time and sit there and chill. That's how I get through it. I change his flowers; I maintain his stone. Wash his stone with soap and water. I do all that kind of detailed stuff. It might sound morbid but it's my way of staying connected to him."

But while a man can be alone and not lonely, a man can also feel lonely in a crowded room. You also can be with people you used to enjoy, but reach a point in your journey when you no longer fit in. And being lonely is not the same as being abandoned. There may be a time when you feel like you've been cast aside or left to your own devices. Worse, you may even feel betrayed.

It's important to learn to live knowing that at some point this may be your reality. Because the further you journey into your destiny, the more difficult some challenges will become and the lonelier the journey will be. For instance, you may find yourself in a place where you're wondering: Why can't I find a job even though I'm qualified? Why can't I get her to come back home to work on our marriage? What has happened to my child and will she recover? How could this happen in our community? Why do I have this disease? How will we ever recover from this natural disaster? Are we going to make it?

And no one can help you. You just have to accept the situation so that you can move forward. Because the truth of the matter is, there are some things every man has to work through by himself. Your partner cannot help you; your parents cannot help you; the fellas cannot help you. Your spiritual journey and life's assignment are different from theirs. You have to go at least part of it alone.

"Losing Faith was the beginning of a spiritual journey for me and some spiritual journeys tend to be packaged in pain," says Leroy. "Here's what came out in counseling. I overspiritualized my grieving process for about a year. I didn't cry much; I just believed that God is good and gonna work it out. But my approach ended up impacting our marriage, because Felicia was emotionally jacked up and I was overspiritualizing. I felt like there was only a finite number of tears for our household and Felicia was using all of them up. I felt like I didn't have that luxury. I actually had a low-grade anger toward her because she was hurting and I couldn't help her.

"On top of that, her deep grieving took me back to when my father and brother had died and left my mother, my two sisters, and me alone. The only message that I knew was that men take care of their families and fix stuff. But I couldn't fix it when my brother and my dad died, and I couldn't fix it for Felicia, and couldn't fix it for us. It became very problematic. And it turned out that Felicia felt guilty for the way she felt. She wished she could have seen me cry, but I was like, 'I can't cry because you *do* cry.' In hindsight, I did cry, I just never let her see me."

As you struggle to make YAC, I strongly recommend that you pray constantly. Many people tell me that they're intimidated by prayer; don't be. When you pray, you don't need to use any special language. God doesn't hear "thee's" and "thou's" any more easily than God hears, "Daddy, I need you to help me!" Just talk to God like you'd talk to the most loving, nonjudgmental friend or father you can imagine. This conversation will not only help to call spiritual resources to you, it will help you to align your thoughts and behaviors with your higher self, helping you to access your Power. After you pray, remember to sit still enough to listen for any answer or sense you may feel in your heart about what you should do next.

You will also have to learn to encourage yourself. Because everyone's not going to want what you want or be willing to sign on to your dream or your program. Other people may just not be willing or able to motivate you or cheer you up when you have a hard day. You're also going to have to learn to speak "life"—motivation and encouragement—to yourself. This means you will have to inspire yourself to think about and do things that do not yet exist as though they already do. Making YAC will require you to progress toward your dream even though you may be the only person who can see it, some people may not believe it's possible, and other people may actively be trying to bring you down. As you strengthen your internal mental, spiritual, and emotional muscles so you can do this, you may discover that you're becoming more like a thermostat than a thermometer. Remember, a thermostat sets the room's temperature; a thermometer merely reads the temperature that the thermostat has set. Similarly, a warrior understands that he will have to create his own positive mental environment.

Sometimes making YAC means deciding that a season is over.

Have you ever watched one of those medical shows where the person is dead and one of the doctors asks the other, "Are you going to call it?" And the other doctor doesn't want to give up on the person and isn't ready to say the person's dead: "I'm not ready to call it." Sometimes they even get into a debate: "Call it." "I'm not going to call it." Eventually the doctor calls what is known as "time of death." Time of death means that life's clock has ticked its last tock; their life is over. Men stay in all types of relationships—friendships, marriages, jobs, business partnerships—that they should have ended already. That season is already over, the relationship is dead and may even be stinking and rotting, but no one will call it. We have to learn to call time of death to release the person and ourselves, so that we can go through the door and enter into our new life.

It's a lot like trading a free agent at the end of the season. Their period of usefulness is over; it's time for both parties to move on so they can be useful somewhere else and the team can acquire the player they need. All of us need to learn to say in a loving and respectful way: "I want to thank you for the role you have played in my life and for the role I played in yours. But I'm preparing to go to a different place and I need to leave you here."

Purpose in Our Pain

Every hardship has a purpose and that purpose is greater than the problem itself.

"In the middle of grieving Faith, I was announcing my call to the ministry. I wanted to minister in places and areas of brokenness in order to create purpose for my and other people's pain," Leory said. In addition to his work at our church and at the children's hospital where he was a chaplain, Leroy and Felicia have created a ministry that helps other couples who have lost children. "One of the biggest lessons I've learned from my own pain is to tell brothers to be vulnerable, to be transparent. Sometimes your folk need to see it. In my work I share that a lot, because brothers, they don't know that. Once they do, they can navigate the man thing and they're not feeling like a chump."

There are some situations where stress helps you to improve. In sports, you can't develop every skill in a winning game. You also have to learn from your losses. A diamond only forms when carbon experiences pressure and heat; a teabag only works when it's placed in hot water. The outcome occurs not just because of the temperature but also because of the nature of the material the heat acts upon. For example, the same heat that melts butter hardens clay.

When I first moved to Philadelphia, I fell in love with the 76ers. That was back during the Allen Iverson years. After that era ended, the Sixers experienced a number of losing seasons. The fans became frustrated. But then a new group of owners came on the scene. At first, the team continued losing; however, the management changed the team's messaging. They told us the team was rebuilding and asked that we trust the process. In time "trust the process" even became the team's tagline. During this phase, the Sixers cut some folks and traded others for better draft picks. They were also changing players' mind-sets—doing things like teaching new systems and putting a few guys into positions they didn't play in college. The new owners had a different vision for them. After several years of struggle, the Sixers became exciting and even made the playoffs again.

Just as blue skies and sunshine are not all that's needed for a plant to thrive, every skill that's required to win cannot be learned in a winning game. Loss, too, can teach us to grow and change. Indeed, what separates many of the world's greatest athletes from other athletes is that they are capable of coming back from behind, working around double and triple teams, and winning "ugly." Their ability to gut situations out is what allows them to rise above the rest. The tough times, not blue skies, make them superstars.

Knowing that struggles take place for a reason can help you stay focused when you're hurt or even down for the count. I encourage you not to throw in the towel during a season of hardship. Nor should you interpret your difficulty as meaning that God is angry with or punishing you, as many men mistakenly believe. I see far too many men give up when the going gets tough, when engaging life's fight is essential to a man's destiny.

Be Made Whole

In order to maximize access to your life's path, I strongly encourage you to be honest about the things that you need to work on within yourself. Most men I know want to feel more powerful. Well, the truth of the matter is that people who have overcome a mortal wound or faced down spiritual, mental, physical, or emotional "death" or demons are among the most transformative people on the planet. So be quick to perform a postmortem on yourself or engage in an autopsy on your own sin. Go back and take a look at what really happened. What did you do? Why did you not do it?

What were you feeling? What were the results? Most importantly, what did you learn? The process will make you more powerful.

For those of us who are addicts, recovery helps us understand that a relapse happens long before we pick up a drink, a pill, a credit card, or our "drug" of choice. In other words, the day you start "using" again is not the day you relapse. The relapse happened three or four months earlier, when you changed your routine, or had a conversation with a person who triggered you, or ran into the folks you'd stopped hanging out with. You may not have gotten high, but that incident was your relapse. Without purposeful interventions, the pickup—whether drugs or alcohol, porn, gambling, shopping, sex, overworking, or another vice—is almost inevitable. Even for men who don't struggle with addiction, the screw-up tends to begin long before the mess-up.

Understanding our areas of weakness is very important. After the fight for my Level 7 CKM test was over, I reflected upon my experience. I thought about my reflex to flinch when I expected incoming blows that hadn't even been thrown. It dawned on me that that's how I've lived my life—expecting a blow and impulsively flinching even though a hit was not necessarily coming. The benefit of that behavioral pattern is that I rarely get hit. But the downside of my impulse to protect myself is huge. For instance, what if I cover up or withdraw from someone who was not going to harm me but help me? What if they had no ill intent at all? I now understand that by assuming that a person will hurt me and being excessively self-protective, I have likely missed out on opportunities to experience rewarding possibilities and relationships—and that this has been something I've been doing to myself for much of my life. Even worse, maybe I unwittingly "hit" other people preemptively before they can hit me, but what if that was never their intent?

It's been life-changing for me to have this level of self-awareness. Now that I know better, I am trying to do better. I know from my studies that John Eldredge, author of the book *Wild at Heart*, writes that a male comes into manhood only after three things exist: (1) he understands what he's been created for, (2) he has connected emotionally with something to protect and fight for, and (3) he has come to grips with what's wrong with himself and is dealing with it. This implies that self-awareness is part of the journey of manhood. I am growing in my understanding of all the things that are wrong with me. The process has been humbling and eye-opening, but also very empowering. I know it could be for you also. Robert Hicks, author of *The Masculine Journey*, examines six Hebrew words meaning "man," each of which correlates with levels of a guy's development. Hicks describes *adam* as being the creational man; *zacar* as the phallic, or sexually potent, man; *gibbor*, the warrior; *enosh*, the wounded man; *ish*, the mature man; and *zaken*, the wise man. While I don't agree with everything Eldredge and Hicks espouse, I do agree with the fundamental principle that every guy has something wrong with him. We've all got some *enosh* "stuff" that at some point we must confront. As we heal our hurts we become more *ish*—able to reconcile who we are and what we are to become. That sets the stage for us to push through to the next level.

Grappling with the difficult parts of himself allows a righteous man to take responsibility for all of himself. Because there is a gap between every man's "is-ness" and his "ought-ness"—that is, between what he is able and unable to do, between who he actually is and who he thinks he should be, between what he wishes he'd accomplished and the mistakes that he's made. There are screw-ups on his record that he wishes didn't exist. Every man has done some things he's not proud of; I count myself among them. And while we may not be able to escape the consequences of our actions, we can still experience meaning and fulfillment. We can learn and grow from them and figure out how to do better. Indeed, the scars we get as a result of our battles can be an important part of our destiny. Scars signal to other people that you've been through something significant. Did you know that people will seek you out because you've overcome the problem they are still struggling with? When you no longer hide your scars—and particularly when you reach the point that it no longer hurts to talk about them—you will be able to support other people. Think of your scars as similar to tattoos that are attached to great stories.

Part of the process of moving to the next level involves synthesizing who you are and who you're not. Hicks's *ish* man has been wounded and survived the storm and the rain. He knows that he's not "all that"; nor has he become who he thought he'd be. Yet he's comfortable with and likes who he is.

"I feel bad that my kids saw me when I was 'the drunk,'" says Rich. "But thank God my son lived long enough to see me make the change. My nineteen- and forty-year-old daughters are still here. They have seen me make this change."

A Man's World

No matter what's going on in your life, if you want to get an idea about where your life is headed, just look at who you hang out with. Who do you allow in your home or apartment? Who do you watch the game, play ball, fix the car, hunt, or meet up with for happy hour? That's who you're probably going to become.

Many guys mistakenly think that they're their own person no matter who they hang out with. We fool ourselves if we actually believe that no one we are with can influence us. Humans were created as social beings. We often fall into groupthink, a psychological phenomenon where people's desire to fit in with their friends causes them, unknowingly, to make irrational or dysfunctional decisions. You know the story: You want to exercise, but your buddies want to go watch the game, so rather than bringing them to the gym with you, you go with them and miss your workout. Or, you want to take a training program so you can go for a promotion or change your career, but your best friend at work discourages you by talking about how much it will cost or how much work it will be. Or, you want to start attending religious services but one of your friends calls you weak so you don't go. This kind of thing happens all the time. That's why it is so important to get the right people in our life. Who you walk alongside will eventually be who you stand alongside and who you eventually will sit down with at the business or dinner table. That goes for how you get in trouble as well. I talk to a lot of guys who say they want to be eagles, but they are hanging with chickens. Both are birds and neither is bad, but chickens can't fly, eagles can. Many men have friends that keep them stuck or even drag them down to engage in behaviors that are beneath them. And sadly, a lot of guys remain loyal to friends who allow them to drift through life without doing anything meaningful. Sometimes we need to let people go.

We need to replace them with men who can help us heal. Only a man can help another guy progress through manhood; a woman cannot help him with that. It's very important to hang out with men who also have dreams and aspirations. Guys who inspire your greatness rather than want you to stay the same for their comfort. Look for friends who encourage you and inspire you, as our group inspired Jerome to participate in the Tough Mudder and held him up even as he struggled in the race and following his surgery; helped Rich rebuild his life; held Leroy and Jerry up in the face of disaster; supported Vernell as he navigated toward his dreams. Every man needs at least one or two people in his life who can live in the tension of what I call his "ugliness" and his "awesomeness." What I mean by that is that none of us are perfect. We need guys in our life who can see the worst parts of us yet know that that's not all of who we are; guys who can see our warts, but don't get hung up on them. Guys who also see our gifts but don't get swept up into the hype. They see the best of you yet know, that's not all there is, and see the not-so-pretty parts yet push you into your greatness.

If you want an eagle assignment in life, find guys who are taking responsibility for their Power, Place, Purpose, and Parameters. Hang out with men who can take up their cross and sacrifice and play hurt and even help you through it. Hang out with fellas who can get a prayer through for you. To walk through righteous manhood, you have to build the right tribe. In the Bible, Jesus ministered to everyone, but he only hung out with his twelve disciples, and only three of them—Peter, John, and James—were in his inner circle. Similarly, righteous manhood involves participating in the larger world, yet having a smaller group of people who support you and a tight-knit crew who sees all of you.

Playing for the Comeback

I have always liked the quarterback Peyton Manning. When I first discovered him, I liked him because he was good yet chose to complete all four years of college, when he actually could have left the University of Tennessee and started playing pro ball before he graduated. Then, not only did he choose to play his fourth year, he set records along the way.

Another reason that I like Peyton Manning is because he transformed the position of quarterback by taking the tactic of calling an audible to a new level. I also like him because in 2003 he engineered a great comeback, leading the Indianapolis Colts from 35–14 down with five minutes left in the fourth quarter to engineer a come-from-behind win over the Tampa Bay Buccaneers. At the time it was the greatest comeback victory ever; however, later in his career, Peyton Manning broke his neck. A lot of people gave up on him and assumed that he'd never play football again. The fans said he was finished. The pundits were certain he'd retire. But it turns out that Peyton Manning was not done. He returned to the game he loved and went out on top after winning Super Bowl 50.

Peyton Manning's comeback reminds me of the journey of a righteous warrior. The righteous warrior knows that he can stumble and fall, but then get back up again and rally from being down. He knows that he can come back from failure, from mistakes, from defeat, from messing up, from hard times and bad times.

He can do this because he understands that life is not just about winning. Life is actually about managing the process. In other words, it's not merely about what you do or what you have, it's also about how you do it or obtain it. Everyone stumbles sometimes, but a man with a warrior mind-set gets up and tries again and again. He shoots for the top, but when he falls short, he keeps trying until he makes it—or gets as close as he's able to get. Even if he's messed up, he knows that he can honor God and himself by getting back on his feet. He knows that even bad outcomes that honor God are good. When he stumbles and falls, a righteous man's goal should be to end up better than he did last time. In fact, a righteous warrior emerges from struggle stronger than he was when he went into it.

After Tiger Woods fell from grace, Nike ran a commercial where the voice of Earl Woods, Tiger's deceased father, asks him, "Tiger, what did you learn?" Not only is the commercial very poignant, it asks a question every man should ask himself when he's picking himself up from a fall. A warrior conducts an autopsy of his mistakes, but he doesn't stay stuck asking "Why me?" He, too, asks the question: What can I learn from this? He wants to know: How can this experience make me better?

There is a saying that slow people don't learn from their mistakes, smart people learn from their mistakes, and wise people learn from other people's mistakes. To improve your ability to learn from both your own mistakes and those of others, it's important to examine your personal history. You may need to examine your history of behavior; your family background looking for blessings and curses that travel intergenerationally; your cultural history, for behaviors that may be common to people who share your ethnicity; and American history, to examine your place within it and what people who are like you have tended to do. You can engage in introspective practices yourself, but you may also benefit from a group of men who can help you look at your life more objectively and hold you accountable. Look for a men's group in your spiritual communities. You may also want to explore counseling, as I did and as Leroy and Felicia did. Nobody can address your deep issues and brokenness but you. A lot of guys shy away from it, thinking therapy is just a thing that women do. Indeed, among men, there's not a tradition of talking about the challenges we face or of seeking help in the way women do. The problem with this approach is if you don't address it, it will happen again—and maybe again and again and again. That's far more embarrassing or damaging than telling your business to a person who has the skills to help you get back on track. Things don't get better unless you change them, so I strongly suggest you not put your head in the sand.

Guys who think therapy is for women couldn't be more wrong—many men seek out help, though often they wait too long. I saw a lot of guys in rehab and see a bunch of them in AA meetings—after they've already made a mess of things. Now I understand that just as you would hire a mechanic as soon as your car makes a funny sound, a plumber when your pipes get clogged, or go to the doctor when you blow out your ACL, every man needs someone objective to talk to and troubleshoot with when he's not getting the results in his life that he wants. For instance, when his relationship with his father or children isn't like he dreams it could be, he has experienced traumatic circumstances or violence, he keeps thinking unwanted thoughts over and over, compulsively repeats behaviors or keeps experiencing the same situations again and again, struggling to put down a substance or stop watching porn when he's feeling overcome by life.

A man is ready to live his best life when he has conquered his wounds and his brokenness lies under his feet. When you can talk about your mistakes, and your scars don't hurt anymore, you also possess the power to use your story to help and minister to others. No longer is there a need to hide or be ashamed of your experiences. You now understand that the process helped you develop the muscles that are required for the next level of your life. You know it opened new possibilities and dimensions of your destiny. Indeed, the best healers are wounded healers. But getting there requires great faith.

No man is judged by any one particular moment in his life. He earns his reputation not because of his best or worst day, but rather because of the sum of all his days. God will give you another and another and another chance. That said, all the news isn't good news. Struggling and especially messing up isn't easy. Though you may repent and say you're sorry, and confess that you didn't mean it, and admit that you goofed, you can't guarantee that everyone will forgive you. Some people will forever remember every mistake, not let go of their hurt, and continually remind you of it. There are things that some folks will just not get over. You could get mad and tell them to be better people. But remember, you did do it. Sometimes a man just has to live with that.

However, just because you have to live with something embarrassing doesn't mean that it has to cripple you. When experts study octogenarians and centenarians—people who make it to eighty, ninety, and a hundred years of age—they struggle to explain why some people live so long. Thus far, they haven't been able to identify anything ethnically, culturally, religiously, or even dietarily that correlates to a longer life. In fact, some people in that population have smoked since they were thirteen, while others have never held a cigarette to their mouth. In fact, you may remember the Delaney sisters, two Black women who lived to be more than 105 years old. In their book *Having Our Say* they claimed that they never drank liquor, but if you read closely you can see they meant that they'd never *purchased* liquor. In fact, they made their own dandelion wine and had a sip of it every day.

But one thing about octogenarians and centenarians is different from many of the rest of us. Many have an uncanny ability to let things go. Because when you walk around always angry, holding on to things you could have moved on from, you are not hurting the person you're angry with, you are blocking your ability to get to your next level. Whether of yourself or others, holding on to old hurts actually weakens you. Forgiveness makes you stronger and sets you up for your comeback.

So don't wait until your life is perfect before you start to walk in your destiny. God can use you, even in the midst of your weakness and mistakes. And as you walk in your destiny, you become your destiny, even though the process isn't easy and may even hurt. A true martial artist isn't fearless; he just demonstrates discipline and focus to help him manage his fear.

Sometimes life feels unfair and as though the world is stacked against you. You may not know how to handle it. Or life's fight hasn't gone the way you thought it would. It certainly hasn't gone how it goes in the movies. It isn't pretty and sometimes it breaks our hearts, yet righteous warriors keep fighting when we're hurt. There's no need to be afraid, run away, throw in the towel, self-destruct, or take your life or the lives of others when you face an overwhelming challenge. You can lose people, places, things, and love, but keep going. As life moves forward, if you keep your head in the game, you will figure how to make things right. The situation will get fixed and you will be transformed. You will come through it. As my grandmother used to say, "Trouble don't last always." The suffering that you are experiencing as you grow can't compare to the wonder that will be revealed through you.

PRINCIPLE 9

Learn, Earn, and Return

*Commit to reaching a high enough level of development that
you fight for others to enjoy the same rights, privileges, and
opportunities that you want for yourself and your loved ones.*

I'D GROWN UP in a time when boys didn't wrestle girls. Times change, and
I thank God for that. But that doesn't necessarily mean that I always know
how to handle them.

I stood on the edge of the wrestling mat feeling very weird and confused. I was staring at a fifteen-year-old Black male laying on top of his female opponent. She had curled herself into a ball. He was wrapped around
her backside with his arms around her waist. The optic alone was making
me uncomfortable. Not only was I struggling with the gender issue, American history is rife with incidents where women have accused innocent Black
males of whistling at, looking at, touching them, and more, with disastrous
outcomes for the guy. And this doesn't even include people calling the police
on Black men for nothing. But this couldn't become that. Or could it?

In addition to my pastoral responsibilities, I share my life experience
and love and knowledge of wrestling by volunteering as the assistant coach
at the neighborhood high school. I was coaching this young man. I knew
that if he wanted leverage, he needed to reach across his opponent's chest.
He had been raised, however, not to touch a young woman's breasts. Was
the wrestling mat a different context? I wasn't sure. What should I tell
him? I didn't know. This situation was outside of both my values and my
experience.

I felt bad for the kid. Because even though this was just a wrestling match, for this young man it represented much, much more. First, wrestling occurs concurrent with basketball season; Philly is a basketball town. Any young man who chooses to wrestle instead of play round ball is cutting against the grain. Wrestling also tends to be a predominately White sport. So any Black male who participates has also chosen, knowingly or not, to place himself in the swirl of dynamics that can cause both racial stress and an uphill battle to be seen for who he is, rather than in terms of the limiting and negative stereotypes that our society applies to Black males—think: dangerous, rapper, baller, not intellectual. If that weren't enough pressure, this young man was up against gender, too. Even if he won the match on points, there was a good chance he would not be awarded the victory unless he pinned his opponent. Either consciously or unconsciously, the ref was likely to award the match to the young woman whether or not she had actually won; not only because she was White, but because she, too, was behaving way counter to societal norms. Indeed, had she stuck to gender traditions, she wouldn't have been on the mat.

I reflected upon what I should tell him. One of the reasons I'd decided to coach the team was because the school's wrestling coach was a White man who was coaching Black kids. There were certain things that needed to be said to the boys because they were Black, but a White man cannot say them to a young Black man—at least not with the same level of credibility. Some things can only be said Black man to Black man. For example, my own high school coach, Mr. McIntyre, a Black man, always taught his Black wrestlers to pin their opponent. "Don't make it close," he told us. Pinning our opponent could help us rise above the referee's subjectivity as well as any racism he may intentionally or unintentionally demonstrate. "A pin is a pin; you can't argue that," Mr. McIntyre would say. I also know from personal experience that, in a society that values mediocrity, being excellent can often provide a Black male with a bit of insulation against racism and bigotry. If nothing else, when you're excellent, you can call racism out and catch people in the act.

Back on the mat, the young people stayed curled in a ball for too long, so the ref made them break and get back up on their feet. I could tell that my guy didn't know what to do. Neither did I.

"Why are you taking this long with this girl?!" I hollered. Not particularly helpful, but the best that I could come up with.

I knew there was a high crotch move that would take her down. But that would require him to touch the young woman's privates. And if he touched her genitals in any other aspect of life, it could get him in a lot of trouble. My guy knew it, too. I could almost see the gears turning in his head; he was frozen. He tried to do a double leg takedown instead, but she reversed it and threw him on his back onto the mat. This wasn't good. How could he touch her without being offensive?

"Come on, man!" I hollered. "You're gonna mess around and get beat."

I knew that nothing good would come from the situation. If he won, it was because he was supposed to win—in fact, he should have won faster. But God forbid that he got beat. Because that wouldn't just be a regular loss; he'd hear about it on the bench, he'd hear about it in the locker room, he'd hear about it in the halls at school, he'd hear it at the barbershop, he'd hear it in the neighborhood. In fact, the whole league would know he was the guy who had lost to a girl. He'd still be getting clowned at his twentieth high school reunion.

I watched as the young woman went for my guy's legs and took him down out of bounds. So much for my good intentions. I was stumped.

The Season Is the Reason

There is a time and season for everything. There's a period in every man's life when he should focus on educating and training himself so that he will one day be able to live as an independent adult. There's a time when he stands on his own two feet, looks for his life partner, and prepares to create a family. There's the stretch when he's wrapped up in earning a living and providing for his children and loved ones. Some men also share their gifts and talents with others along the way, doing things like coaching the soccer team or teaching Bible study.

Certainly, by the time a man is well into his forties or is nearing his fifties and beyond, he has developed enough wisdom that giving back to others becomes a prime responsibility of his life. He can easily do this by identifying younger people who he is drawn to or have similar interests and abilities, and then pouring everything he knows into them. By sharing his knowledge, he ought to be able to walk them up to and push open the doors of opportunity for them, easing the way for younger people to walk through and follow along a path that may be similar but not the same as his, as they access their own destiny.

In other words, once a righteous warrior achieves a certain level of development—once he reaches a mature season in his life—he stops living just for himself and his small circle of loved ones and starts living with humanity in mind. Indeed, whether he slows down long enough to think about it or not, every man is part of something greater than himself and his nuclear family. For instance, if we pull up to ten thousand feet, as I do when I fly, we can see that all of us are members of our gender, racial, ethnic, religious, national, and socioeconomic groups. But then, the higher up you fly, the more you begin to see that we're all very similar. Increasingly, I engage in extreme adventures or work in my ministry that takes place internationally. When I'm on an airplane at forty thousand feet, geographical boundaries blend away and I can even see the curve of the earth. Whether I'm in Italy, Israel, Palestine, India, Kenya, or South Africa, once I'm on the ground, it is clear that people all over the world care about very similar things. We are all members of the family of humankind. So I'd like to suggest to you that rather than merely focusing upon taking care of himself and his family, the well-developed man shares his wisdom, gifts, and talents with that larger social context. This requires a righteous warrior to be reflective.

Indeed, whether CKM, Naphtali, or the U.S. military, the highest level of any warrior art challenges the fighter to use what he knows to liberate someone else. This principle also exists in many spiritual traditions, including Christianity, where, as we have discussed, Jesus Christ "took one for the team" by dying at Calvary. The righteous warrior frees other people by embracing his destiny full out—no matter how imperfect his is, what mistakes he has made in the past, his age, the size of his wallet, or even the state of his health. Similar to the world-class athletes he admires, he goes for it no matter the score, the quarter, who his teammates are, or how well they are playing. He's willing to win ugly. And as he leaves everything he has on the field of life, he inspires the men, women, and children around him, who witness his commitment, to become better themselves.

Unfortunately, even though lots of guys long to experience their greatness, only a handful of guys challenge themselves to develop to this level. Lots of lanes of opportunity are wide open and unoccupied because so few men accept the call. Indeed, there's a huge opportunity for men to up their game, lay their lives on the line, and becomes heroes in their own right. This is exciting! Because, let's be honest, what man doesn't fantasize about making the buzzer-beating shot, the game-winning catch, or the winning goal as the clock winds down? What guy hasn't wished he was LeBron James, or Roger Federer, or Mariano Rivera, or David Beckham, or Manny Pacquiao, or Mike Trout? What man doesn't want to be idolized by his woman, children, and community? I'm here to tell you that any man can accomplish that by how he chooses to live his own life. It's not like we live in a world that's short on challenges that could benefit from a guy's gifts and leadership—that could benefit from your gifts and leadership. So what better time than now to roll up your sleeves and begin to think of how you can serve others?

If you haven't been giving back already, at some point during middle age I suggest that you begin to package and share your stories with younger family members and other men and women in your community who might benefit from them. Because by the time you move into the third quarter—in other words, by the time you hit forty—you have overcome some challenges and difficulties and survived some wars and lived to tell about them. You have something to offer to other males and to humanity—whether that involves battling through cancer, a nasty divorce, the death of a child, or just the times you wish you'd been a better parent. Certainly, by the time you reach your fifties, start to talk about the challenges you've overcome, not keeping secrets or holding back about your most difficult ones.

Telling your story is extremely important because there are people right now who are wrestling with the very challenges you have struggled to overcome. They don't yet know what it takes to win those fights. On the other hand, you've scaled the wall; you've climbed over the mountaintop; you've developed a toolkit that could help another person conquer it. You have something to offer someone else—even what you learned from your mistakes can help someone. So why not give another boy or man or another human being the information they need so they don't have to bleed where you bled, suffer where you suffered, lose a part of themselves where a part of you died?

For instance, in our band of brothers, although he could have chosen to focus on preaching, Leroy decided, instead, to create meaning out of the pain he and Felicia experienced when they lost Faith. Among the ways he does this is as a chaplain at a local children's hospital, where he works with families during some of their most difficult times.

"When I work with men whose children are very ill or dying or who have otherwise experienced loss, I always ask, 'Has your wife (or daughter) ever seen you cry?' And often I hear, 'No. I cry alone in my room when she doesn't know what I'm doing. She just thinks I'm okay and I don't cry.' Now, knowing that that's what Felicia once thought about me, I tell them,

'You gotta let her see you struggle.' These are lessons I've learned from my own pain and that I can share to help men to be vulnerable, be transparent. I help them understand that sometimes your folks need to see that." Together, he and Felicia also lead a ministry for people who have lost children early in the child's life.

After being addicted to cocaine, methamphetamine, heroin, and alcohol at some point over the course of thirty-five years and joining our church high on cocaine and drunk, Rich is now clean and sober.

"I'm just straight and on the narrow and it's just been fabulous," he says. "The best times in my life have been these last four to five years. I'm comfortable where I'm at. My ride's been a good ride. You never know when God's gonna touch you or bless you. Now I think that my grandmother's and mother's prayers that I would be okay have been answered. I pray that they can see where I'm at and where I stand now."

Today he openly shares his testimony to encourage others who are struggling with addiction and grief.

In other words, whether on the wrestling mat or in other areas of life, over the course of his lifetime, a righteous man learns; he earns and then he returns to others some of what he's learned and earned, so that they can thrive in their own lifetime. Among the most important understandings of mature life is growing to grasp the significance of seasons and seasonal change. So, if you are middle age or older, ask yourself: What young man's (or young woman's) feet are beneath my table, so to speak? You can also ask yourself this question if you are still a young man and have learned something you can share with your peers or kids who are younger or less experienced in an particular area than you, or even your elders.

Love Is the Bridge

There is a famous African proverb that states: "When I was a child I thought my village was the world, but when I became a man I learned that the world is my village." This saying encapsulates in just one sentence the mind-set of a well-developed warrior who is also seasoned in what life demonstrates.

A righteous warrior not only cares for his own nuclear family and raises his own children, he also helps out with other people's children, spends time with his elders, and contributes to his larger community, his country, and even the world. This runs contrary to popular culture, which tries to convince us to look out for ourselves; that everyone else is our competition. But if I were a betting man, I'd wager that you've already practiced this principle within the context of your family. When you were a child, it's quite likely that some of your caregivers gave you chores. Those chores weren't just for you; they helped the entire family. You probably didn't clear just your own knife, fork, and plate from the table but also cleared the serving dishes. You probably helped put all the dishes into the sink or dishwasher. When you needed clean jeans or sweats, you didn't just wash your own, you washed the dark clothes for the whole house. As an adult, you don't earn money just for yourself but for your entire household.

In similar fashion, a well-developed man takes care of more than just himself but conducts himself as a vital member of the larger human family. When he's at his best, he looks beyond his own needs, trusting that as he extends himself his needs will be covered, in order to see how he can help others. Recall that one very important part of a righteous warrior's Purpose is to create an atmosphere in which everyone else's Purpose can be achieved. He helps others develop and share their gifts so they can walk in and fulfill their own destiny. Indeed, one way he reaches his own next level is to help someone else get to their next level.

Don't just take it from me; this concept is universal. Indeed, every major world religion as well as most spiritual traditions professes some version of what's called the Golden Rule. In Christianity, the Golden Rule states: "Do unto others as you would have them do unto you." When I put on my theologian's hat, I notice that this passage of scripture contains both an active verb tense and an active sentence construction. In other words, Christians are called to do more than live passively trying not to hurt other people. We are to follow the example that Jesus set—to go out into the world actively looking to help other people. Indeed, our goal should not merely be to make sure we don't hurt others but to proactively set out to find somebody to help. I also know that a Christian who is mature in their belief looks for somebody to assist even at their own expense or inconvenience. Moreover, they serve them without being celebrated.

But Christianity isn't the only religion to embrace this outlook. Other major religions convey their equivalent of the Golden Rule. Many use a more passive sentence construction, essentially: "Don't do what you don't want done to you." And that interpretation makes sense also—if I don't want a thing done to me, I shouldn't do it to others. Both sets of interpretations can help us create a better world. However, in highlighting the distinction in phrasing, I want to draw your attention to what I believe is a warrior's choice. The Golden Rule is conveyed so actively in Christianity because— whether we're talking about *eros, storge, phileo,* or *agape* love—love is an empty word until it's put into action. The righteous warrior puts love into action. He leans into it and he stands on it. By way of an analogy, if I point you to a footbridge over a deep gorge in the wilderness and tell you that it is strong enough to hold your weight, but never walk across it myself, what I've told you isn't going to mean very much to you. But when I put my own weight on it and walk across that bridge first, my claim has meaning. Similarly, a man's faith doesn't mean much if it can't support his weight.

Love is the bridge; I invite you to cross it.

As best as we know, human beings are nature's crowning achievement. We have the power to do amazing things—from creating the pyramids, to climbing Mount Everest, to sending the Hubble telescope into outer space. We can also do great harm, such as destroying the climate and dropping the atom bomb. Many of us say that we love other people, but a righteous warrior not only says he loves people, he also does things to help them. In fact, helping others lies along every man's spiritual pathway to becoming significant and it's a requirement for being heroic. Men who achieve significance live for others rather than just for themselves and their immediate circle of loved ones. Whether on the basketball court or as a humanitarian, part of how they develop the "A game" that others admire is by sharing themselves so generously. Their openheartedness and unselfishness not only capture other's attention, they also create access to larger platforms and higher levels. So, while they never set out to be famous, they often become well known in their community or beyond.

The righteous warrior values significance over success. Remember, success is about material things—such as how much money you have, what kind of car you drive, and where you live. But life is about more than money and possessions. Indeed, significance has nothing to do with possessions. At a man's funeral, people won't talk about how much money he had; they'll talk about what he did with his life. You'd be surprised how many older and dying men are pained not by money but by relationships they didn't attend to, the time they didn't spend, the attention they didn't give, the heart they didn't show sufficiently. A man becomes significant when he does things for others, when he makes the world a better place in ways large and small, everywhere he goes. By showing your heart and demonstrating love and making a difference in the lives of the people you touch, you can move from being a good guy to a great guy.

What might being significant look like in the real world? First, make sure you're being the best man you can be with the people you are responsible for and who are closest to you. A righteous man's power begins at home and moves outward in concentric circles. So solidify your home front by being the best partner and father you can be, honoring your parents and doing things like checking in on your elders. Begin sharing first in your inner circle. As you demonstrate your Power, occupy your Place, and demonstrate your Purpose and Parameters with your Partner and in your household, you will get clearer about your story and strengthen yourself in ways that allow you to expand your influence into your community. After you've solidified your base, pay attention to the things in society or the world that you repeatedly notice, or that disturb or call out to you. Pay particular attention to things that trouble your spirit but that don't seem to bother others. The reason these specific issues attract your attention or disturb you is that a part of you notices the fact that your gifts are missing from that situation. If you have a gift, it bothers you when you see areas in which it's deficient; if you don't have a gift, you may not even notice its absence. The hole where your gift fits cries out to you. You are the missing puzzle piece. Your destiny is to share in ways that help to fill it.

Though he's in his mid-forties now, Vernell still remembers what it meant to have the love, discipline, and guidance of the grandfather who helped his mom raise him, as well as his other grandparents, uncles, and extended family members who sowed into his life. He also recalls what it was like to be "a scrawny dude who used to get picked on, who turned into a skinny dud with a lot of mouth" but who felt scared and vulnerable. Today he leads several training programs for young people, many of whom don't have the same kind of support that he did as a child.

"I run a boot camp program for wayward kids, fourteen to seventeen," Vernell says. "They may have issues around truancy, they may be on probation, so they come to this program. I don't try to be a disciplinarian but just try to be a structured male, because they're used to doing and saying whatever they want. So I meet them where they're at. You wanna cuss? I'll cuss back at you. You don't wanna do what you're supposed to do, then I'm gonna ignore you until you learn how to do it." In this way he helps to teach discipline, respect, self-care, and crucial manhood skills.

At our church Vernell also teaches self-defense skills to children.

"The idea is if some adult pulled up in a car and tried to kidnap you, or if you were inside a store and somebody grabbed you, what would you do to get out of the situation?" he asks. "We do a simulated training where I put on headgear, a mouthpiece, overalls, and protective pads, and I'm the one the kids have to fight to get away," Vernell says.

You, too, can extend yourself; volunteer to take on a difficult issue in your family, community, city, our nation, or even the world, just as Vernell does. In our band of brothers, he's not the only one.

"I can say with all sincerity that the Lord took Devon from us but gave us Malika," says Jerry, who with his wife, Francina, adopted the elementary-school-aged child of a relative who was struggling with substance abuse, even as their broken hearts were still mending. "We just came and kind of scooped her up. We saved a life! So now everywhere we go she's there. My Saturday mornings are spent at ballet class."

These are not things that either of these guys have to do; they choose them because they are right and lift all the parties involved to the next level, including themselves.

So reach out to other people or organizations that are taking on challenges that interest you. Volunteer to come alongside them and roll up your sleeves and get your hands dirty, so to speak. And not only help people but consider doing the work yourself and letting someone else who was also involved and worked hard get the credit. This is the opposite of what is prized in popular culture, where everyone wants to be the celebrity or the star. You can also do something as simple as listening to somebody else's dreams. Help them think about their life, support them as they identify their goals, then cheer them on, steer them around roadblocks, and celebrate their success. Remind them that they are capable and worthy. Also let them know that you're there to pick them up when they fall. A fall is only a failure if you don't dust yourself off and get back up.

Though many of us imagine courage as involving heroic acts— administering CPR to a man who has had a heart attack, pulling people out of a car accident, or plucking a child from a fire—in actuality, demonstrating courage can be as simple as extending yourself beyond where you are now without being certain of what the outcome will be. Think about things like offering to read in the neighborhood elementary school, teaching the kids in your neighborhood how to play chess, inviting a struggling relative to live with you. Unfortunately, many guys limit themselves because we will only scratch another person's back if they also scratch ours. We wonder, "If I do this for them, what will they do for me?" While these may be the ways of the world, on a spiritual level this is not how life works. Viewed spiritually, the person you're able to help might not be in a position to reciprocate. That's why they need you. That's where your maturity comes in. When the mature man gives, what he needs is not for the person to give back to him, but for God to have his back. By this season of life, he has enough experience to understand that God works in ways that no man can comprehend. Indeed, no matter your spiritual belief system or religion, the way the principle universally works, when you give to others God gives to you. And the more you do for others the more God does for you.

And here's the piece that many people just don't understand: You never know where that blessing will come from. If you're expecting the person you help to reciprocate, that may in fact happen, but you'll miss something greater. If you're looking for lightning bolts or listening for choirs of angels, you will probably miss it as well. God works through humanity in general, so keep your heart and mind open and your eyes peeled. Your blessings could come in the form of someone being as generous to you as you were for another person and in the exact same way that you were for that person. But don't limit God. Your blessing could also come in the form of money, favors, opportunities, services, networks, resources, educational opportunities, mentoring, miracles, and more. This type of spiritual favor, as we call it, knows no limits, surpasses human ways of understanding, and often occurs when you least expect it. And while

God may not show up right when you want, your blessing will always arrive right on time. You can't beat God's giving no matter how hard you try. Plus, if everybody pays it forward even just a little bit, things will handle themselves.

But maybe I'm getting a little bit ahead of myself. Because in order to make a difference, you have to believe in who you are and that you have something really special to offer. Maybe you're not quite there yet—or perhaps you worry that you will be perceived as arrogant. Perhaps the question "Who do you think you are?" reverberates in your head. Either way, how do you find the sweet spot? You ought not think too highly of yourself, but you ought not to think poorly of yourself, either. In other words, live with humility. Being humble doesn't mean you have low self-esteem, it means you have an accurate understanding of both who you are and who you're not. You don't have a big ego. You have a balanced understanding and appreciation of yourself.

When a righteous warrior looks in the mirror, he sees somebody worthy, deserving, and capable. He knows that he is so special that no one in history who has ever existed is like him and no one ever will be. But even though he is unique and beloved, the same thing is true about every other human being, so he shows up where he is needed and he meets people at their level of need. He doesn't care whether the person is of the same educational or socioeconomic background; he doesn't care if they share his religion; he doesn't care whether the person is of the same race or ethnicity. As he shares and serves, he doesn't question people's political party. He doesn't question their creed, color, sexual orientation, or nationality. He doesn't worry about whether they say thank you or reciprocate. The righteous warrior knows that God will cover him. He helps other people because they are human beings. Each time he shares his gifts and extends himself into the world in order to help someone else, he comes face-to-face with his own destiny.

Men Need Men

But if we are to maximize our impact upon others, many of us have to take a step back in order to heal our broken places.

No matter what has happened in your life, you can be made whole again; however, you have to choose it. I don't believe that any man ought to live forever as a wounded human being. To fulfill your destiny, it's important to embrace your *ish* identity; the mature man essentially says "Yes, I've been wounded; yes, I've been through the storm and the rain. No, I'm not who I thought I would be, but I am comfortable with who I am." The *ish* man has reconciled who he was with who he has become. He accepts this situation and is determined to share everything he has to offer.

But a warrior doesn't stop at his *ish* stage. If he's blessed to live long enough, he grows from *ish* to *zaqan,* the older established man. The *zaqan* man has more sense than strength, so he looks to connect with the young and virile *zacar* who has more strength than sense. The "old head" then tells the "young buck" about how life has been for him. This relationship helps the young man reach his next level and allows the old man to share the best of himself. And by this point, *zaqan* man should be comfortable enough with himself to create a safe space where a less experienced man can share what's going on in his world and he can share back.

"Master Robinson was like my Mister Miyagi, and he helped to rebuild some things," Vernell says of the years when Master Robinson helped him develop as a martial artist and Vernell helped Master Robinson become more physically fit. You may remember Mister Miyagi as the karate master in the *Karate Kid* series of movies. "He's been a friend to me. He's a man of a different age group who reminds me of some of the men in my family. And he's a man of his word, which I'd been seeking."

Then, as life would have it, the seasons changed; Master Robinson became ill. Not only did he recover more quickly because of the strength training he had done with Vernell, but Vernell was by his side to help him recover.

Every man needs a place to talk about his areas of weakness, fear, uncertainty, bad feelings, and lack of knowledge. Indeed, the spiritual teaching "man was not meant to live alone" is not merely about marriage—men also need other men. For there is something about one man affirming another man that a woman's praise cannot satisfy. We need safe places to have relationships with each other. The members of our band of brothers have found both peace and power in that.

Having said that, I also want to acknowledge that it's often not comfortable for men to develop friendships within our society's limiting definition of manhood. Sadly, many of us have been taught the false narrative that as long as we have the comfort of a woman we can go through our life without any male friends. And while there's nothing wrong with talking to women, a woman cannot feed the soul of a man when what he really needs is another man's support. All too often our narrow masculine socialization, which includes homophobia, gets in the way of men's ability to develop sincere friendships. The loneliness and isolation that develop when men become disconnected from meaningful friendships with each other often lead to tragic results. Far too many of us try to earn more money, buy material things, chase women, abuse drugs and alcohol, or engage in other unproductive or destructive activities in order to fill the hole where our relationships with other men ought to be. Our band of brothers filled these holes for each other.

I hope I don't offend anyone by saying this, but connections with other males are particularly important for young men who have been raised primarily by women. Because not only does every male require the role modeling and boundary setting that only a father or father figure can provide, but in my experience it seems to take an accumulation of female voices saying "you're the man" in order for him to believe what one man can accomplish through his mere attention and presence and in fewer words. I can't tell you how many guys I've seen attempt to collect enough affirmative female voices in order to feel confident. There are never enough, though, because women's voices never become baritone in the literal and metaphorical sense. There are times when males of all ages need a man to tell them that they're good and to help them work through problems so they know everything is going to be all right.

The Corner Man

There is a story I tell sometimes when I preach about an Amish man who was driving a horse and cart full of pigs into town to the market. As he was driving, a car drove by and ran him into a ditch. When the sheriff arrived on the scene, he noticed that the horse had a broken leg, so the sheriff pulled out his gun and put him out of his misery. *Boom!* Then the sheriff saw that the cart had fallen on a few of the pigs. He noticed that one pig had a broken leg and another pig had a broken neck, so he shot the two pigs. *Boom! Boom!* Then he walked over to the driver, looked at the driver, he said, "Sir, how are you?" The driver looked up at him and said, "I'm fine—everything is fine!"

In order for a man not to quit, he needs some men in his corner. But if I'm going to be honest, men tend to shoot the wounded. We tend to view a man as weak, or a punk, or by a number of politically incorrect epithets if he admits that he's down. Too often we tell guys to "man up," when what we really need is to sit down alongside him. Men need to learn how to support and encourage each other so we can make it to the other side. We need someone who we can tell "No, I'm not fine, I just need somebody to talk to" or "I need somebody who will pray for me" or "I need somebody who will help me." We need someone who will tell us "I will walk alongside you" or "Here, take what I've got," knowing that God will bless us. When the righteous warrior sees another person in a weakened state or overtaken with a fault, he doesn't leave him there alone—and he darn sure shouldn't shoot him with gossip, self-righteousness, or judgment. The man with a warrior mind-set understands that his destiny is linked to the well-being of his fellow human being, whether that person is in his biological family, his geographic community, or elsewhere on the planet. He doesn't laugh at, disparage, or feel superior to any man who has fallen. He believes that another man's struggle is his struggle as well. To him, it really doesn't matter who falls because the failure of one is the failure of all.

One way you can begin to tend to your wounds involves deepening your spiritual life, ideally by attending a church, synagogue, or mosque or participating in a spiritual community. Many men don't develop their spiritual life because they fear the judgment they will receive from others. Spirituality seems feminine to many men, largely because in Christianity in North America, houses of worship tend to consist of disproportionate numbers of women. Between guys' traditional masculine socialization and the demographic reality of many spiritual communities, lots of men don't see a place for themselves. I get it. Complicating matters, the demographics being what they are, many ministers design their message to speak to a feminine audience. In the meantime, men can tell that the minister is speaking to women and excluding them. We ministers have to do a better job of crafting messages that resonate with both men and women and push harder to get men to participate in spiritual activities.

Another place that guys often get stuck is feeling that they aren't good enough or that they will be judged. If you have this feeling, trust me, you're right. Someone will judge you, just like they judge me. But so what? There is no behavior present in the world that does not also take place in a spiritual community. That is as it should be. A church is like a hospital; it's where you come to heal. Related to this, lots of guys don't want to come because they've messed up in some significant way—they've been an imperfect father, fooled around on their wife, feel guilty about their relationship with their own dad, got locked up, have been through a divorce, lost their license, were molested as a child, hit their child's mom, and so on. Then someone wrongly tells them that the guys in the front of the church are not those things and that they can never live up to who the men up front are. Wrong! The truth of the matter is most of us in leadership have some sort of junk that we have been working through. We are merely stepping further into our destiny by trying to lead and give back to others.

Spiritual leaders also need men to push us to create contexts where men can just hang out and chill. One time, at Enon, we set up a large-screen TV in our gym so the men at the church could watch a football game where my home team, the Cleveland Browns, played the Philadelphia Eagles. I put my chair on one side of the room and two hundred chairs on the other side. Sadly, the Browns lost, which Eagles fans never let me live down. Honestly, creating an environment where men feel comfortable takes a lot of work. Even with all the men's emphasis we do, my own church is still almost seventy percent women. This isn't women's fault. As part of our spiritual growth process, we men have to make up our mind to push our way through our discomfort and roll up our sleeves to create the contexts and communities we need.

Forgive Your Father

Many men also need to do the emotional-warrior work necessary to reconcile their feelings toward their father.

Whether at home or in the workplace, the best model of leadership and teamwork follows that of a healthy family. In theory, of course, our families of origin should be like a practice facility where we learn how to treat people out in the world. According to this ideal, every older man in my life should receive the benefit of the (presumably) healthy relationship that I had with my father. Every older woman should receive the benefit of my relationship with my mother. We should treat our male and female peers as though they were our blood brothers and sisters. So ideally, we practice in our family of origin and then perform what we've learned on the stage of life.

But many (and perhaps most) people's family life isn't ideal, including my own. So our healing work is necessary. If we find ourselves struggling to relate to others in a healthy manner—if we have problems with authority figures, or are angry at women, or find ourselves asking forgiveness for repeated offenses—it's probably because we have to go back to examine and fix the thing that went wrong in our family. Doing this will free us to access more of our destiny. In my family, my older brothers got the dad and I got the father. Subconsciously I wondered if I was good enough for him and sometimes I've driven myself in unhealthy ways because this tape was running quietly in the back of my head. I've had to go back and forgive my dad, especially as my own ministry has grown beyond my wildest imaginings, at which point I began to experience the same types of conflicts between my own wife and daughters and my work that my dad certainly did with my mom and us kids.

In addition to other folks you may want to settle your differences with, it's essential to reconcile your relationship with your pops so that you can be whole and the best father or leader possible. Your relationship with your dad informs who you are. Whether your father was present in your life or not, you may need to forgive him. Carrying anger or resentment toward your dad increases the odds that you will repeat his behavior. Forgiving him is important because having a healthy relationship with the previous generation helps unlock the possibilities in your generation—not to mention your children's generation and the generations that follow them. When you forgive your pop (or any person), you let somebody out of prison. Most people think forgiveness frees the offending party, but the person you actually let out of prison is yourself.

We've certainly experienced this in our band of brothers.

"There was a period where our group was reading *Wild at Heart* together and reached a section about forgiveness," says Vernell. "I'm like, forgive my father? I have nothing to forgive my father for. My father died; that wasn't his fault. He didn't wake up one morning and say, 'I've got a three-year-old child, I've got a wife I just got married to, I've got bills, I've got responsibilities, but you know what, God, I'm ready; come on take me today.' "

But as he reflected, Vernell began to remember pivotal points when his father wasn't there.

"I blew through the forgiveness chapter the first time, but another chapter told me to read it again. As I did I was like: 'Dang, he wasn't there to see me fight. He wasn't there to see me be on the team. He wasn't there to see me go to my prom. Wow!' I was reading on the subway and remembering some of the things that I wanted to be a part of with my boy's life and my dad's life and I'm like, 'Dad, I forgive you.' All of a sudden I started crying. It's seven, eight o'clock in the morning and I'm on the train on my way to work, yet I'm sitting there crying. I'm like, 'Wow! This is crazy!' "

One of the most powerful experiences I've ever had as a pastor took place at a church function, a men's retreat. I taught about fathers and forgiveness, then asked all of the men ages sixty-five and older to come to the front of the room. I knew there were many young and middle-aged men in attendance who needed to tell their fathers that they loved and forgave them. I also knew there were many men in the room who needed to hear that same message from their own sons. So, for the purposes of this exercise, I invited them to be each other's pretend family. One group of men asked for apologies and the other offered the forgiveness or hug that was needed. You should have seen all the guys crying and weeping and melting into the arms of men they didn't even know. They didn't actually need their fathers; they could gain some relief from a substitute dad. After we finished, many of the guys realized, "I've got to forgive my pop. I've got to get this sadness and anger out of me." They began to realize how many unexpressed emotions they had and that those emotions were undermining their possibilities. We can do our forgiveness work with each other.

Men have to forgive so we can move forward. It's one of the most difficult things we need to do. One of the hardest parts is naming the thing you're forgiving your parent for. You have to say: "I'm mad that you did X, Y, and Z, and here's how it affected me." "I'm hurt that you worked all the time" or "It broke my heart that you didn't come to my football games" or "I'm upset that you put your other children over me." Or "I forgive you for doing X, Y, and Z. Here's how it affected me, but I no longer want to carry that with me." In other words, "I've been mad at you for working all the time. But I forgive you. I realize now that you were just trying to provide for our family in the best way you knew how, but it left me feeling as though I didn't matter to you. I've been hurt for a very long time, but I no longer want to carry that with me." Real forgiveness cannot take place unless you name both the mistake and its impact.

And if you're the father being approached by a son who says you've hurt him, take a deep breath and listen to him. Don't be defensive and deny what he's saying. He's talking about the impact of your behavior upon him. That's different from your intention. So when you respond, don't just stop at "I'm sorry" and allow your son to say "Okay." Find the courage to say why you're sorry, what you would do differently now, and how it feels to know how hurt he is. Either in that moment or after you've had a chance to reflect and gather your words, say, "I'm sorry that my choice to work such long hours made you feel as though I'd abandoned you. At the time I was doing my best to provide for the family in the only way I knew how. But today, I understand that a child needs more of his father's attention. I didn't understand that then in the way I do now, because my own father worked all the time. If I had to do it all over, I would have cut back in other areas, or taken you with me, or taken what little time I had to make sure you understood how much you meant to me, even if it was just fifteen minutes of alone time when I tucked you in at night. I didn't do that then, but if you'll allow me, I'd like to try to be a better dad now." That's the kind of thing you need to say. Not trying to squirm out from under his anger and hurt, but taking responsibility and committing to change. Also, don't just let him say "No problem." Ask him to say more than that. You need him to tell you in detail how the behavior or incident impacted him. It will be uncomfortable, but a warrior sits there and listens. Real forgiveness cannot take place unless you name the mistake and name the impact.

The truth of the matter is, lots of guys are mad at their dads. But anger is a secondary emotion. There's another emotion beneath your anger: fear. Once you clear out the anger, it's time to speak to the fear. As you progress through the healing process, it's important to develop the ability to say, "It hurt me when you did A, B, and C. I was afraid that X, Y, and Z." For example, "It hurt me when you promised you'd come pick me up and spend time with me but would cancel or wouldn't show up. I was afraid that I wasn't good enough for you and that you didn't love me and that your other children were more important to you than I was." Or "I was afraid that if I didn't work late that I would be fired and our family would be worse off"—that kind of thing. But be honest.

If you can develop the ability to communicate like this, you will experience a completely different level of healing than if you just speak in generalities like "It made me mad" or "It turned me off" or "It made me feel some kind of way." We tend to use these types of phrases when we want to protect ourselves. But while they may protect us they also put a cap on our healing—and consequently our growth. When you can become vulnerable enough to admit that you hurt and that the hurt has led to anger and callousness, that creates a space where the other party can say in a nondefensive way, "I understand that and I'm truly sorry." When this occurs, real healing and forgiveness and even reconciliation can begin. Once this occurs a weight will come off of you and you will be free to travel even further into your destiny. Churches, synagogues, mosques, and other spiritual communities need to create safe spaces for that conversation to open up. Men can also decide to engage in this work among themselves. As a man does his emotional healing work, he opens up the opportunity to truly trust other men.

Get Your Life

Men who have gone back to engage in their healing work develop the ability to experience opportunities that can be accessed only by those who trust other men and women enough to team up with them.

When two or more people come together in a partnership or team, not only can you accomplish great things that you would be unable to accomplish alone, you can achieve a level of significance that inspires other men and women, including your own children, to be their best. Righteous warriors are responsible for creating an atmosphere where everyone's Purpose can be achieved; however, no man can accomplish this by himself. Every human being is like a puzzle piece that interlocks with another. Your gifts and calling and destiny are connected with the destiny of others, as our band of brothers has discovered as we've come together.

But we will only be able to get a glimpse of what is possible for us as we deepen our ability to work collectively. Right now, too many men talk about problems but don't do anything meaningful to solve them. In fact, we have become a society of commentators, talking heads, and Monday-morning quarterbacks who critique everything but don't have the courage to stick out our necks or roll up our sleeves to fix anything of substance. We watch the highlights and instant replays but never step off the sidelines and into the game. Far too few of us go after the life we want and were created for, then we wonder why we find ourselves feeling unfulfilled.

"I've found a purpose for the pain," says Leroy. "Ministering in these places and in these areas of brokenness is where I feel called. Most guys, when something happens, run from it. Now I can see the pain and I run toward it. We've become a group of guys who run toward it on a number of different fronts. And that's a big piece of who we are as a team."

As you mature spiritually and emotionally, you will have to decide for yourself what you are going to get involved with and where you will roll up your sleeves. I urge you to commit to making a difference in your immediate community, whether by mowing the infield, volunteering to read at the elementary school, becoming a mentor or Big Brother, serving at your place of worship, or teaching business or chess at your local Y. Also consider getting involved in a way that helps to fix one of society's many broken systems—political, public education, health care, criminal justice, or economic, for instance. Also look for ways that your work can be both local and global, or "glocal." In other words, as you help in your own community also consider the implications for people on the other side of town, in your region, in your state, in your nation, and even in other parts of the world. If your child is well fed, don't other children deserve to be well fed? If your wife and daughter are safe, don't all women and girls deserve to be safe? If your son is going to college, doesn't another young man deserve that as well? The work we do in the United States we must also do abroad; the work we do abroad we should also do here. We must do good for all of humanity.

Ultimately, the righteous warrior wants the world to be fair to everybody. This should be particularly true of Christians, for the Bible consists of sixty-six books that were written while people were living under oppression. Indeed, the Greco-Roman period when Jesus lived was one of the most oppressive periods in human history, resulting in many problems similar to those we are struggling with today: corruption, wealth gaps, hunger, homelessness, sickness, oppression, and so on. Jesus was a political figure who stood up against injustice. The fact that he upset the existing order of things was what resulted in his death, as he took one for the team. Earlier, I wrote about how Jesus ran the money changers out of the Temple. But the fact that he did this wasn't because they were selling things in a place of worship, he ran them off because they were being unjust toward vulnerable people. Every day, Jesus worked to fix broken systems—

whether social, financial, religious, or political. As the righteous warrior grows and develops, he ought to do the same.

Indeed, I believe that if more men stepped up, we could make meaningful inroads toward solving stubborn problems like hunger, poverty, homelessness, joblessness, fatherlessness, sex trafficking, immigration, the refugee crisis, and many of the ills that plague society today. Men can play a powerful role in conversations about how to make our society better, and actually take it upon themselves to engage in that work. Rather than seeing what's wrong but being cynical or vindictive or going along with the program, we need to learn to speak the truth to powerful people, offer them a more imaginative future, and stand up for what's right.

But will we?

Churches and other spiritual organizations can play an important role in helping to fix broken systems. Though we are far from a perfect church, Enon tithes ten percent of our budget back into the community. In addition to the traditional work we do to feed and clothe people who are struggling, this also allows us to fund both the music teacher and music program at our neighborhood high school, where budget cuts had caused music to be removed from the curriculum. As increasing numbers of after-school activities were eliminated from public school budgets, we decided to field competitive football, basketball, baseball, cheerleading, track, soccer, chess, and martial arts teams. None require that the young people who participate be Christian or even belong to our church. As they participate, the kids do learn foundational Christian principles; what they choose to do with that information is up to that child and his family. Hundreds of children in our community are involved. At competitions, we are almost always the only church team and many of our teams are ranked nationally.

How do we do this?

A few good men step up to help. From Vernell leading boot camps to the many fathers who coach the various sports teams, and many men lend their help in other ways. In the process, they participate in developing the next generation and find tremendous meaning and satisfaction. Enon also does community work. In one neighborhood in our church's catchment area, a number of men in our church came together to create safe corridors for children walking to school in a section where there's been some street violence. Many of our guys even reach beyond that to help our city. For instance, on several weekend evenings during the heat of the summer, Enon men have worked with the police department and stood on some of the highest-crime corners of the city. On the days when our guys were out there talking to young men—often in the same neighborhoods they'd grown up in—crime dropped. Now that we know we can have an impact, we also have to ask ourselves why boys and young men are slinging drugs on the corner in certain urban neighborhoods. And we must also ask ourselves why kids from the suburbs are coming to these inner-city neighborhoods to buy the drugs they smoke, snort, and shoot up. Why are men in small towns and rural areas cooking meth and shooting heroin—or coming to places like Philly so they can find those drugs? In large part, because powerful men are taking advantage of the vulnerable, and guys who could speak truth to power in order to protect them are either out of position or lack the backbone to stand up to them out of fear that they might have to take one for the team. The nation needs men to tackle these situations. It's not always up to the police or the sheriff. Some of this is more about, "Dude, where are *you*?"

We also need guys who are going to think about the world. In our church and many others, we have a great number of men who roll up their sleeves and help to lead missionary work in other nations. In the traditional missionary model, people in other parts of the world are asked what they need and told that it will be done for them; in our church, we ask the communities in which we work what sort of support they need, then we send capable bodies and minds to help the local people do for themselves what it is they need. Our guys do things ranging from planning and building a drinking well in Kenya to rescuing young men from drug addiction in partnership with Teen Challenge in South Africa. Many of these men are older and could have "retired"; instead, they have taken on a new assignment and are now sharing their gifts and talents globally as they work on issues they really care about. Of course, as we help other people, we must also support them to help themselves. There are some things we must do and some things people need to do for themselves. But as we set high expectations for the people we help, it is our responsibility to have a clean heart—and to make sure that our behavior and systems at home don't make things more difficult for them.

As a righteous warrior helps to lift others up, he leaves them better off than when he found them. I no more have all the answers than I did when I was coaching that young man on the wrestling mat who had a female opponent. But I know that he is better off for having me in his life and I am better off for knowing him.

Don't Quit

Persevere and strive for excellence even during the difficult, exhausting,
and unfair phases of your life—you will obtain results that men
who give up early do not know are possible and cannot access.

I WATCHED AS Leroy's feet flew way up in the air and he hit the mat on his back. *Boom!* He started laughing, but he'd been foot swept, a move that martial artists use to trip their opponent. On the inside I was laughing as well. I'm short, but Leroy is more than six feet tall. In fact, he's the tall and handsome type. I'd secretly hoped he would take one on the chin.

Leroy, Jerry, Vernell, and I were at the Muay Thai Institute in Rangsit, Thailand, where Leroy and I had traveled to get certified in that martial art. Jerry had never done a martial art before; he just wanted to leave proficient. We could have attended a more glamorous facility, but we wanted to study in the location where the art originated and have an authentic experience. The floors and stands were gray cement and the ring and body bags were frayed and worn. As we walked through the gym, we could sense that many great fighters had come before us. In the dorms, our beds consisted of a foam mattress just an inch or two thick. Each room contained just a bed, a TV, and a shower. Then again, we'd come here to get certified in an ancient fighting art; we hadn't come here to get spa treatments and Godiva chocolate on our pillows.

The history of each martial art is very fascinating. In each culture, there tends to be a base art centered in the body types and physical threats that are found in that region. People develop derivations on that art with subtle nuances. For instance, Koreans practice tang soo do and tae-kwondo, both of which are centered in a lot of kicks. When you're a boxer, being short doesn't really work in your favor. Korean martial artists tend to be short, so they tend to perform kicks, which creates space between a fighter and his opponent. Thai people are shorter than most Americans as well; however, Master Moy, a former world champion with a 100–3 record, is almost Leroy's height. He took on each of us in the ring one-on-one and during each fight he didn't hold back. As accomplished as we are in the martial arts, we always knew who was boss—and it wasn't us.

On Day One of our training on the Institute campus, we had to run a 10K. After that, we'd trained from seven a.m. to nine a.m. The training was so tough that the shirt and shorts we worked out in were completely drenched in sweat. We could barely drag ourselves up the five flights of stairs to our dorm rooms. When we finally got there, we wrung out our shirts and shorts, put them on a hanger, and crawled right into bed. When we finally awakened several hours later, we put our dirty shorts and shirts back on and walked downstairs for our three p.m. to five p.m. session.

For the ten days that we trained at the center, our life was about simplicity. We ate, we slept, we ran, we trained, and we wrung out the same sweaty clothes; that was it. Keep it simple, son. Our training involved repeating the same moves over and over. We kicked two-hundred-pound body bags until our shins and feet were raw. At this point in our development, we knew enough to hold at bay any thoughts we may have had of quitting. Eventually, our feet became so sore and torn up that Master Moy felt sorry for us and told us to wear our fighting shoes. We were exhausted and never knew how we would make it through the next workout. Our clothes were so funky they could have walked home on their own. In spite of all that, none of us threw in the towel. This was good for us, and we knew it. For instance, I needed to be treated like an ordinary guy, not someone who needs his water poured for him. I needed to get my butt beat.

The elder men sat in the stands and watched us train. If we weren't doing something right, they would pull Master Moy aside. We never knew quite what they were telling him. They only said two words in English: "automatic" and "balance." "Automatic," as in we had to repeat the moves over and over until they became second nature. And "balance," because our stances had to be right. We weren't novices. At this point in our martial arts development, we knew our feet were our Truth. "Balance, balance, automatic!"—the elders would say those words to us for hours. They upheld their standards and we did our best to rise to the occasion and live into them.

When we were tested for each level of certification, the elders were strict and scored us harshly. If we didn't do something right, they noted it. We didn't have to be told that it was to maintain their integrity. We had come from America to learn a Thai art. What they required of us was that we protect its purity and authenticity; they were not going to allow outsiders, who didn't understand either the craft or the culture, adulterate or water down their art. They also wanted us to walk away having mastered the craft they had committed to teach us.

We were bruised, we were chafed, and we bled on the mat. We hurt all day, and we wanted to just give up. But we were determined to return home with both the knowledge and experience we'd come for. We'd need this discipline in the world. Leroy, Jerry, Vernell, and I each left twenty pounds in Thailand, but all of us brought home our Level 2 Muay Thai certifications.

Finish It

There are times when every man wants to throw in the towel, but to achieve his greatest victories, he has to learn not to quit. A righteous warrior always persists.

I think a lot about my father and the men of his generation—the guys former anchorman Tom Brokaw has labeled "the greatest generation." Guys who struggled through the Great Depression; men who defeated the Nazis in World War II; fellas who fought back against the Ku

Klux Klan and Jim Crow segregation. Men who raised their sons not to roll over and die.

When I look at the world through the eyes of my father, one of the worst things you could be was a quitter. To my dad and men of his age, quitters lacked character, quitters lacked integrity; quitting was just awful. Finding the courage to stand up for yourself and fight back was, to them, just part of what it meant to be a man. So the men of my dad's generation taught the men of my generation that if you tried out for the team and realized you didn't like it or wouldn't be the star, you didn't have to go out for the team next year, but you did have to finish the season. You had to complete what you'd started; whatever you did you could not give up; quitting was not an option. We didn't always like it, but we all had to do it. As a result, we learned that you kept coming back and standing up whether you wanted to or not. Standing during the difficulty was just part of what it meant to be a male.

But not every man my age internalized or even agrees with that lesson. And between my generation and the young men of today, society's values about persevering have changed. In fact, it amazes me how quickly some guys throw in the towel, especially if something's hard or they don't get a pat on the back. Everyone may get a trophy in your Pee-Wee League, but you don't get a medal when you walk out the door of your family home. In the real world, the man who gets the reward is the man who can create a plan and carry it through to completion.

It's taken twenty-plus years of preaching and teaching, a decade-plus of competing in the martial arts and extreme experiences, and more than six decades of life for me even to begin to understand the power of perseverance. Because at midlife—and after ministering to and counseling hundreds of people—it has become very clear to me the price men pay—in lost possibilities, depression, and dissatisfaction with life—when they raise the white flag and pack it in too soon. When we don't fight our way through difficulty, we cut short the chance for all our possibilities to unfold. We cut off our spiritual journey far too soon. As a result, we never attain the greatest achievements and satisfaction that would have been possible for us had we journeyed more of the path to our destiny.

In order to reach the level where we truly thrive, we cannot quit, no matter what obstacles we face or how unfairly our fight unfolds.

Six months after his son passed away, Rich fell down the front steps of his house and was unable to get up. Given his history with drugs and alcohol, the neighbors figured he was just drunk, but when he tried to move his legs he couldn't. His wife, Cindy, took him to the hospital.

"The next day my right leg was paralyzed from the knee down and the right one was from the thigh down. Two days later I was paralyzed to my waist on both sides," he recalls. "A week after that, nothing's moving at all. My whole body. Two weeks after that, one side of my face drops. Now I'm on the feeding tube.

"Over the course of the next month, they treated me for Bell's palsy, they treated me for a stroke, they treated me for Reye's syndrome, a rare disease that makes the liver and brain swell.

"I told my wife, 'Listen, if it comes down to it, pull the plug. I'm not doing this.'"

But members of the church would come visit Rich to comfort and encourage him.

"One of the deacons said something that I'll never forget. I'd told him, 'Fred, they said there's nothing they can do,' and Deacon Fred said, 'That's good; the doctors just submitted the situation to the Lord.' Then he told me that the MRI machine would be like Jesus's tomb and when I went in it I would basically be naked, so I should confess everything that I've ever done that I've been holding back from saying. 'Pray to God with your heart and just wait until you come out of that tomb,' he promised."

When Rich came out of the MRI machine nothing was different. The doctors still couldn't figure out what was going on, so they tried their last resort: plasma.

"This doctor was the best in the business, but after I received the plasma he told me that I might not walk for two or three years."

The next morning, as the doctors made their rounds, a large crowd of doctors and interns and residents in training came into Rich's room to see what affect the plasma had had.

"Move that leg," the doctor told me. "Just try to lift it for us."

"I said, 'Doc, you know I can't move nothing.' I'd been laying there unable to move for over a month. But then I heard a different voice: 'Raise your leg.'

"'Did anybody hear that?' I asked. The roomful of people said no. My wife asked, 'What's wrong?' Then I heard the voice again: 'Raise your leg.'

"So I tried to raise it and my leg jumped up about a foot off the bed.

"'*Oh!*' I shouted.

"'It was just a spasm,' the doctor said. 'Don't get your hopes up.'

"'No, I just raised my leg,' I insisted. Then I raised it again. From that day on I really began to understand the power of prayer. My recovery was on!"

Be Made Whole

The final spiritual principle that we will discuss is Professor Schreck's concept of Integrity. The question of Integrity essentially asks, "How do I make sense out of life and take each day as it comes without allowing everything to stress me out or drive me crazy, so I can live as a whole human being?"

A man must have integrity to endure life's challenges. In math class you learned that an integer is a whole number—one with no decimal points or fractions. Similarly, a righteous warrior intentionally sets out to transform himself into a whole and integrated man—a man who is fully developed and who has filled in the places where he started out weak. When a man has Integrity, what he believes lines up with what he says, and what he says lines up with what he does. He is consistent in his actions. His yes means yes and his no means no. The tongue in his mouth and the tongue in his shoes both head in the same direction. In other words, he anchors himself in timeless ideas that are bigger than himself and lives his life accordingly. He possesses Power and Purpose, he occupies his Place in the world, he stays within his Parameters, and he finds a Partner who helps him be an even better man. In other words, he understands his Identity, he demonstrates great Industry, he has Intimacy with his loved ones, and he lives in Integrity.

The great poet Maya Angelou used to say, "When you know better, do better." A righteous warrior both knows and does better than the average man. In *Webster's Dictionary*, the verb "to know" has several connotations. One means being aware of things, another means having a relationship with a person; there's also an archaic definition that means having sex with another person. In the Old Testament of the Bible, the word "know" often had sexual connotations. But in the New Testament, which was written in Greek, the verb for knowledge, *pisteo,* underscores the relationship between knowing and doing. Consistent with this definition of the word, a well-developed person's intellect connects to his heart and his hands. In other words, if you understand something you don't just get it intellectually or conceptually, you are also able to do it in the world. If you can't do it, you don't really get it. You don't just talk the talk but you also walk the walk. Or "don't just talk about it, be about it," as some folks say.

As Jerome struggled with his weight, he fought to be in Integrity, where his actions aligned with what he knew to do to take care of himself. Choosing bariatric surgery, for him, gave him accountability and hope that forced him into a lifestyle where he had to eat less. Even then, that fight wasn't easy.

"I had to lose weight so I'd be approved for the surgery. I was doing water aerobics with the old ladies; I didn't care. You gotta find your own path; it was working," he says. "When I got approved, I found out that I had to go basically two weeks without eating. My stomach was the size of a football and I had to get it down to a tennis ball. After surgery it would be the size of a golf ball. I didn't tell a lot of people except the fellas. I could drink nothing but protein shakes. I hated it. I had to make it through a retreat where everyone was 'Are you eating?' And I was like, 'No, I'm cool. I'm just gonna drink my shake.' Then we went fishing and there was fried chicken and mac and cheese. I couldn't touch any of it and I was starving. I fussed for two weeks."

Jerome's surgery went smoothly, but he had complications and for several weeks his life was quite unbearable.

"Then once I got home, I was supposed to drink more protein shakes. I didn't wanna eat, I didn't wanna swallow, I didn't wanna do anything. Just leave me alone. But you had to drink. Then you add clear liquids, then dark liquids, then baby food, then solid food. That period was really rough; you're talking basically six weeks. I got gout; I had diarrhea; the first time I tried solid food I threw up. Things bother your stomach and you have to lay down a lot. I was struggling to walk up into the pulpit and everyone witnessed it. I wouldn't wish any of it on anyone."

At various points during his recovery journey, Jerome wondered if he'd made a mistake and if the surgery could be reversed. He even went to the emergency room and ended up back in the hospital for several days because he'd become dehydrated.

"They gave me some medicine that got rid of the nausea. That ended up being a turning point. For the first time I started thinking I was going to make it," he recalls. Fortunately, his Partner, Lestonia, was right by his side. Slowly, Jerome started figuring out what he could safely eat.

"You go through experiments, what you can eat, what you can't eat," he recalls. "But then I became the incredible shrinking man. I just kept going until I was 15 pounds past 180. I was supposed to end up at 180. I had to deal with people thinking that I was dying, I had cancer, I had some major disease, that it wasn't looking good for me. We even had to make an announcement that I was okay."

Ultimately, through his struggles, a righteous warrior seeks to achieve self-mastery. In other words, he knows it because he can do it. As a spiritually mature person, his practice of discernment allows him to see through situations and prevent his emotions from clouding the way he handles each moment. Indeed, a mature man considers all of his options as he engages in life's combat. And depending upon the situation he's in, he knows that he has a number of options: He can choose to run for his life to protect himself and his loved ones, roll up his sleeves to create the family and world he believes in, or take one for the team by standing up for a cause much greater than himself. He is able to play a long game and fight for a victory he may not even live to see, even though he knows that it will appear to some that he is losing. In reality, he's overcoming everything in the world.

Because he believes that he is part of something larger than himself, he stays in constant communication with the source of his Power. He then allows that connection, rather than popular culture or other people's opinions, to dictate his decisions. As a result, the man who embodies Integrity doesn't try to impress other men, win contests, or attain society's definition of success. Instead, he remains faithful to his higher calling and follows the path toward the furthest reaches of his destiny. As he perseveres through difficulty, people witness him triumph over his struggle and he not only wins their admiration and inspires them, he also attains significance.

This—not acquiring material things, or stacking your loot in a bank account, or meeting the most beautiful woman, or owning the biggest toys—is the safest form of living: You know God, God knows you, and you follow God's direction. On a day-by-day, moment-by-moment basis, a righteous warrior takes his direction from a Power higher than himself. He allows that Power to tell him what to do. A man who demonstrates this level of self-mastery can overcome any challenges the world presents to him and translate his intellectual knowledge into results. His closeness to God frees him to access more and more of who he has been created to be. He becomes free to be more and more himself in its awesomeness and wonder.

And just as the greatest warrior fights to the finish—and just as Christ conducted his father's business until it was done—a righteous warrior doesn't just start a thing, he finishes it.

This is True Integrity.

"Fast forward twelve years after Faith passed away. It's my first day on the job at a children's hospital, where I've become a chaplain. I'm meeting with my supervisor, the head chaplain, and she says, 'Hey, I have this interesting experience, might you be interested?'

"'Okay, yeah, what's up?'

"'I've been here for three years and I've never had to go to the morgue, but I need to go because a child died and the parents are of a faith where they don't embalm,' she says. 'They want me to go look at the child just to see if they can have a service for her.'

"Of course, my supervisor has no idea what I've experienced, so I say to myself, 'God, you've got jokes.'

"So I go to the morgue, not knowing if I will be okay, and when they show us the child, I see this beautiful little girl, a beautiful child. It was only in that moment that I could see God's glory at work and say, 'I'm good. I'm good.'"

Go the Distance

In the closing seconds of the eighth round in his 1980 rematch with Sugar Ray Leonard, Roberto Durán turned his back to the fight and told referee Octavio Meyran "*no mas*"—no more. Then he threw in the towel and ended it. Today, his decision to walk away from that fight is the greatest regret of a man who is one of the most feared and highly respected boxers we have ever known. But as public as his washout was, Roberto Durán isn't alone in his experience of giving up too soon. I wish I could tell you how many conversations I've had with guys who have limited their own opportunities because they packed it in before they'd given it all they had.

Sometimes it's because they smoked weed and couldn't pass the drug test to get the job, or chose not to take the promotion because they would have to relocate, or walked away from the chance to develop a relationship with their son because his ex was humiliating him when he couldn't keep up with child support. The guy who cuts out of the battle and sells himself short misses out on the opportunity to develop the skills to reach the next level. In the process he unknowingly benches himself, places himself on the sidelines of life when he actually wants to be out on the field.

The sidelines certainly have their place, but no guy wants to ride the pine. Yet far too many men permanently bench themselves while they watch the guys who persisted through difficulty and developed themselves get all the playing time. They, too, could have been on the field if they had just stuck around, pressed on, and developed the muscles they needed to become a starter. In the meantime, some men are where they are merely because they just kept showing up, not necessarily because they are that much better or smarter than the other guys who didn't make it. The ball bounced their way mainly because sometimes part of being in position requires that you keep showing up.

Once Rich got movement in his leg, he threw himself full force back into the game of life.

"I immediately started physical therapy," he says. "I just started boom-boom-boom-boom. Within two weeks I was able to use a walker and roll myself home. Then, after about two more weeks of therapy, I put down the walker. I put down everything. Then I jumped right in with Vernell and them. I started doing the heavy stuff. It was hard but it was amazing!"

One of the things I value most about the martial arts is that they teach you not to quit no matter what an opponent throws at you. You are trained not to allow anyone else to make you give up. Whether in Muay Thai camp, or in the Amazon, or alone in the Negev Desert, I can tell you from personal experience that a man can do more than he ever thought possible. Every human being has more in the tank than they know. If you give up, you never discover that. And if you never discover that, you cannot get to the next level. And not only will you not get to the next level, you won't get to the level after that or the level after that. As a result, instead of experiencing life's upward spiral, far too many men keep circling on the level they're already at; still others spin in circles as they're being sucked down the drain. Whether talking to the men who attend my own church or interacting with friends and competitors at martial arts tournaments or meeting new guys during extreme experiences, I hear a lot of stories about men's frustrations and regrets over their inability to reach their goals.

What a high-level martial artist knows is that he must repeat the principles of his art so often that they become a part of who he is so that he does the moves automatically. He must practice each kick hundreds if not thousands of times so that he no longer has to think about it; he's embodied the move and can execute without thinking. This is true of any high-level performer. No musician thinks about every note when he sings or plays; there's a point at which he's rehearsed so much that his body just plays or sings it. When LeBron or Stephen Curry hits a three at the buzzer with two defenders in their face, it's not because they got lucky. They have worked on their shot over and over and over again. They practiced during practice and they practiced long after other players had left the gym. By clutch time their shot had become second nature. As a matter of fact, if they stop to think about it, that's when they'll get in trouble.

In a similar fashion, if you center your life around the spiritual principles you've been learning—in other words, if you acknowledge God as the source of your Power and Identity, seek to identify your rightful Place in the world, carry out your Purpose within the Parameters where you are most powerful, and do this in relationship with the right Partner—you will practice them so often that you do them naturally. They will not only become part of who you are, they will equip you to go the distance and to end up victorious.

When you master the principle of Integrity, you do not need or even expect life to occur in a textbook fashion. You know that things will not always be pretty; in fact, you expect that you will have to win ugly, so you don't give in when hard things happen. No matter what life may throw at you, you are committed to withstand it. Because you stand for something greater than yourself, when the going gets tough you figure out how to keep going. You finish life's fights, neither surrendering nor allowing others to stop you.

Difficult battles develop your mental, emotional, and spiritual muscles. The more developed you become, the more of your destiny you can fulfill. This happens because staying in the game not only develops the skills you need to navigate from level to level, it simultaneously strengthens your ability to go through the doors toward the far reaches of your destiny. Your tenaciousness helps you integrate both the smooth sailing and the rough times. Becoming a man of greater Integrity will prepare you to experience the joys of living that less-determined men do not.

"Back when I retired from the military, my wife had encouraged me to start cycling," says Jerry. "I'd ride with Leroy and some of the other fellas. So after Devon passed, Leroy brought up the idea of doing a memorial ride; I agreed. And because recently a group of eleven hikers had gotten in an accident and one had gone through a car's windshield, we thought it would be a good idea to help cyclists who had gotten involved in an accident with a motor vehicle where their bike was totaled get financial assistance to get back on a bike with a community of support, so they wouldn't be gun-shy and say, 'I'm not riding again.'

"So the community donated the local park. We got a bike shop on board. And for our first ride, more than fifty-five people from Pennsylvania, New Jersey, Delaware, and Maryland got on board. Lots of folks came out to support us. We had a state police escort so we didn't have to deal with traffic. We even created two one thousand dollar scholarships for criminal justice students at church in Devon's name."

Keep Your Head in the Game

Finishing what you've started requires you to stay in the present moment.

I never will forget when I stopped playing football. I'd started playing just like any other boy, on the flag-football field competing against kids who were all about the same size. I played quarterback well against the boys in elementary and middle school, and again they were roughly my size. But the summer before high school it seemed like everybody grew. Well, everybody but me. Suddenly, dudes who had been close to my size seemed six inches taller and fifty pounds heavier than I was.

In the tenth grade, during the middle of the game against Shaw High School, we were receiving the kickoff and my friend Beano caught the ball. His runback went uneventfully, but when Beano got tackled, I saw his leg break. His shin broke in half and seemed like it was bent to a ninety-degree angle. Beano was on the ground writhing and screaming—I had never seen anyone in that kind of pain before. Beano was my friend and part of me wanted to help him, but another part of me just wanted to run away from what I'd seen. Today I know that I was just having a fear response. My thinking became cloudy, my legs became weak, and the voice inside my head said, "This is not the sport for you!" The game resumed, but from that point on my body was on the field but my head was somewhere else. After I threw or handed off the ball, I would intentionally run away from the play. I had mentally checked out and was praying for time to run out!

Maybe there is an area of your life where you, too, have metaphorically left the building and checked out. At work, maybe you have a difficult boss or an impossible assignment. Once Friday comes you "phone it in" as you wait for happy hour. Perhaps you're the guy whose work life didn't go down the way he'd planned and you are just counting the years, months, or even days until retirement. Or maybe you're hoping to get fired so you can get unemployment or severance. At home, perhaps you haven't left, but your marriage isn't working and you're not working on it.

Or you had children with your first wife, but that ended and you remarried, and now life with your new family keeps you on overload, so you don't show up for your first family like you know you ought to. Eventually, both your ex and the kids are mad and the guilt weighs on you, so it just becomes easier to fade out of your first family's life, leaving your kids to figure their future out for themselves.

There are a whole lot of really good guys whose bodies are present but who have mentally, emotionally, and spiritually vacated the premises. I know how it goes. I've been there, done that, bought the T-shirt, designed the cap, and showed off the sweat suit! When life gets too hard, sometimes we retreat to our cell phone, man cave, porn, alcohol, weed, or some other distraction or addiction when we would be better off rolling up our sleeves and doing the work that life and our relationships require. Sometimes we just retreat into our man cave to process, regroup, and or get it together. That's fine as long as we're not doing destructive things—and assuming we return in a timely manner. But the stepping back momentum can be difficult to stop. Especially if we've adopted bad habits, it can be tough to step forward and get back on track. If we wait too long, we not only have to return to the problem we were avoiding, but so much time has passed that now it not only has snowballed, it has whipped cream, sprinkles, and a cherry on top. If we had just stayed when the problem developed, we could have figured it out and handled it. Not letting our thoughts get too far ahead of us and taking the day one moment at a time can help us manage each moment.

Beat the Clock

To persevere it really helps to have a productive perspective on time.

There are more ways of understanding time than merely what the clock or calendar measures. In Greek, the word *chronos* translates into the English concept of clock or calendar time. *Chronos* isn't the only Greek word that denotes time, though. There's also *kairos,* which means God's time, or the most opportune time for something to happen. Indeed, *kairos* represents everything everywhere working together in order to create the best outcome for everyone on the planet. Many people who interpret the Bible are unaware of this. As a result, during their spiritual education, they unknowingly reduce a word that was intended to convey God's time to the human—and easier to comprehend—clock time. Though we may want something to happen on our human time frame, we can't put an infinite God on a limited timetable. Though humans tend to believe that we are in charge, we deceive ourselves if we believe that an infinite universe runs on our *chronos*. The greatest scientists don't even understand ultimately what causes the planets to orbit the sun, the seasons to change, or many of the ways the natural world demonstrates the passage of time. Though science can tell us what happens, science can't tell us what causes those phenomena. Though we experience the clock and the calendar as real, on a more profound level life runs on God's *kairos*.

A warrior understands that sometimes he must wait for the right, or most opportune, time for a thing to unfold. Some things only happen if, when, and how God says they will. The sun does not set from west to east; our solar system does not revolve around Earth's moon; snow does not fall during the heat of summer. Some things are bigger than us. As inconvenient as waiting may seem in that moment, the warrior understands that *kairos* time is not just best for one man, it is also best for every living being; indeed, everything that ever was is now and will be, a world without end.

So don't give up merely because either the clock in your head or society's clock says that something is taking too long. Don't give up just because you, in your limited human way of seeing the world, are feeling discouraged and afraid that something's not going to happen when you want it to. Everything God intends for you will take place, so first make sure that you're in touch with your Power, on Purpose, and within the right Place and Parameters. Even then, everything won't unfold on your timetable. All things do work together for good; however, other people, places, and things are involved—and the good that is being worked out benefits everyone.

It's also important to have the right perspective because today we live in an always on, twenty-four/seven, everything-at-your-fingertips, throwaway culture. Every couple of years we think we need a new phone. Even if we don't think we need one, the manufacturer will "update" it so that it no longer works. A year or two after that we think we need a new computer. But our society's throwaway approach doesn't support a man's growth. Throwing things away can translate into a lack of appreciation for things that endure, are resilient and durable. All of us can learn a thing or two from our parents' and grandparents' generations; they valued longevity. For instance, I remember how our elders bought pants that were just a little too big. They sewed seams and cuffs into them and let them out as we grew, so that rather than getting one year of wear out of them we might get two (or more). Rather than being embarrassed by the fact that we "repeated" our clothes, the creases and faded lines that marked where the seams and hems had been provided proof that we were growing.

Just as some devices are designed to wear out, some things in life are unapologetically designed in order to make people quit. There is a weed-out class in every college major whose goal is to separate the serious student from the slacker. Military boot camps are intentionally designed to generate a certain proportion of soldiers as well as a smaller percentage of washouts. Every level of a martial art draws a line between those who have practiced the moves enough to know or embody the principles and those who have not lived up to the process. A whole lot of people buy a martial arts uniform and step onto the mat, but only a handful of folks ever become a black belt.

Back when I was in the military, in the days before everyone had GPS on their phone or another navigation device, I learned that one of the most common mistakes soldiers made when reading a map was underestimating the distance they'd traveled. They didn't get lost because they went in the wrong direction; typically, they just didn't judge their distance correctly, or they gave up too soon.

It's important to correctly judge the distance between where you are and where you are headed. If you're fortunate, your destiny will unfold over the course of sixty, seventy, eighty, or perhaps even a hundred years. To get there, you have to brave difficult situations for long enough that you grow to the point that you can handle the next level. Staying in the struggle instead of choosing to bail out is the mental, emotional, and spiritual equivalent of lifting weights in the gym. At first, lifting weights is hard. You have to find the time, join a gym, get over your embarrassment about your gut. You may struggle to complete more than just a few reps. Your muscles burn. In a nutshell, it sucks. But over time, you get stronger and can handle more reps. You go from ten reps to twelve, from two sets to three. And before long, you're ready to up the weight. Similarly, remaining engaged in difficult mental, emotional, and spiritual circumstances even when you want to quit helps you develop the wherewithal to handle them.

It's okay if you decide, after trying, that something's not for you after all. But whether a job, a certification program, or a marriage, you ought to fight long enough to develop yourself, graduate from your current level, and learn what you can from the experience. By lifting life's weight, you may strengthen yourself so that you can handle the problem and manage, overcome, or even transcend it. That prepares you to pass through the door to the next level. Here's another way of thinking about it: When life overwhelms you, rather than walking away from the problem, bring some additional support to it by practicing a spiritual discipline or getting other help. Consider practices like prayer; meditation; studying a self-help, motivational, or inspirational text; demonstrating intentional discipline with your diet, like removing meat, juicing, or even fasting; or speaking with a therapist or spiritual counselor. That said, many men need to spend more time on the front side of situations asking, "Should I even start this?"

When Beano's leg broke, the best solution I could come up with was to run away. Today I know that there's no need to retreat from things just because they are scary or hard, or give in when there's more that I could attempt and learn. Instead, we ought to try so hard that we fail from time to time. Trying and failing is not the same as quitting. When you fail you can walk away knowing that you gave it an honest effort. You also learn a lot in the process and take what you've learned with you. In fact, failing's not personal. Every man should expect to have some ups and some downs in his life. Your "up" is not where you should hang your hat, nor is your "down" where you need to stay and wallow. Neither your good days nor your bad days should have the final word. If today has been the worst day of your life, it's important that you don't throw in the towel. And don't attempt to rest on your laurels if it's been your best day.

As you progress through life, you will need to persist. Men who give up both deprive themselves of learning and miss out on the satisfaction of knowing what they could have accomplished. In addition to helping to build the muscles to handle life's difficulties, sticking out the tough times makes the good times mean more when they roll back around. Your good times and bad times actually complement each other. As they do, your life makes more sense and you become more whole—you develop greater Integrity. The times you cried, your heartaches, and your late nights mean a lot more once the situation has worked out. Indeed, allowing yourself to sit in your feelings of humility and even heaviness makes it easier to feel grateful when you reach the other side. You will look back on how you made it through and are still here to talk about it. You will also appreciate the simple things in life. In the meantime, the bad times become material for the testimony you share about how your faith and diligence brought you through to the other side. And when the next difficulty arises on life's horizon, you will carry the confidence and strength you developed while riding out the last challenge.

"Once I started turning the corner, I preached a sermon about metamorphosis and lifestyle change and told my story," says Jerome. "After that, I discovered that watching me lose weight was helping others get through it. I started sharing war stories with people who had been through the surgery and talking with other people who were considering it. I would never say that surgery is the answer for everyone, but I can now see how I can encourage others. And every time I walk past the mirror, I look in it and go, 'That's me?'"

Eventually, even when life becomes difficult, you stop getting hysterical and get historical as you reflect upon all the things that you've made it through. So I strongly encourage you to play all four quarters of every challenge you encounter. It's also important to play through all four quarters of life, as Rich is doing. In fact, play for the overtime win if necessary. In a culture that values temporary things, you will distinguish yourself from everyone else by shooting for permanence and longevity.

Sadly, our society is also undermining our ability to do this because it's destroying our ability to pay attention. Digital life has shortened the average person's attention span from twelve seconds in 2000, which was bad enough, to eight seconds in 2015.* Today, young people dislike reading books and even older folks, who weren't brought up in the digital age, are easily distracted. This is just devastating because no matter how old he is, a man who cannot pay attention or who needs to be entertained will be unable to persevere. When companies control your attention span, they also control you. You can be controlled because you cannot persevere past eight seconds. Once companies control you, they own you. When they own you, you sacrifice the free will that is the gift that distinguishes all of humankind. That is a high price to pay for convenience.

---

*Kevin McSpadden, "You Now Have a Shorter Attention Span Than a Goldfish," Time.com, May 14, 2015. Accessed at http://time.com/3858309/attention-spans-goldfish/.

Don't Start None, Won't Be None

Understanding where along your journey you are can really help you to hang on.

One of the most dangerous reasons that men quit is because society tells them that they're getting too old. They turn fifty and start to experience age discrimination; turn sixty and are told to pull out the rocking chair; turn seventy or more and told they should just hold on until death because they have nothing more to offer. Yet during the fourth quarter of a man's life—between the ages of sixty and seventy-nine (eighty and up is overtime!), a man's time *is* winding down—you need to finish what you've started and work with greater intention and perhaps even a sense of urgency.

The fact that we live in a society that pushes its elders to the side is part of the opposition an older man must war against. As you move into your more seasoned years, I encourage you not to allow other people's narrow and limiting definitions of age and aging to sideline you and make you irrelevant. Do not buy into society's projections that older men are less virile and useless. Instead, embrace your *zacar* identity. The life of a man in his sixties and on should involve standing in the grace you've experienced throughout your life and imparting knowledge and sharing your testimony—all of your testimony, not the edited version—with younger men. You've made it this far; you can let go of your need to look good or win others' acceptance.

The time has come to become an elder in the African sense of the word. Traditional African culture views a person's senior years differently from the ways the Western world uses the word "elderly." The African elder is both highly regarded and revered. He has succeeded in taking on life's challenges, raised his family, and built a community of friends and connections. That is priceless. An elder has also amassed a lifetime of loyalties and relationships, which remain intact no matter what kind of physical or mental condition the elder is in. Indeed, in some cultures, young adults are viewed as being too inexperienced to carry the full responsibility of rearing their children. So, while the young adults do more of child rearing's physical labor, the elders, who have more wisdom and patience, handle the spiritual and emotional lift.

If things have gone smoothly during the first three quarters of your life, you may be able to settle into your *zacar* role and hold the ball until the clock runs out. Perhaps you can kick back and sow into your children, grandchildren, and, if you're really lucky, your great-grandchildren. But that ought not to be all. Share your skills and advice with younger men, mentor at the Y, encourage the boy next door, or share your professional acumen through an organization like the Service Corps of Retired Executives.

If your life got off to a slow start—or if you made a lot of turnovers and now need to throw a bomb or Hail Mary to finish strong—use the wisdom you've garnered in order to score. Rich's life didn't get great until he was in his sixties.

"Pastor had been watching me and offered me an opportunity to travel with him and help him," says Rich. "I got a lifetime opportunity to go to South Africa. Then I told my story to the church and that helped other people and other drug addicts. People speak to me now who would never have talked to me before because of my background. And I'm comfortable now because I have what I never had: brothers. Now I have family, people that I trust—Pastor, Vernell, Leroy, Mark and Jerry and Jerome. I've got somebody and we've got each other."

As in Rich's case, you may find yourself working longer or harder than you'd planned. Even if that is your struggle, there's honor in an honest day's work even during the golden years. Men like Rich, who are on the comeback trail, need to be wary of people who would knock them off of it by mocking or discouraging them. Because whether at the gym or the barbershop, guys are full of stories of things we started, but there are also a lot of stories of things we did not finish. Many guys have a strange relationship with the idea of what they almost did. It's like some of us will sabo-tage our own efforts and live for the next forty years telling the story about how close we were to it. Or of what we used to do or who we used to be. Don't let them discourage you.

Because the goal in life is to complete your assignment and finish life strong. Almost anyone can be a freshman, but who is going to graduate?

A man in the *zacar* stage should ask himself whether he has done all his living. This question can be painful no matter where he is in his life, and it can be particularly painful during the fourth quarter or overtime. There is no crime and no shame in losing or dying; however, dying can be particularly painful if you have never started living. If you count yourself among those who haven't started living, then play for the late score or even overtime win. Don't be too proud to throw up a Hail Mary! Even at this age, you ought to ask yourself questions like: Have I actually started the things that I'm supposed to do? Have I been afraid of them? What do I need to do to overcome my fear? How do I finish them?

Know When to Fold 'Em

A righteous warrior doesn't quit, but he does understand the need to strate-gically decide to move on. Use the same introspective thought process that you use to decide when to run, fight, or take one for the team to help you figure out when it makes sense to quit.

It can be difficult to let people, places, and things go, so we may be in-clined to keep them around past their sell-by date. There comes a time when you have to tell the truth and be able to acknowledge that a thing is dead. When I used the word "dead," I mean it's no longer inspiring, it no longer energizes you, no longer has life, no longer has meaning to you. When you give your best effort yet doors remain closed or the gentle nudgings of your spirit say stop, listen; it may be time to change direction, do something differently or even move on. Developing this awareness is essential. Because you can't start a new thing until you acknowledge that the old thing is dead. I suggest you always remember: Your destiny awaits you in the new season.

I'll use myself as an example. The season of having children at home is over for Ellyn and me. We called that phase of our life dead several years ago, once both of our daughters were successfully living their own lives. Both Ellyn and I have stepped into new seasons. During this phase of our life, I am not the only one traveling. In fact, if either the girls or I need Ellyn, we may have to wait until she returns from some part of the world where she's helping to lead a movement against human trafficking. An I'm as likely to be following her somewhere as she is to be accompanying me. Our daughters are not our little girls anymore. We cannot treat them like they're children, and they cannot interact with us like we're the parents we used to be.

Indeed, a man's life is best understood retrospectively. The longer you have lived, the more you can look back in a way that makes what has happened over the decades make sense. The old church hymn many of our grandparents sang reminds us that "we will understand it better bye and bye"—it will make sense to us eventually. Until then, we must wait for more pieces on life's grand chessboard to move into place. Eventually, every man must answer for his choices. At life's end, each of the major religions and many spiritual traditions teach that everyone will experience a reckoning. In Christianity, God calls us into account both for our actions and our inactions—the choices we made and the choices we didn't make. But no matter your religious or spiritual beliefs, every human being will have to account for what he or she was given and what we did with it.

From *Legion* to *The Book of Eli* to *Mad Max: Fury Road*, many of the things we watch about the end of the world are scary. But in the Christian context, God's judgment isn't a scary thing. To the contrary, God's judgment gives us hope because in the end what matters is not what other human beings think of us, but what God thinks about who we've been and what we've done over the course of our entire life. For men who are not Christian, the thought that they've lived a moral and principled life that honored the people who came before them, the loved ones with whom they've shared their life, and the children and grandchildren they'll one day leave behind can be a source of great comfort and joy.

In Thailand, Leroy, Jerry, and I gained great satisfaction by living into the standards of the elders at the Muay Thai school. Their reminders that we needed to diligently practice so that the fundamentals of that art become automatic merged with the reminders that we must simultaneously maintain our balance. The balance and reflexes we were building were two sides of the same coin; they were part of the same thing. As you practice these principles, they will become instinctual. And as they become who you are, you will be more balanced. Being more balanced will free you to reach further into life's possibilities than you have ever imagined. I'll be the first to admit that the work is hard. I'll be the first to apprise you that it requires great discipline. You will have to reach deep into the warrior you are deep down in your heart. But as you do this, no matter what the world serves up to you, you will fight with Integrity and you will win. Indeed, the Integrity is the win.

After a very difficult battle, Jerome has won his weight-loss war.

"Before I had surgery I'd told the guys that I wanted to celebrate when I'd lost a hundred pounds by jumping out of a plane. Everyone but Jerry said, 'We ain't jumping out of no airplane.' And I'd tell them, 'I've done Tough Mudder; I've followed you through the jungle. We're brothers, remember?' "

Oh, yes, we remembered.

When Jerome underwent surgery, he weighed 304 pounds. We celebrated with him and he rapidly began losing weight.

"I started telling them, I'm at 260. I'm at 240. I'm at 220. Oh, guess what? I lost another three pounds.' Finally, I was like, 'Guys, I'm here!'"

So Jerry signed us up to jump, then Rich hired a videographer and we went.

"When the plane takes off, you start thinking, 'I gotta jump out of this thing and there's nothing down there but air,'" Jerry recalls. "When you're at seven thousand feet you're like, 'Okay, we're really going to do this. Oh my god, what did I get myself into?' The fear builds up."

And boy, did it! When we reached 13,500 feet, they opened this huge garage-like door on the side of the plane and you look out and there's just nothing there.

"In my imagination, I'd wanted to stand up and fly out, but my knees are bad and as I scooted forward I got stuck. I think we just fell out. It was the craziest thing I'd ever done in my entire life! I was praying for the parachute to opened but my jump coach was pointing out things on the ground."

"'Philadelphia is over there!' my jump instructor told me.

"I was like, 'Okay, this is cool. But you haven't pulled the chute yet!'"

Jerome will be the first to tell you that he's not jumping out of a plane ever again.

"But that jump was the great equalizer," he says. "I hadn't seen these guys' weaknesses. But you know how Superman's weakness is Kryptonite? I saw Leroy's Kryptonite. Vernell's and Pastor's, too—all of them. It was the first time I'd seen that they're just like me."

Jumping out of a plane was an amazing experience, but as many extreme things as I've done, I, for one, have never been so happy to have both feet back on the ground.

During my youth, one of the things that I used to enjoy most about wrestling was the period between the end of the match and the moment when the referee raised the winner's hand. Indeed, there were times when the competition was over and I knew that I'd won, but it hadn't yet been announced. We would stay out on the mat as the ref checked the score before coming to lift up my hand. The feelings I had during those moments were ones of tremendous satisfaction. I had stepped onto the mat confident that I had prepared myself for that particular match but, not knowing what exactly would take place, I had to rely on the knowledge that engaging in that contest was also preparing me for my next match. With the raising of my hand, the referee merely confirmed my diligence, my sacrifice, and my courage.

The righteous warrior lives on life's wrestling mat. He never knows what life will throw at him, yet he prepares himself to engage in every battle regardless of where that combat comes from. He knows that he gains Power, gets clearer about his Place and his Purpose, better understands his Parameters, and becomes stronger as a result of the life and family he builds with his Partner, if he should choose to marry. He gets clear about his Identity, commits to exhibiting great Industry, engages with others with deep Intimacy, and lives with tremendous Integrity. Though he will certainly lose many skirmishes as he journeys through life, he never gives up because he understands that, as he lives out the Code of the Righteous Warrior, the clash is both a victory and a test along the path to his long-term destiny.

No matter what challenges, difficulties, or humiliations he encounters, the righteous warrior never throws in the towel. He stays on the battle-field, uses his weapons, plays all four quarters, and never says "*no mas.*" Because he knows that everything will be okay In the end. And if it ain't okay, it ain't the end. . . .

Acknowledgments

I PARTICULARLY APPRECIATE the men who have made covenant with me to grow and stretch to be the best men we can be and who have opened up their lives in this book: Rev. Leroy Miles, Mr. Vernell Bailey, Mr. Richard Walls, Mr. Jerry Pendergrass, Mr. Marc Corbin, and Rev. Jerome Glover. Thank you for pushing me to be the man that I am and helping me complete this project. Your stories will inspire many men to become Righteous Warriors. Like Caine did in the series *Kung Fu*, we have snatched the pebbles from the hands of life. It is now time for us to go and help others to become righteous warriors. This book is not the only way to become a man nor are my ideas the only valid way to see the world. However, I do believe our collective life experiences offer much wisdom and insight into God's creational intentionality for men

I am grateful to the martial arts for informing my view of how to live biblically and righteously in the world; my cousin Lonnie, who first taught me how to fight; my high school wrestling coaches, Mr. McIntyre and Mr. Morgan, who gave me a great martial foundation; Master Hamilton C. Robinson, who taught me Naphtali; Coach Washington, who allowed me to teach in his gym, Washington's Gym, in Ardmore Pennsylvania, and Moni Issacs, who taught me CKM. All of these men have helped to shape my understanding of martial arts and informed some of the ideas I've explored in this book.

I am thankful for Steve Ross for seeing the book's possibility while the concept was still in development and for his extremely capable representation. The support I've experienced from the staff at Simon & Schuster has been remarkable, beginning with Todd Hunter, formerly at Atria, who, remarkably, had already attended Enon and so had experienced firsthand the book's promise, and extending to Beth Adams and the team at Howard Books, whose care, attention and eye for nuance and detail have not only made the book ready for prime time but have also made it possible for people to actually read it.

This book is a compilation of the teachings and experiences that I have gained from Southern Baptist Theological Seminary and Eastern Baptist

Theological Seminary. I have had the privilege of serving four churches in my lifetime: Shiloh Baptist in Cleveland, Ohio; Canaan Christian Church in Louisville, Kentucky; First Baptist Church of Donora, Pennsylvania; and Enon Tabernacle Baptist Church in Philadelphia.

Rev. Rosemond C. Kay, Rev. Nathan Simon, Rev. Dr. G. Thomas Turner and Rev. Dr. Walter Malone all have provided me with the foundation for my understanding of manhood ministry and mission.

This book would not be possible without the genius that is Hilary Beard. As a pastor I have thoughts, ideas and theological convictions. I am trained for people to hear my words. Hilary has taken my words and put them in literary form. Most books written by ministers are difficult to read because our words are meant to be heard more so than read. I am grateful to Hilary for making my thoughts accessible to a larger audience.

I am immensely grateful to my wife of twenty-nine years, Dr. Ellyn Jo Waller, for her love and support. It has taken a lifetime for me to live into the teachings of this book. I am a Righteous Warrior but I have become this over time. My wife has seen the best and worst of me and has helped me to become who I am today. I, ultimately, want to be the man I am writing about in order to be he husband that she deserves.

I am grateful for the many men I have had in my life who have given me an example to follow. My father, Dr. Alfred Waller, is my ultimate role model. I am grateful to have grown up with an old-school dad.

Ultimately, I give glory and honor to God for God's superintending presence in my life. Through all of the ups and downs of life, the successes and failures that I have experienced, God has brought me to the conclusions of what it means to be a Righteous Warrior.

Hilary Beard's Acknowledgments

LITTLE DID I know when I first walked into Enon more than a decade ago that I would not merely find the church community I'd been seeking but years later I'd be called to help you, my brother's childhood friend—all grown up and successful now!—to bring your book to life. Yet here we are decades removed from Woodbury Junior High School, Home Slice. How fun!

It has been a blessing to grow spiritually under you as well as to have this opportunity to test and deepen my understandings of our faith within our writing partnership. I pray that our words help readers gain the clarity they need to become the fully developed men that God has created them (and that they desire) to be—and that other men and women, families, communities and the world so desperately need. Thank you to the fellas, both for being so courageously vulnerable and for trusting me enough to share your personal stories with me.

Madeline Morel, I can't tell you how much I appreciate you. Your presence in my life has allowed me to have an amazing writing career. Thank you for always having my back! Home Team Steve Ross, how fun that we're all three from Cleveland. It's been great working with you once again. Thank you to the folks at Simon & Schuster, especially Todd Hunter at Atria, who first saw our vision, and Beth Adams and the editorial team at Howard, who saw our book through.

I will forever be grateful to Jonathan, Alison, Jennifer, Kailey, Jadon, and Alex for always supporting and being there for me. Your loving presence makes it so much easier to push past my limit lines, knowing that when I fall short I always have people and places to call home. Uncle Ray, thank you for your decades of love, wisdom and guidance, especially during the years since my father passed away. Aunt Carol, thank you for being the keeper of the Lanton family homestead. Words don't adequately express how much the two of you fortify me. Thank you as well to the rest of my Beard, Lanton and Carson extended families, including the many fine examples of manhood our families have produced. I will forever be grateful to my deceased parents, Charles and Peggy Beard and to Aunt Bonnie Morgan, who for decades stood in as my surrogate mom, but recently made her transition.

Thanks to my church family at Enon for taking me in and giving me a place I call home. I particularly appreciate Valerie Harrison, who for years nudged me to help Pastor Waller write his book; the ever-growing community of people who I sit with on Sunday mornings; my FaithWorks friends; and the many ministers who have mentored me as I grow in my faith walk and relationship with God, to whom I am forever grateful for this amazing journey that I call my life.